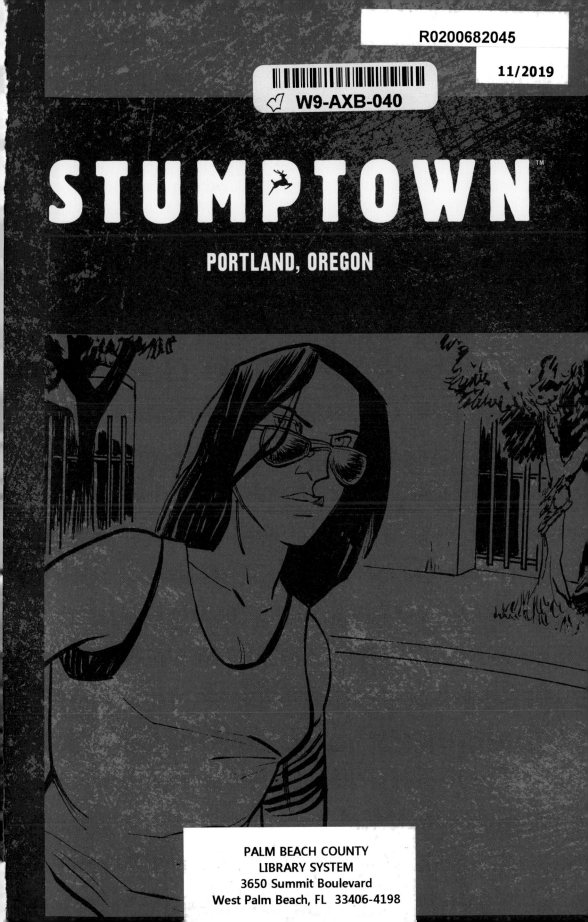

STUMPTOWN™

PORTLAND, OREGON

STUMPTOWN™

INVESTIGATIONS • PORTLAND, OREGON

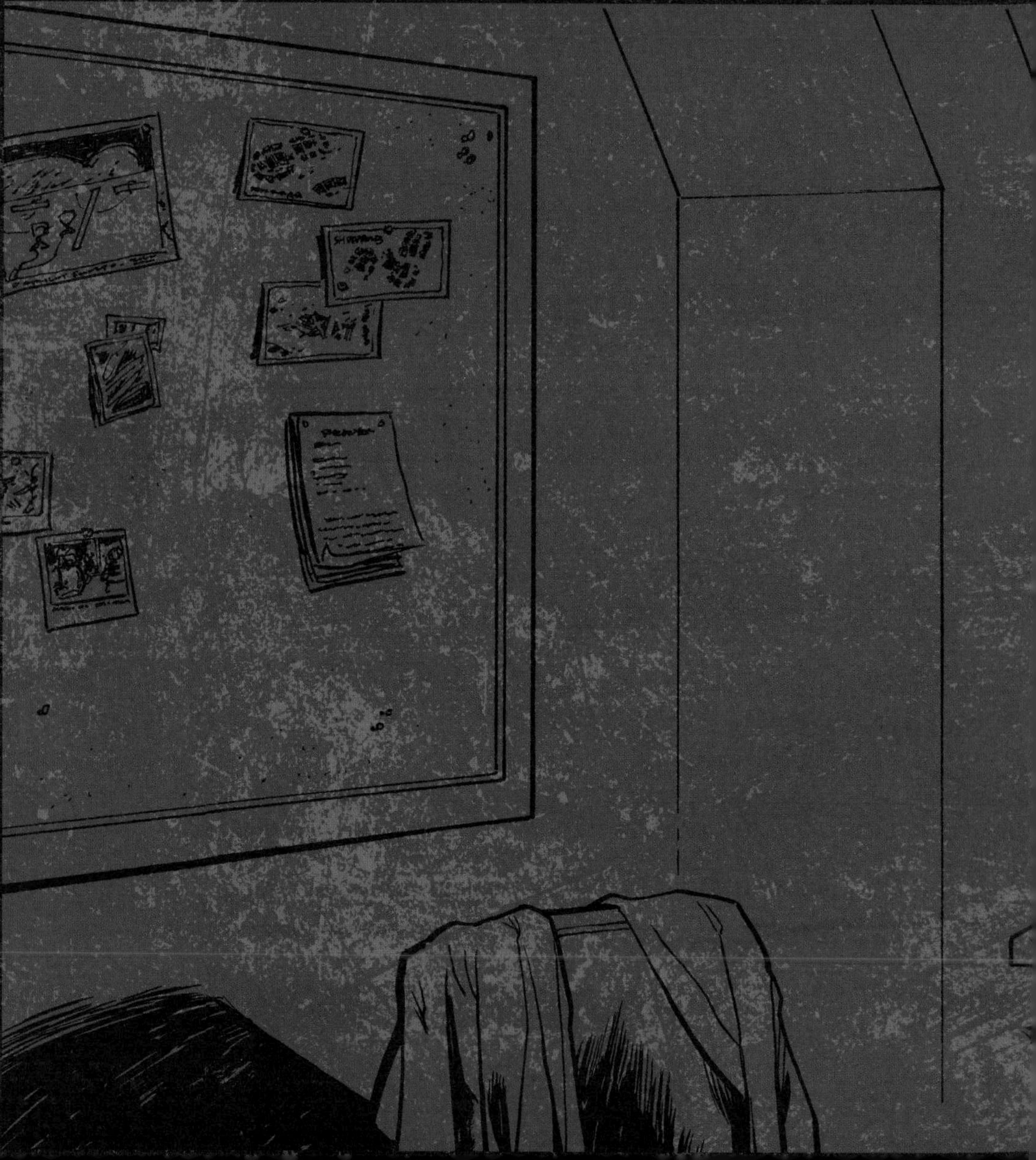

The Case of the King of Clubs

written by
GREG RUCKA

illustrated by
JUSTIN GREENWOOD

colored by
RYAN HILL

lettered by
CRANK!

Edited by
JAMES LUCAS JONES and ARI YARWOOD

Designed by
KEITH WOOD with HILARY THOMPSON

AN ONI PRESS PRODUCTION

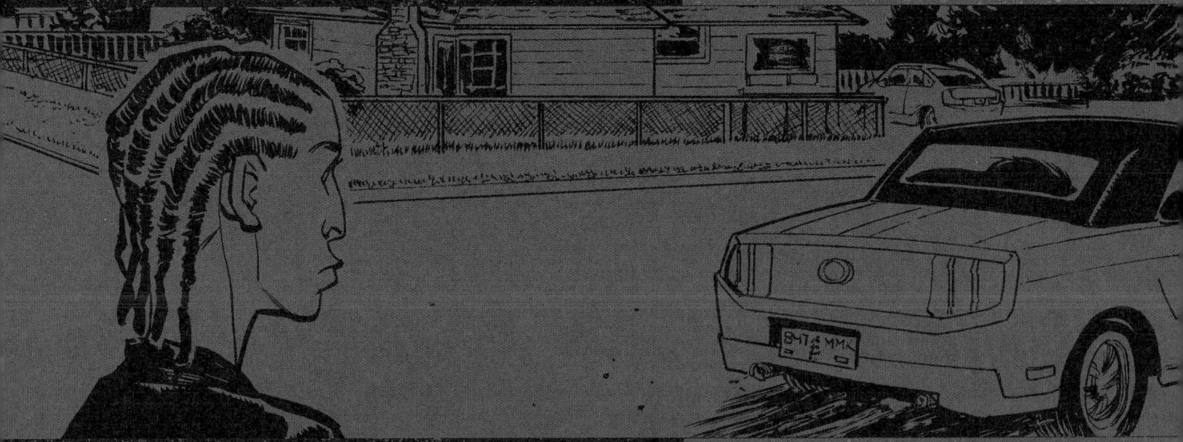

PUBLISHED BY ONI PRESS, INC.
Joe Nozemack, founder & chief financial officer
James Lucas Jones, publisher
Charlie Chu, v.p. of creative & business development
Brad Rooks, director of operations
Melissa Meszaros, director of publicity
Margot Wood, director of sales
Sandy Tanaka, marketing design manager
Amber O'Neill, special projects managertt
Troy Look, director of design & production
Hilary Thompson, senior graphic designer
Kate Z. Stone, graphic designer
Sonja Synak, junior graphic designer
Angie Knowles, digital prepress lead
Ari Yarwood, executive editor
Sarah Gaydos, editorial director of licensed publishing
Robin Herrera, senior editor
Desiree Wilson, associate editor
Alissa Sallah, administrative assistant
Jung Lee, logistics associate
Scott Sharkey, warehouse assistant

ONI PRESS, INC.
1319 SE Martin Luther King, Jr. Blvd.
Suite 240
Portland, OR 97214

onipress.com
facebook.com/onipress
twitter.com/onipress
onipress.tumblr.com
instagram.com/onipress
onipress.com

@ruckawriter / gregrucka.com
@jkgreenwood_art / justingreenwoodart.com
@josephryanhill

First Edition: September 2018
ISBN 978-1-62010-539-9
eISBN 978-1-62010-202-2

1 3 5 7 9 10 8 6 4 2

Library of Congress Control Number: 2018938815

STUMPTOWN, VOLUME 3: THE CASE OF THE KING OF CLUBS, September 2018. Published by Oni Press, Inc. 1319 SE Martin Luther King Jr. Blvd., Suite 240, Portland, OR 97214.

Chapter One

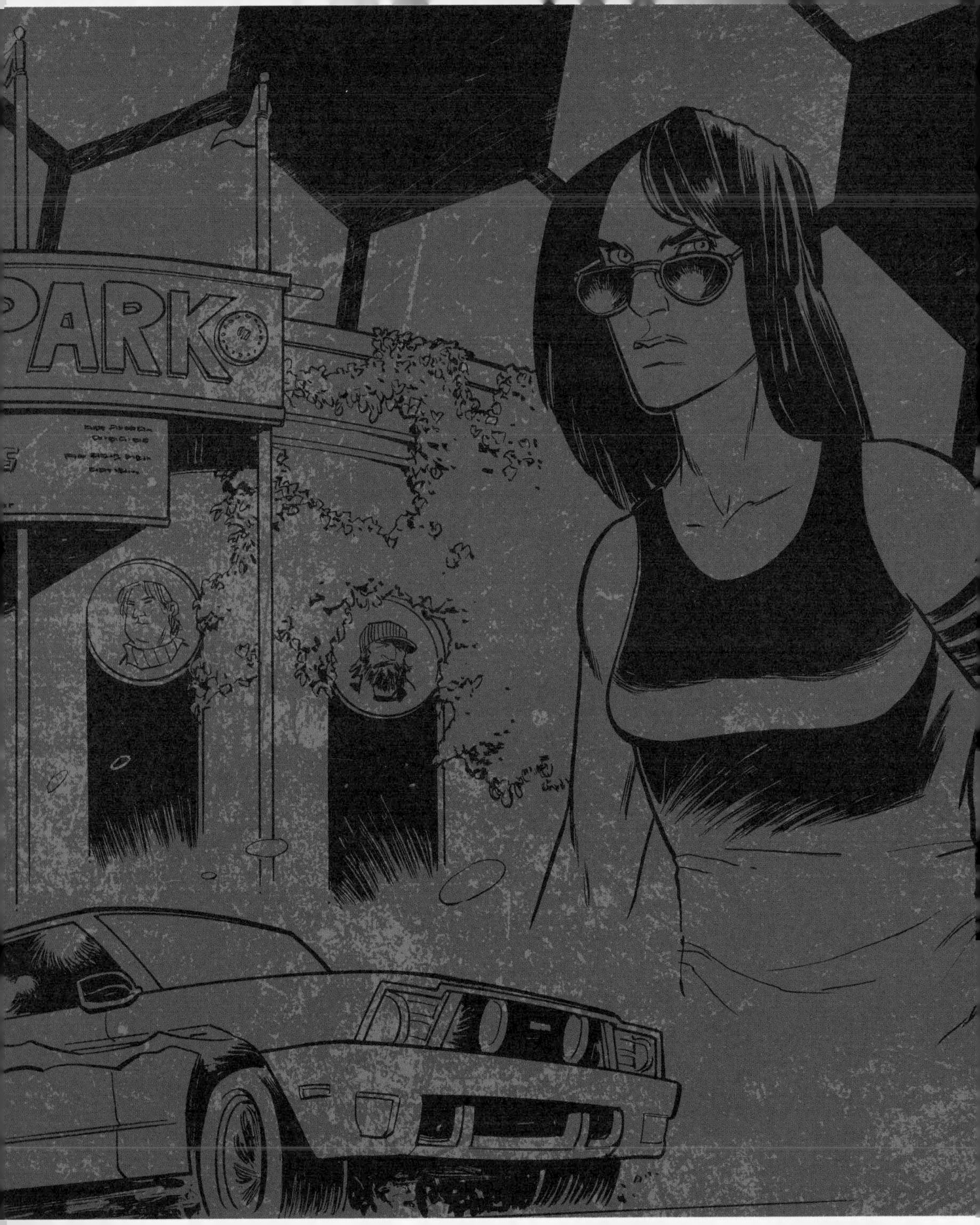
PARK

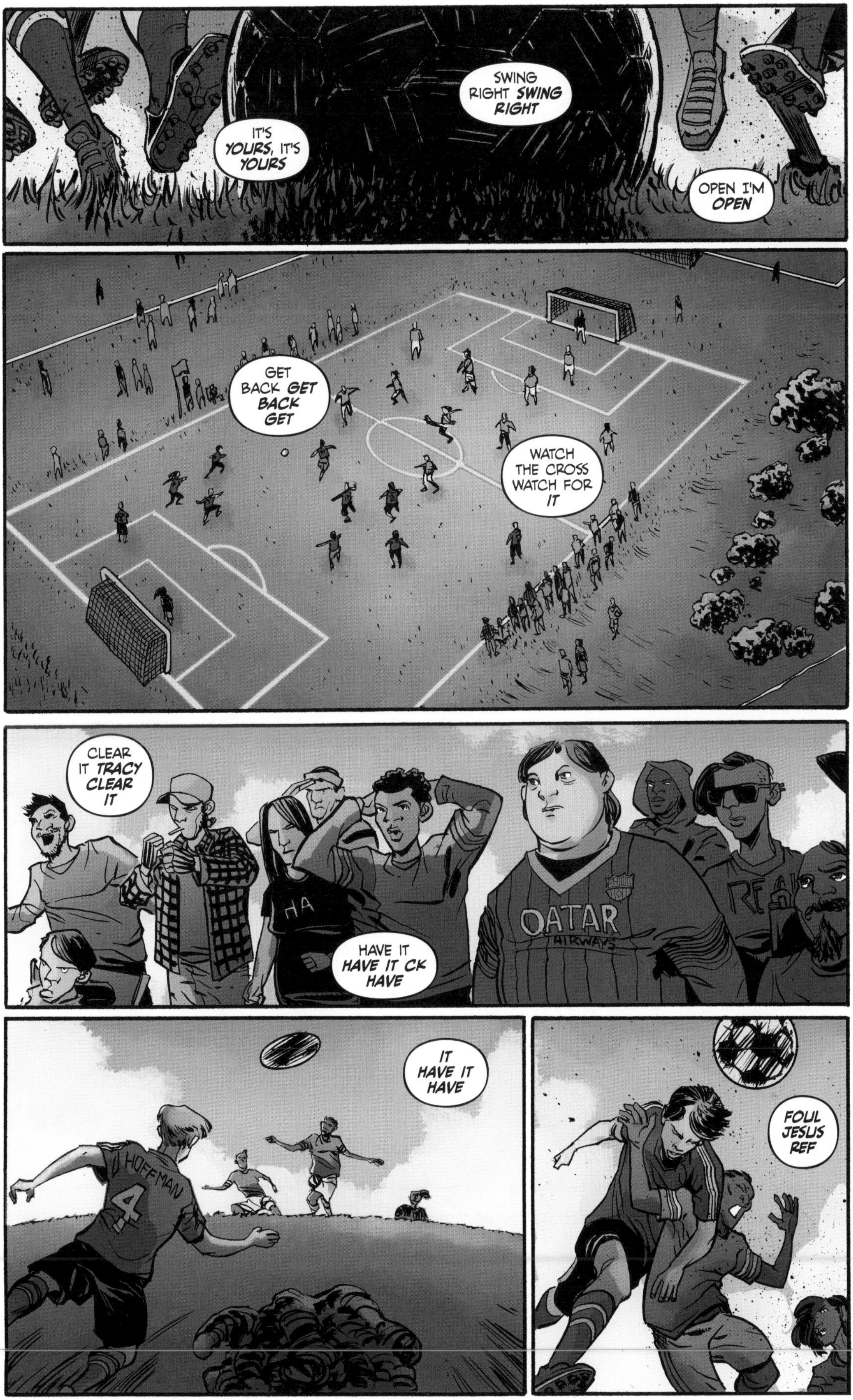

IT'S YOURS, IT'S YOURS
SWING RIGHT SWING RIGHT
OPEN I'M OPEN
GET BACK GET BACK GET
WATCH THE CROSS WATCH FOR IT
CLEAR IT TRACY CLEAR IT
HA
QATAR AIRWAYS
HAVE IT HAVE IT CK HAVE
IT HAVE IT HAVE
HOFFMAN 4
FOUL JESUS REF

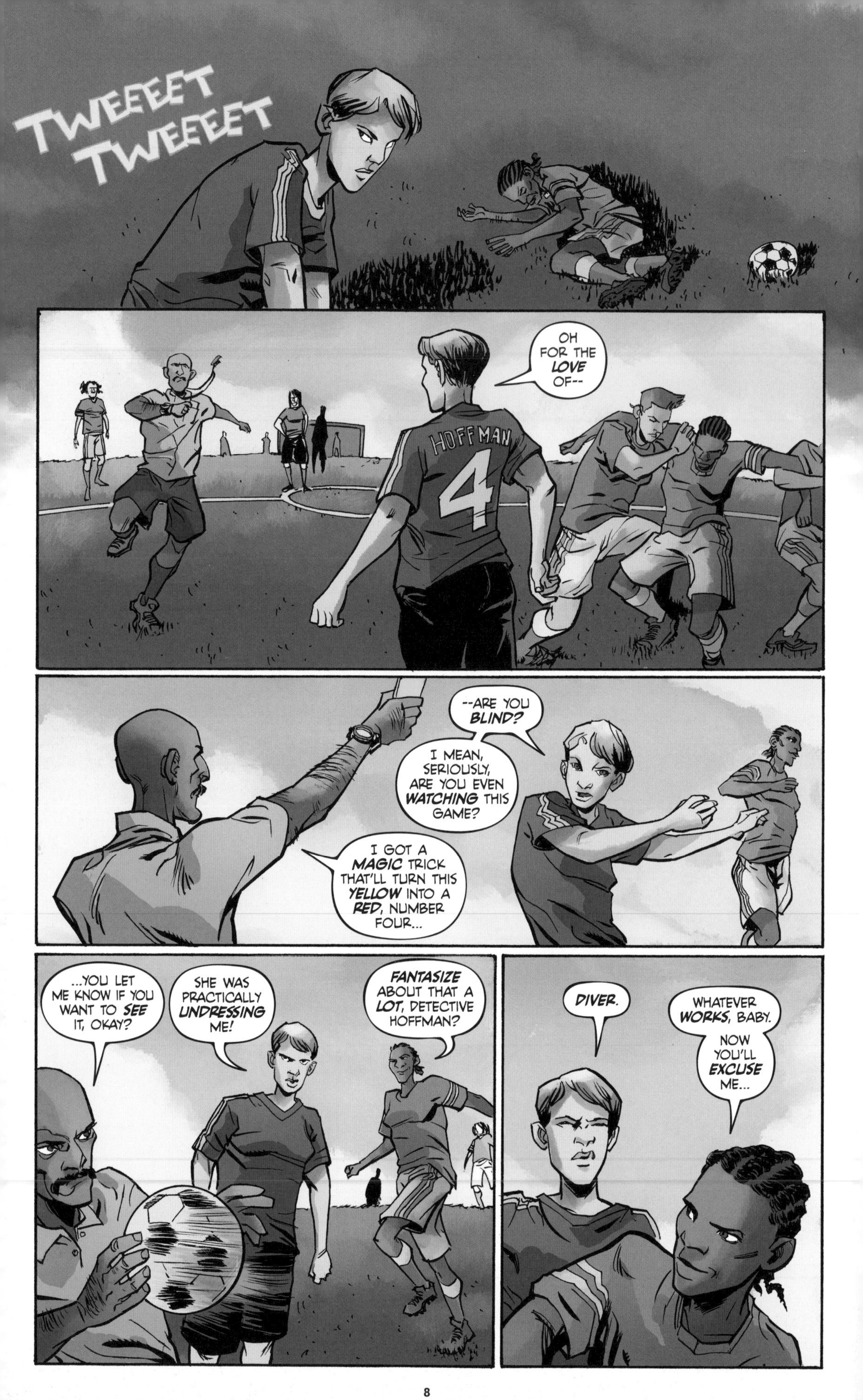
TWEEEET TWEEEET
HOFFMAN 4
OH FOR THE LOVE OF--
--ARE YOU BLIND?
I MEAN, SERIOUSLY, ARE YOU EVEN WATCHING THIS GAME?
I GOT A MAGIC TRICK THAT'LL TURN THIS YELLOW INTO A RED, NUMBER FOUR...
...YOU LET ME KNOW IF YOU WANT TO SEE IT, OKAY?
SHE WAS PRACTICALLY UNDRESSING ME!
FANTASIZE ABOUT THAT A LOT, DETECTIVE HOFFMAN?
DIVER.
WHATEVER WORKS, BABY.
NOW YOU'LL EXCUSE ME...

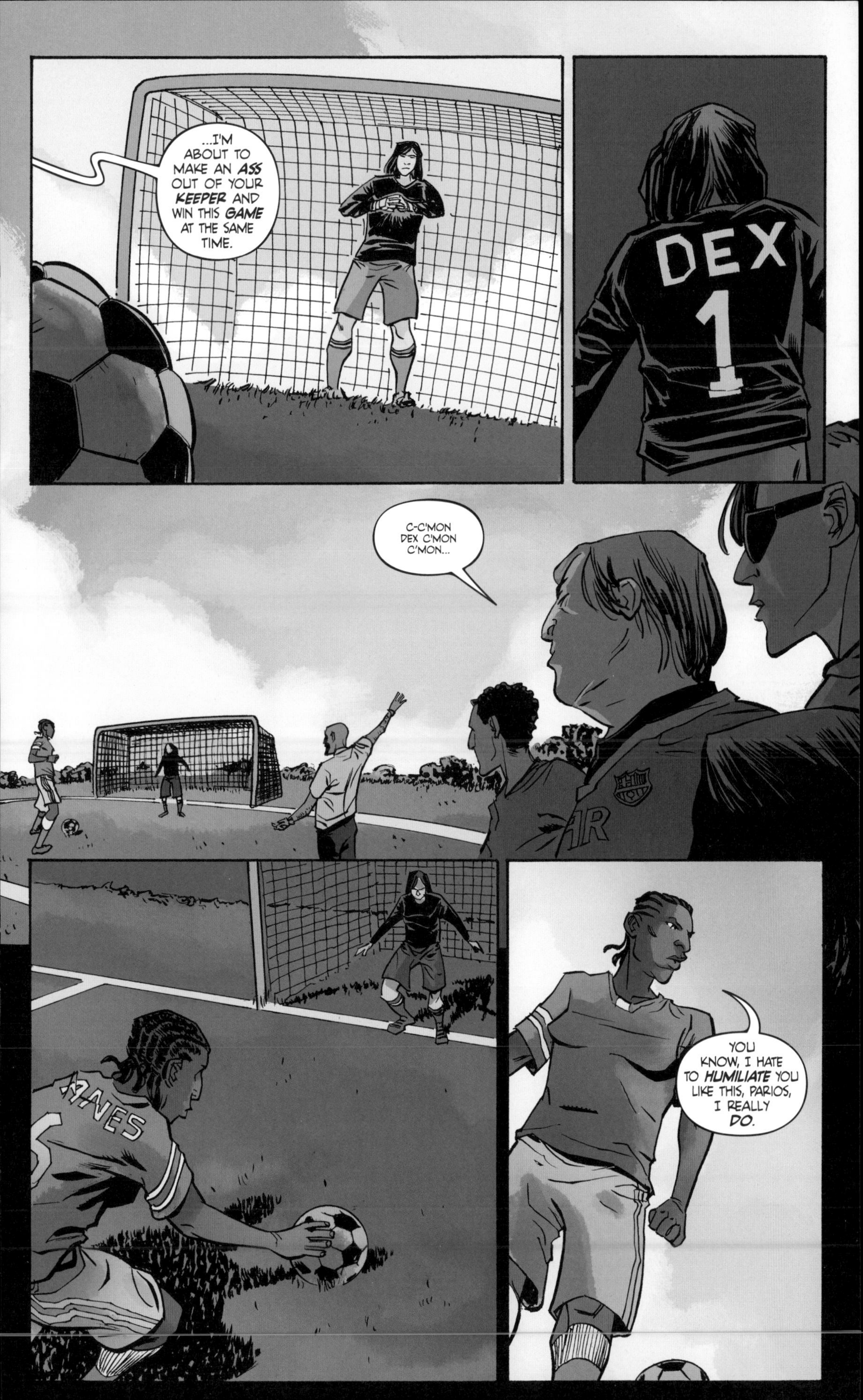
...I'M ABOUT TO MAKE AN ASS OUT OF YOUR KEEPER AND WIN THIS GAME AT THE SAME TIME.
DEX 1
C-C'MON DEX C'MON C'MON...
YOU KNOW, I HATE TO HUMILIATE YOU LIKE THIS, PARIOS, I REALLY DO.

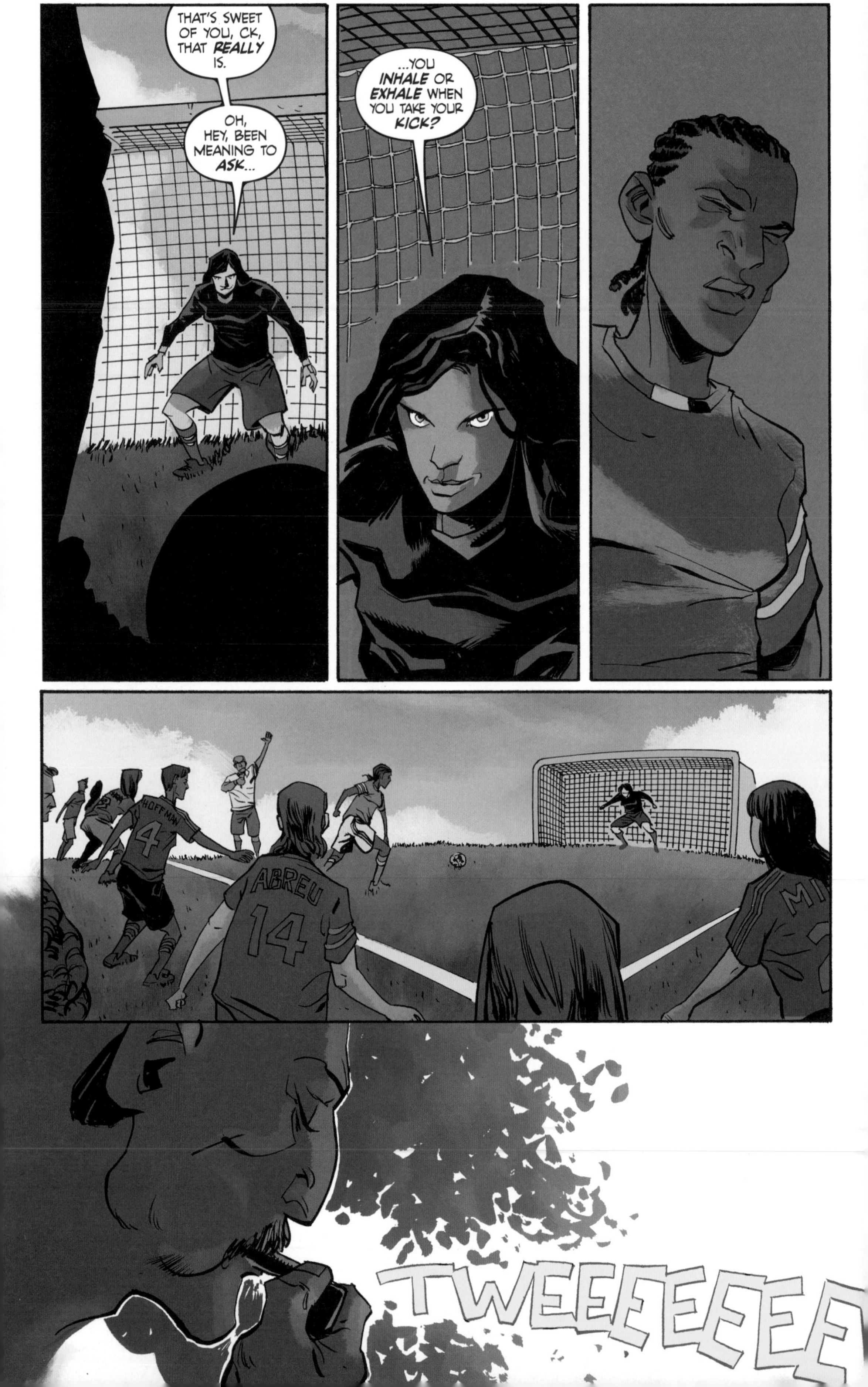
THAT'S SWEET OF YOU, CK, THAT REALLY IS.
OH, HEY, BEEN MEANING TO ASK...
...YOU INHALE OR EXHALE WHEN YOU TAKE YOUR KICK?
HOFFMAN 4
ABREU 14
TWEEEEEEE

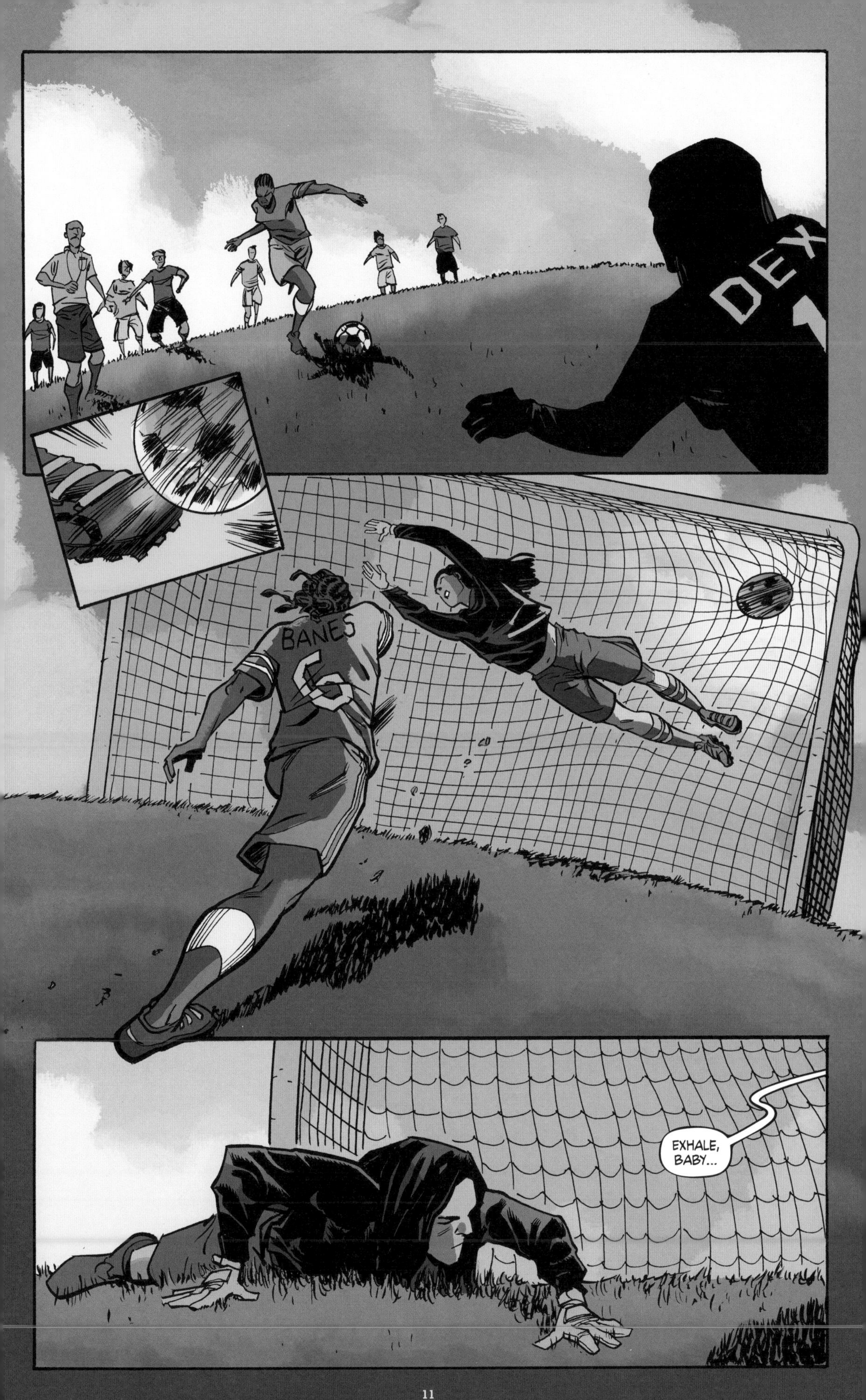
DEX
BANES
EXHALE, BABY...

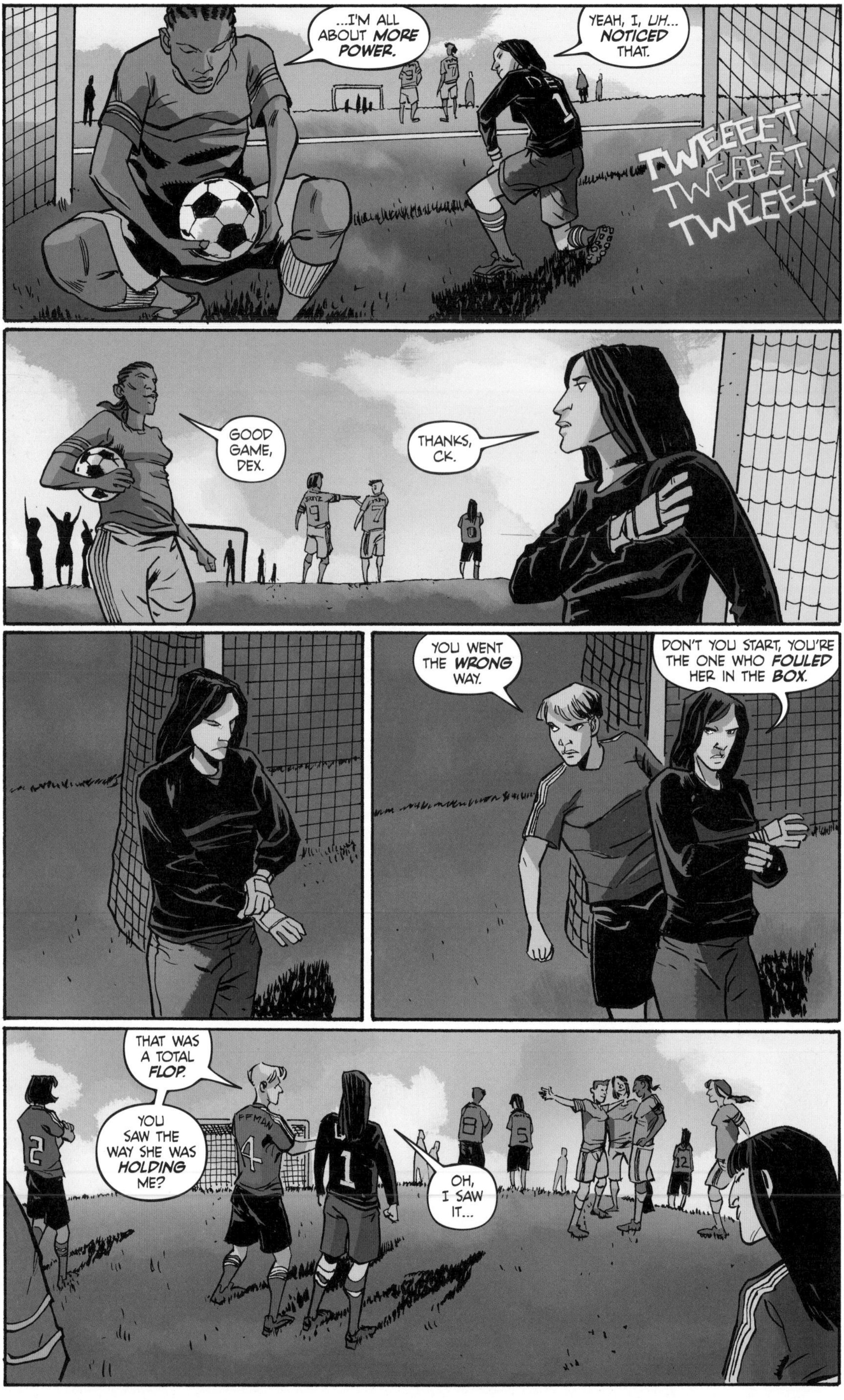
...I'M ALL ABOUT MORE POWER.
YEAH, I, UH... NOTICED THAT.
TWEEEET TWEEEET TWEEEET
GOOD GAME, DEX.
THANKS, CK.
YOU WENT THE WRONG WAY.
DON'T YOU START, YOU'RE THE ONE WHO FOULED HER IN THE BOX.
THAT WAS A TOTAL FLOP.
YOU SAW THE WAY SHE WAS HOLDING ME?
OH, I SAW IT...

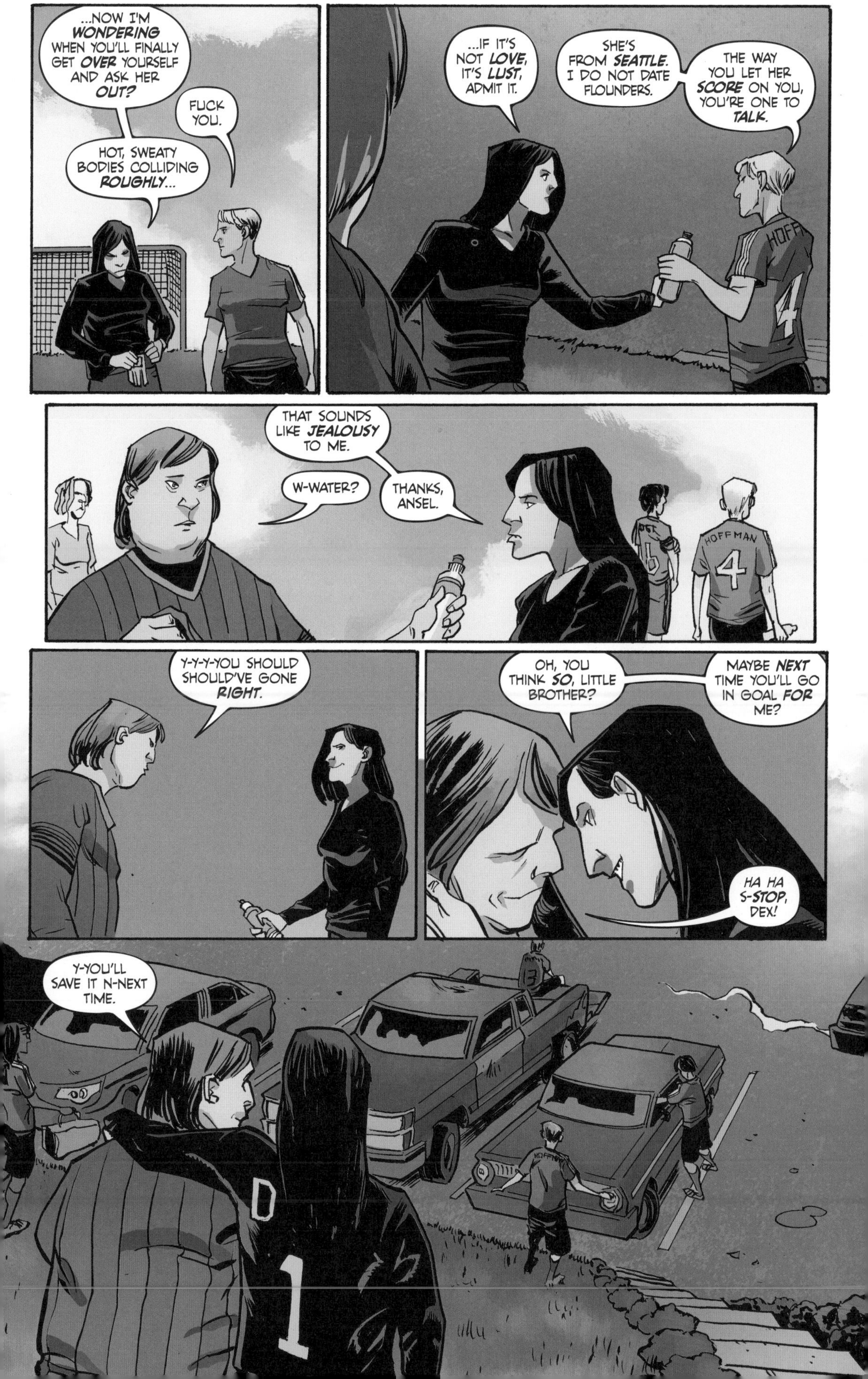

...NOW I'M WONDERING WHEN YOU'LL FINALLY GET OVER YOURSELF AND ASK HER OUT?
FUCK YOU.
HOT, SWEATY BODIES COLLIDING ROUGHLY...
...IF IT'S NOT LOVE, IT'S LUST, ADMIT IT.
SHE'S FROM SEATTLE. I DO NOT DATE FLOUNDERS.
THE WAY YOU LET HER SCORE ON YOU, YOU'RE ONE TO TALK.
HOFF
4
THAT SOUNDS LIKE JEALOUSY TO ME.
W-WATER?
THANKS, ANSEL.
HOFFMAN
4
Y-Y-Y-YOU SHOULD SHOULD'VE GONE RIGHT.
OH, YOU THINK SO, LITTLE BROTHER?
MAYBE NEXT TIME YOU'LL GO IN GOAL FOR ME?
HA HA S-STOP, DEX!
Y-YOU'LL SAVE IT N-NEXT TIME.
D
1

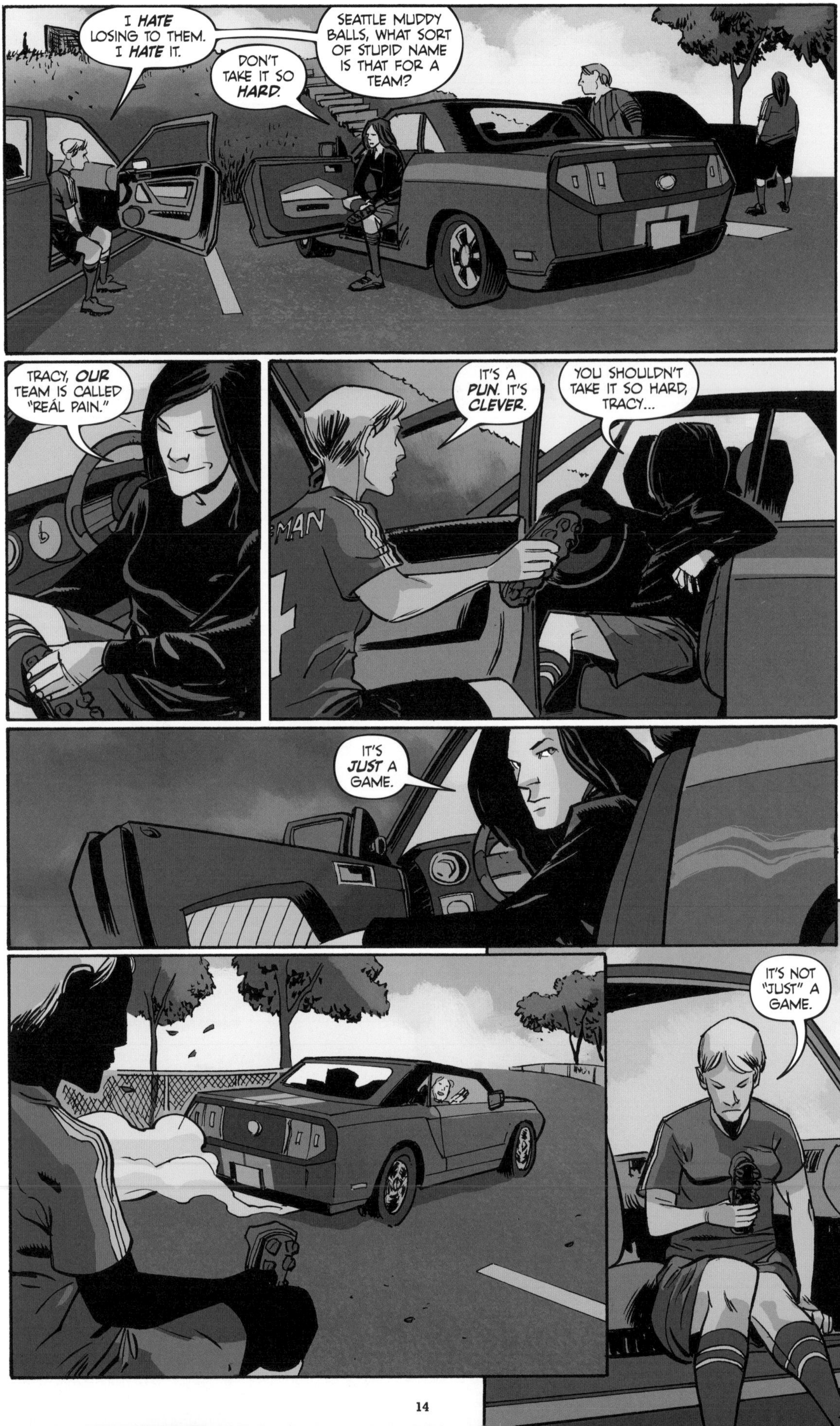
I HATE LOSING TO THEM. I HATE IT.
SEATTLE MUDDY BALLS, WHAT SORT OF STUPID NAME IS THAT FOR A TEAM?
DON'T TAKE IT SO HARD.
TRACY, OUR TEAM IS CALLED "REÁL PAIN."
IT'S A PUN. IT'S CLEVER.
YOU SHOULDN'T TAKE IT SO HARD, TRACY...
MAN
IT'S JUST A GAME.
IT'S NOT "JUST" A GAME.

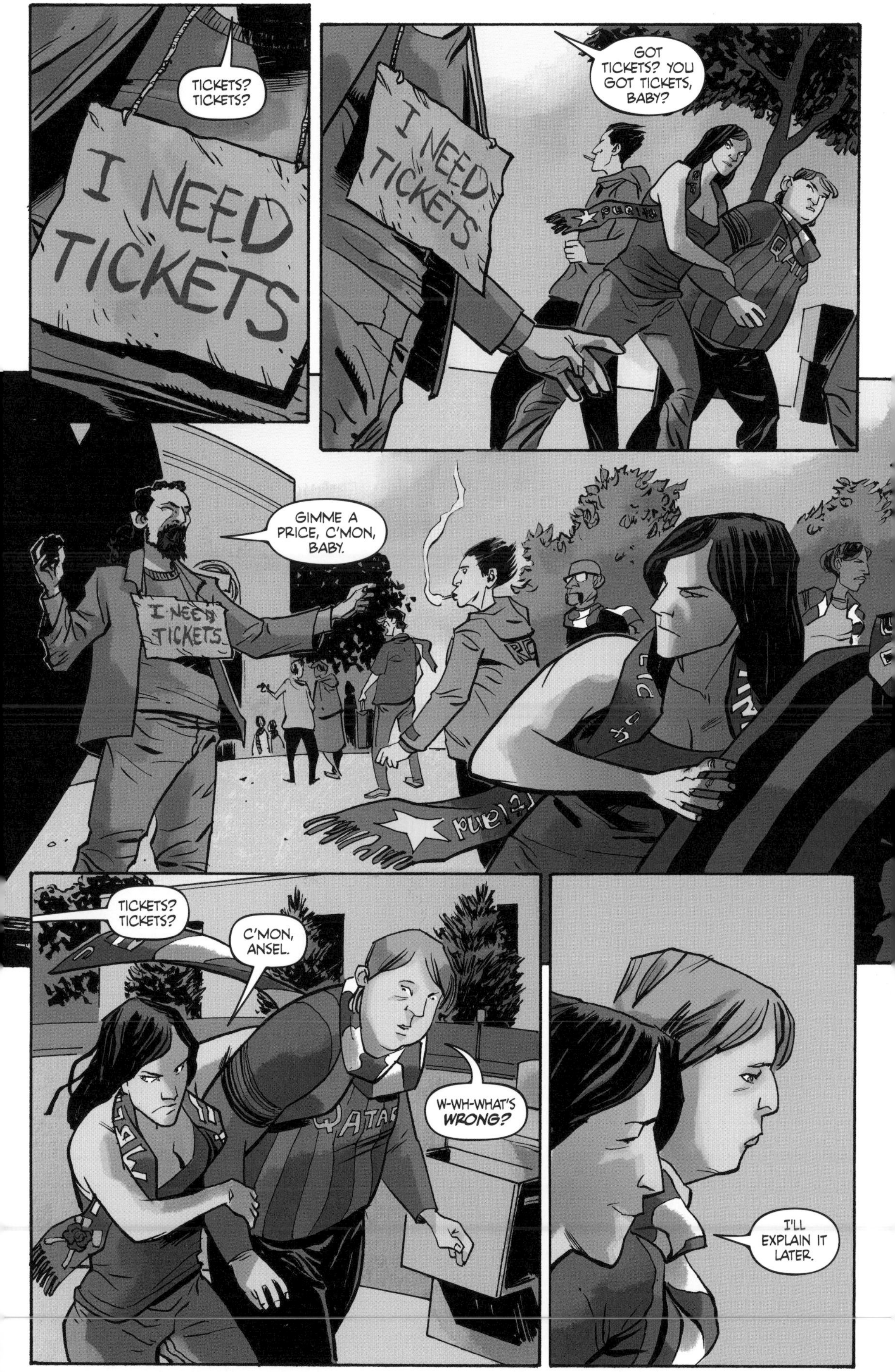
I NEED TICKETS
TICKETS? TICKETS?
I NEED TICKETS
GOT TICKETS? YOU GOT TICKETS, BABY?
GIMME A PRICE, C'MON, BABY.
I NEED TICKETS
TICKETS? TICKETS?
C'MON, ANSEL.
QATAR
W-WH-WHAT'S *WRONG?*
I'LL EXPLAIN IT LATER.

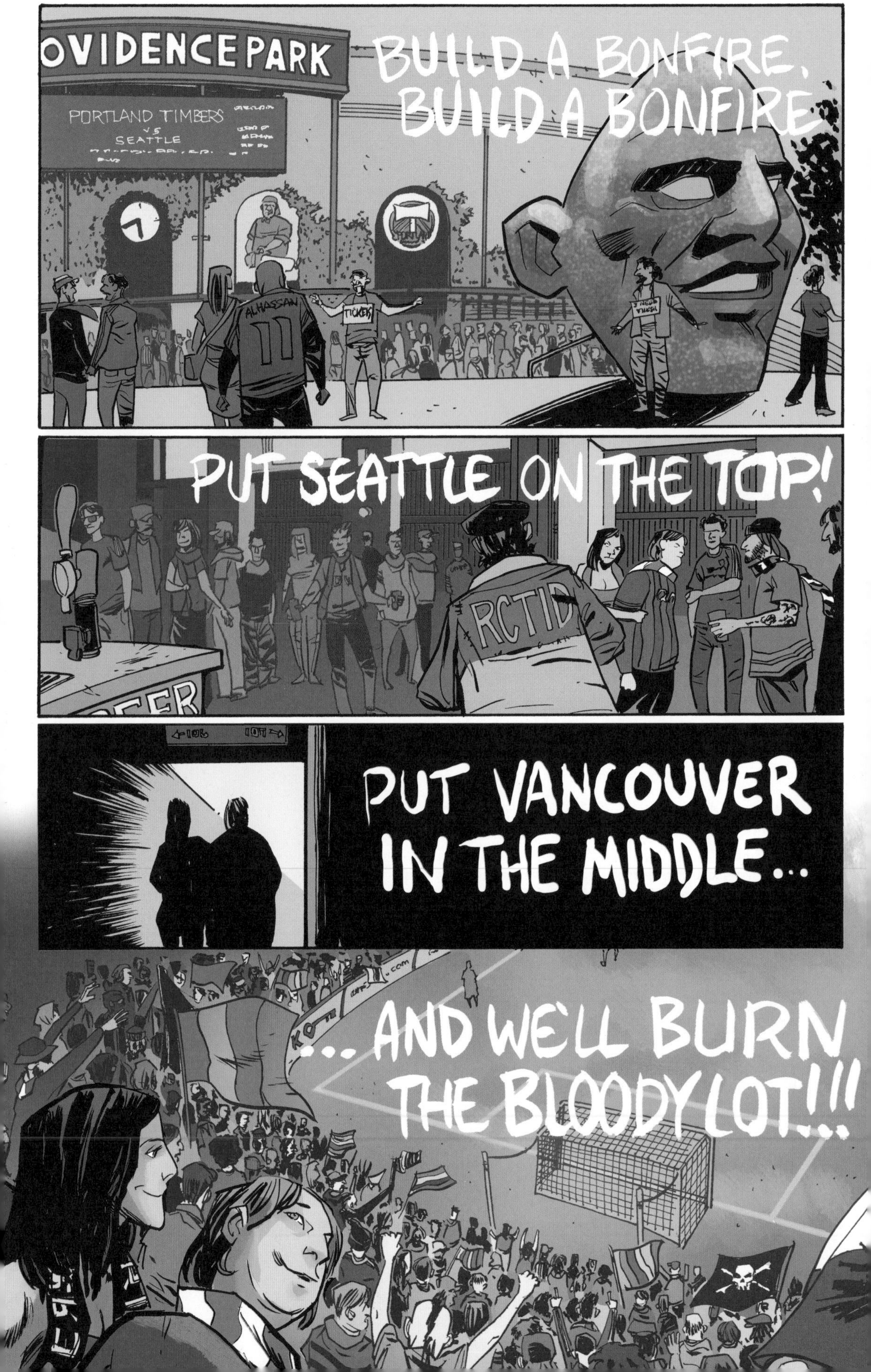
OVIDENCE PARK
PORTLAND TIMBERS
VS
SEATTLE
BUILD A BONFIRE,
BUILD A BONFIRE
ALHASSAN
11
PUT SEATTLE ON THE TOP!
RCTID
PUT VANCOUVER
IN THE MIDDLE...
...AND WE'LL BURN
THE BLOODY LOT!!!

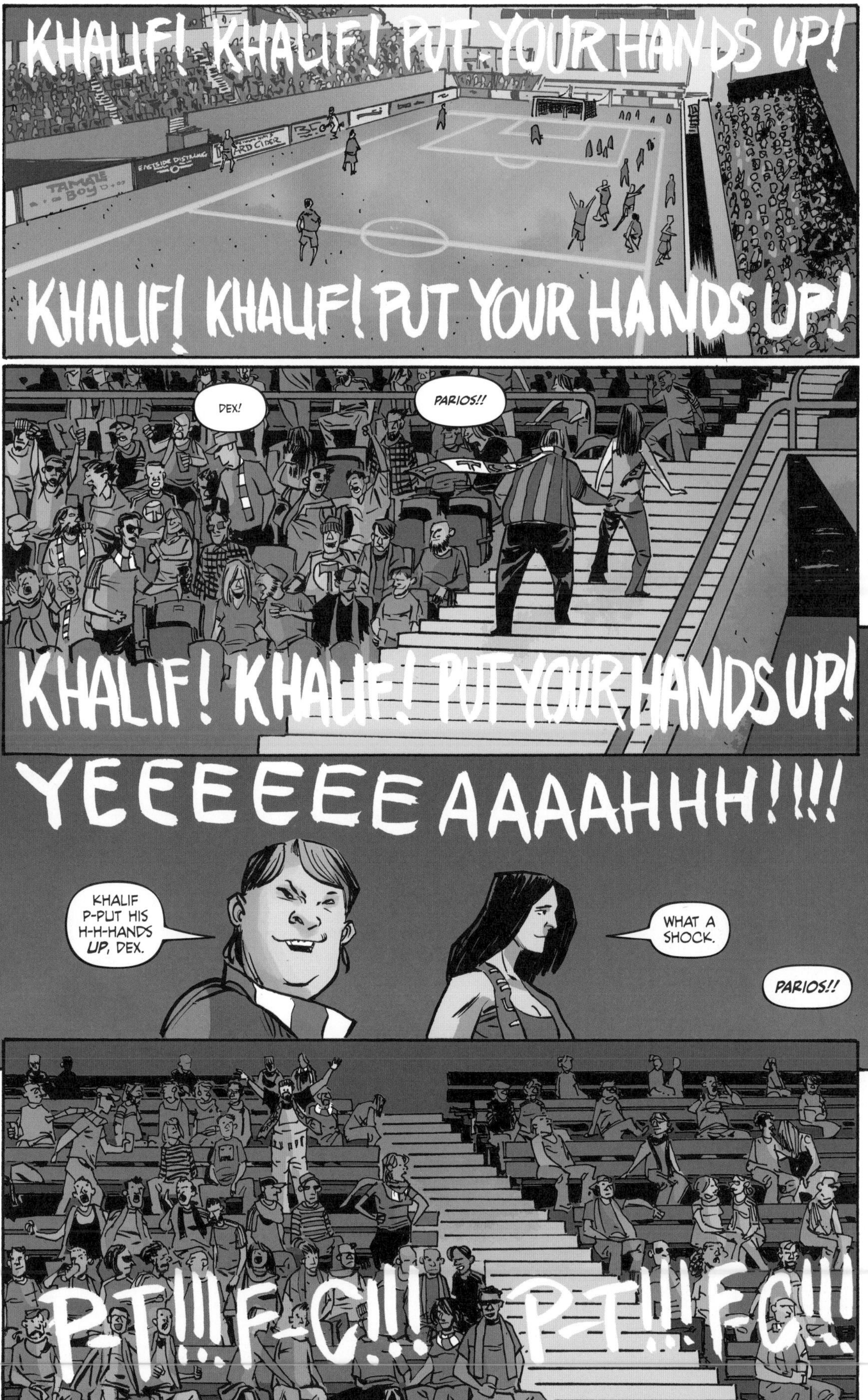
KHALIF! KHALIF! PUT YOUR HANDS UP!
KHALIF! KHALIF! PUT YOUR HANDS UP!
DEX!
PARIOS!!
KHALIF! KHALIF! PUT YOUR HANDS UP!
YEEEEEE AAAAHHH!!!!
KHALIF P-PUT HIS H-H-HANDS *UP*, DEX.
WHAT A SHOCK.
PARIOS!!
P-T!!! F-C!!! P-T!!! F-C!!!

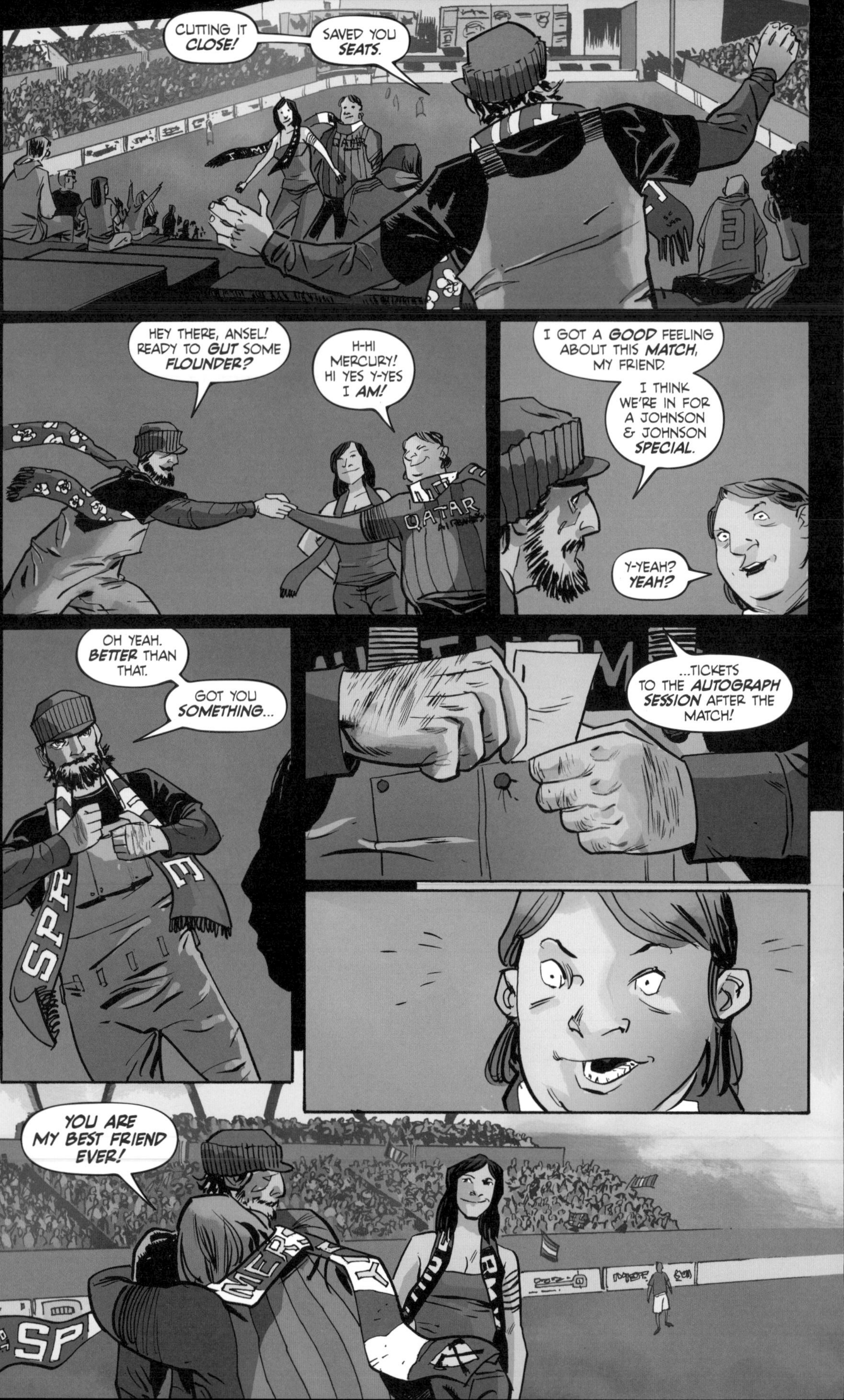
CUTTING IT CLOSE!
SAVED YOU SEATS.
HEY THERE, ANSEL! READY TO GUT SOME FLOUNDER?
H-HI MERCURY! HI YES Y-YES I AM!
QATAR
I GOT A GOOD FEELING ABOUT THIS MATCH, MY FRIEND.
I THINK WE'RE IN FOR A JOHNSON & JOHNSON SPECIAL.
Y-YEAH? YEAH?
OH YEAH. BETTER THAN THAT.
GOT YOU SOMETHING...
...TICKETS TO THE AUTOGRAPH SESSION AFTER THE MATCH!
YOU ARE MY BEST FRIEND EVER!

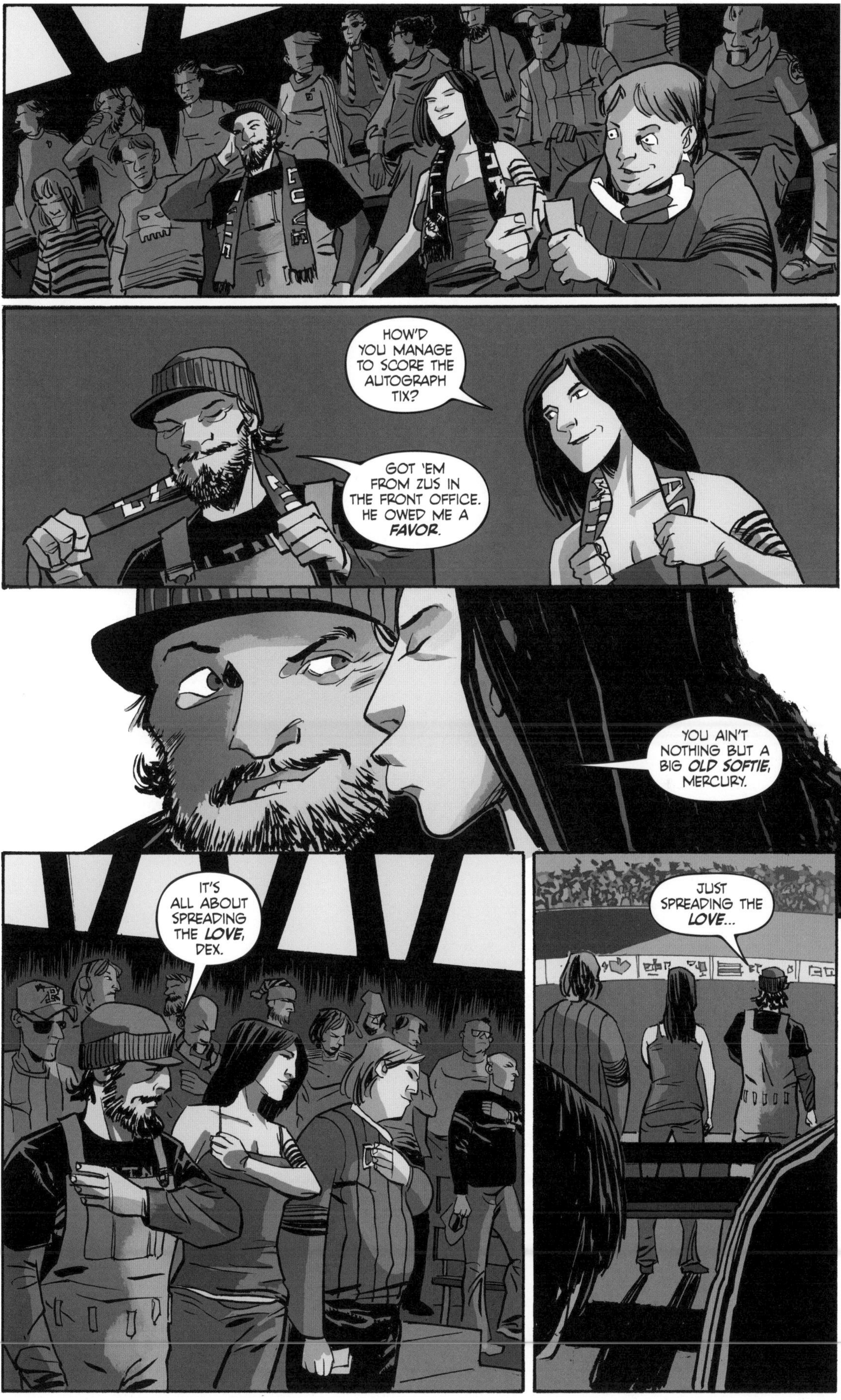
HOW'D YOU MANAGE TO SCORE THE AUTOGRAPH TIX?
GOT 'EM FROM ZUS IN THE FRONT OFFICE. HE OWED ME A *FAVOR*.
YOU AIN'T NOTHING BUT A BIG *OLD SOFTIE*, MERCURY.
IT'S ALL ABOUT SPREADING THE *LOVE*, DEX.
JUST SPREADING THE *LOVE*...

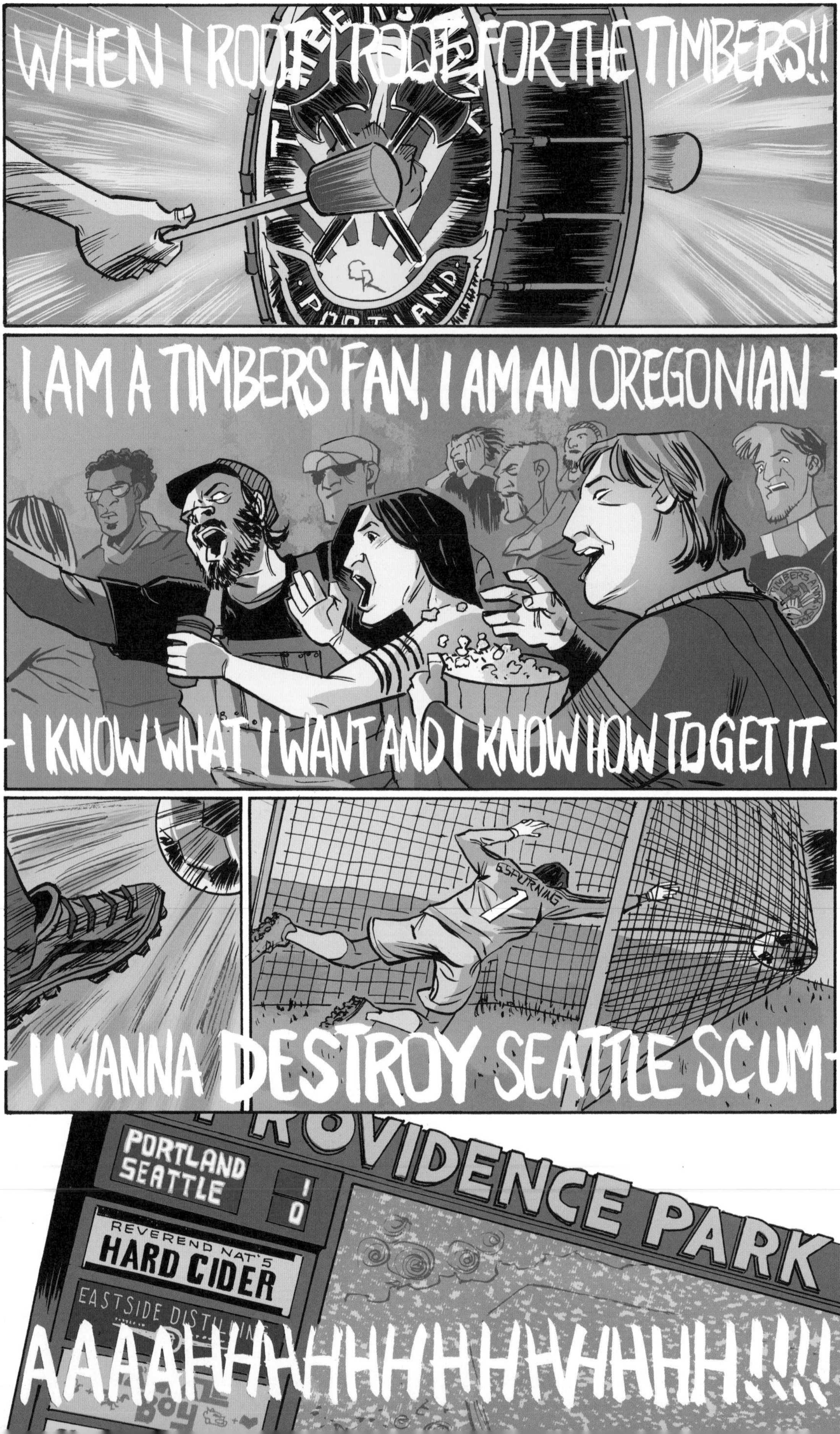
WHEN I ROOT I ROOT FOR THE TIMBERS!!
I AM A TIMBERS FAN, I AM AN OREGONIAN -
- I KNOW WHAT I WANT AND I KNOW HOW TO GET IT -
- I WANNA DESTROY SEATTLE SCUM -
ROVIDENCE PARK
PORTLAND 1
SEATTLE 0
REVEREND NAT'S HARD CIDER
EASTSIDE DISTIL
AAAHHHHHHHHHHHHHH!!!!

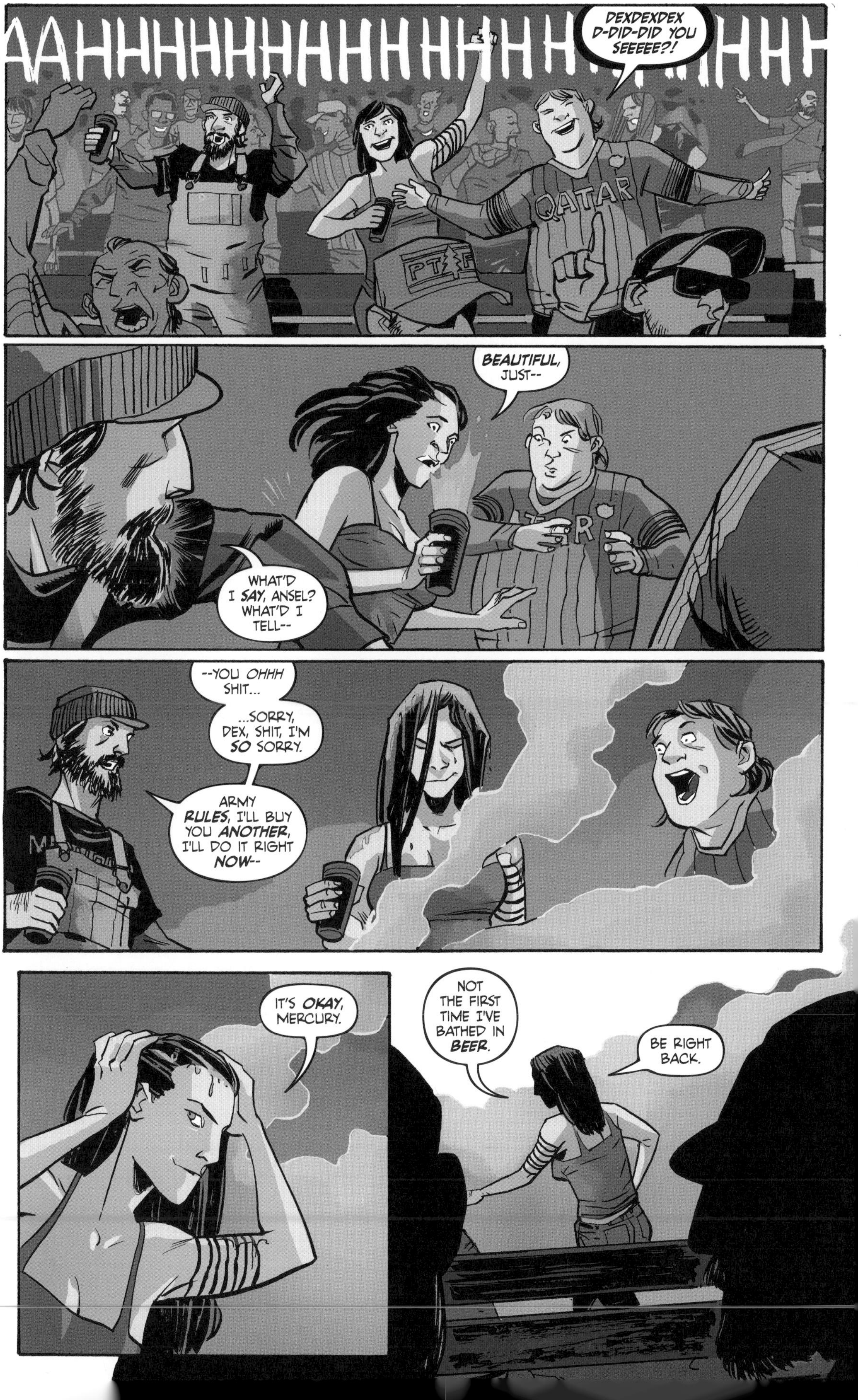
AAHHHHHHHHHHHHHHHHHHHHH
DEXDEXDEX D-DID-DID YOU SEEEEE?!
BEAUTIFUL, JUST--
WHAT'D I SAY, ANSEL? WHAT'D I TELL--
--YOU OHHH SHIT...
...SORRY, DEX, SHIT, I'M SO SORRY.
ARMY RULES, I'LL BUY YOU ANOTHER, I'LL DO IT RIGHT NOW--
IT'S OKAY, MERCURY.
NOT THE FIRST TIME I'VE BATHED IN BEER.
BE RIGHT BACK.

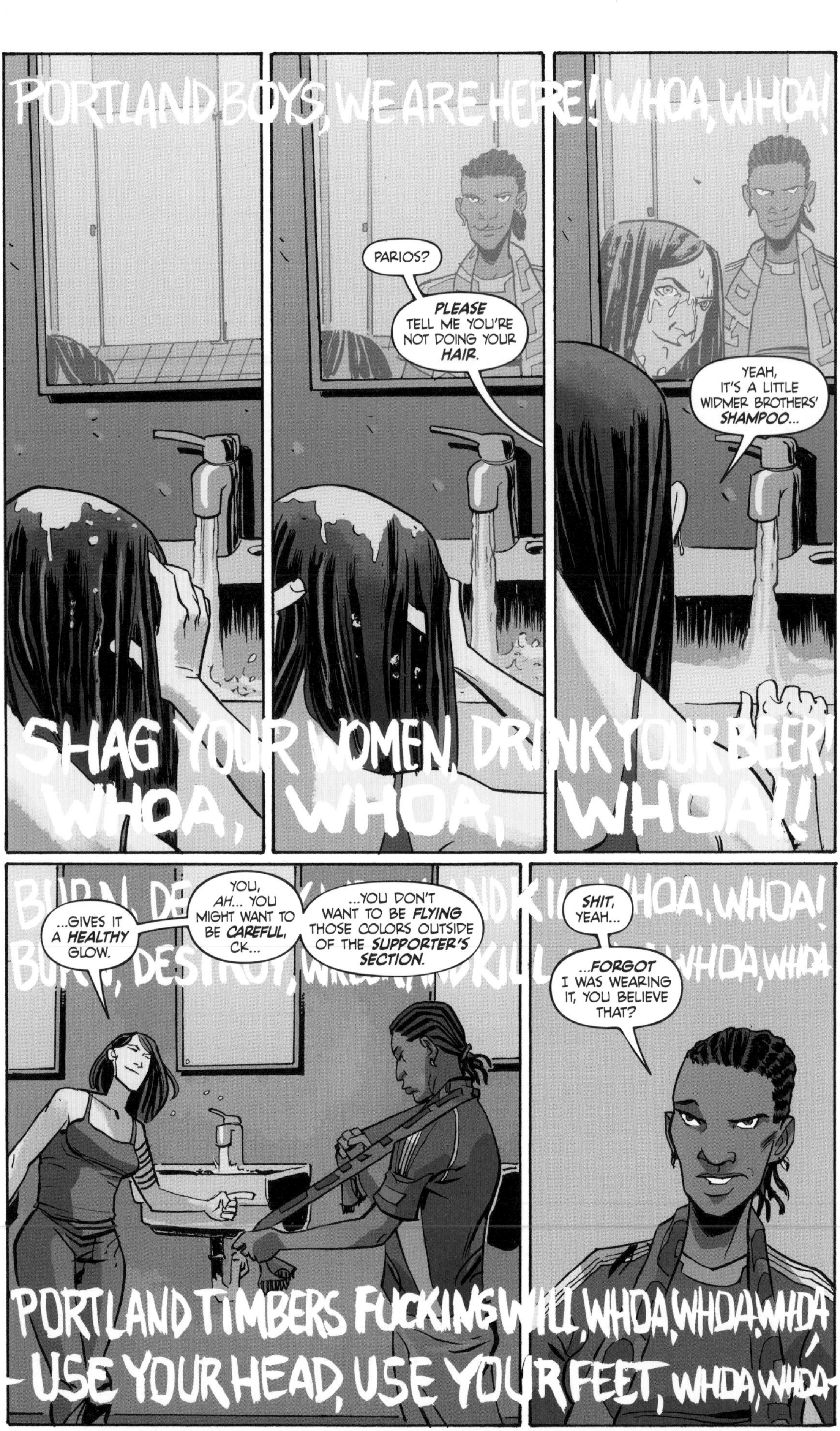
PORTLAND BOYS, WE ARE HERE! WHOA, WHOA!
PARIOS?
PLEASE TELL ME YOU'RE NOT DOING YOUR HAIR.
YEAH, IT'S A LITTLE WIDMER BROTHERS' SHAMPOO...
SHAG YOUR WOMEN, DRINK YOUR BEER! WHOA, WHOA, WHOA!!
...GIVES IT A HEALTHY GLOW.
YOU, AH... YOU MIGHT WANT TO BE CAREFUL, CK...
...YOU DON'T WANT TO BE FLYING THOSE COLORS OUTSIDE OF THE SUPPORTER'S SECTION.
SHIT, YEAH...
...FORGOT I WAS WEARING IT, YOU BELIEVE THAT?
PORTLAND TIMBERS FUCKING WILL, WHOA, WHOA, WHOA
USE YOUR HEAD, USE YOUR FEET, WHOA, WHOA

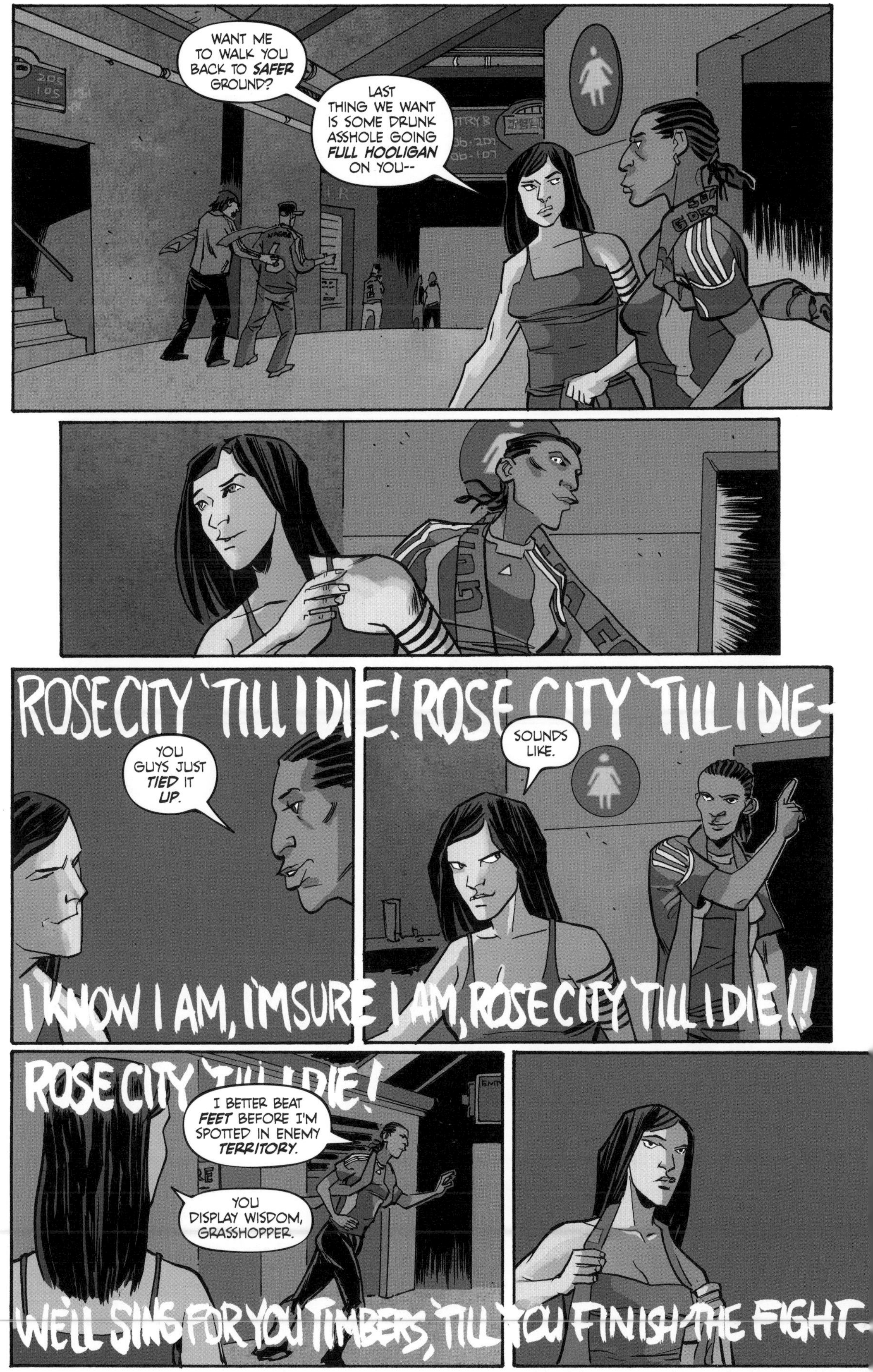
WANT ME TO WALK YOU BACK TO SAFER GROUND?
LAST THING WE WANT IS SOME DRUNK ASSHOLE GOING FULL HOOLIGAN ON YOU--
ROSE CITY 'TILL I DIE! ROSE CITY 'TILL I DIE-
YOU GUYS JUST TIED IT UP.
SOUNDS LIKE.
I KNOW I AM, I'M SURE I AM, ROSE CITY 'TILL I DIE!!
ROSE CITY 'TILL I DIE!
I BETTER BEAT FEET BEFORE I'M SPOTTED IN ENEMY TERRITORY.
YOU DISPLAY WISDOM, GRASSHOPPER.
WE'LL SING FOR YOU TIMBERS, 'TILL YOU FINISH THE FIGHT-

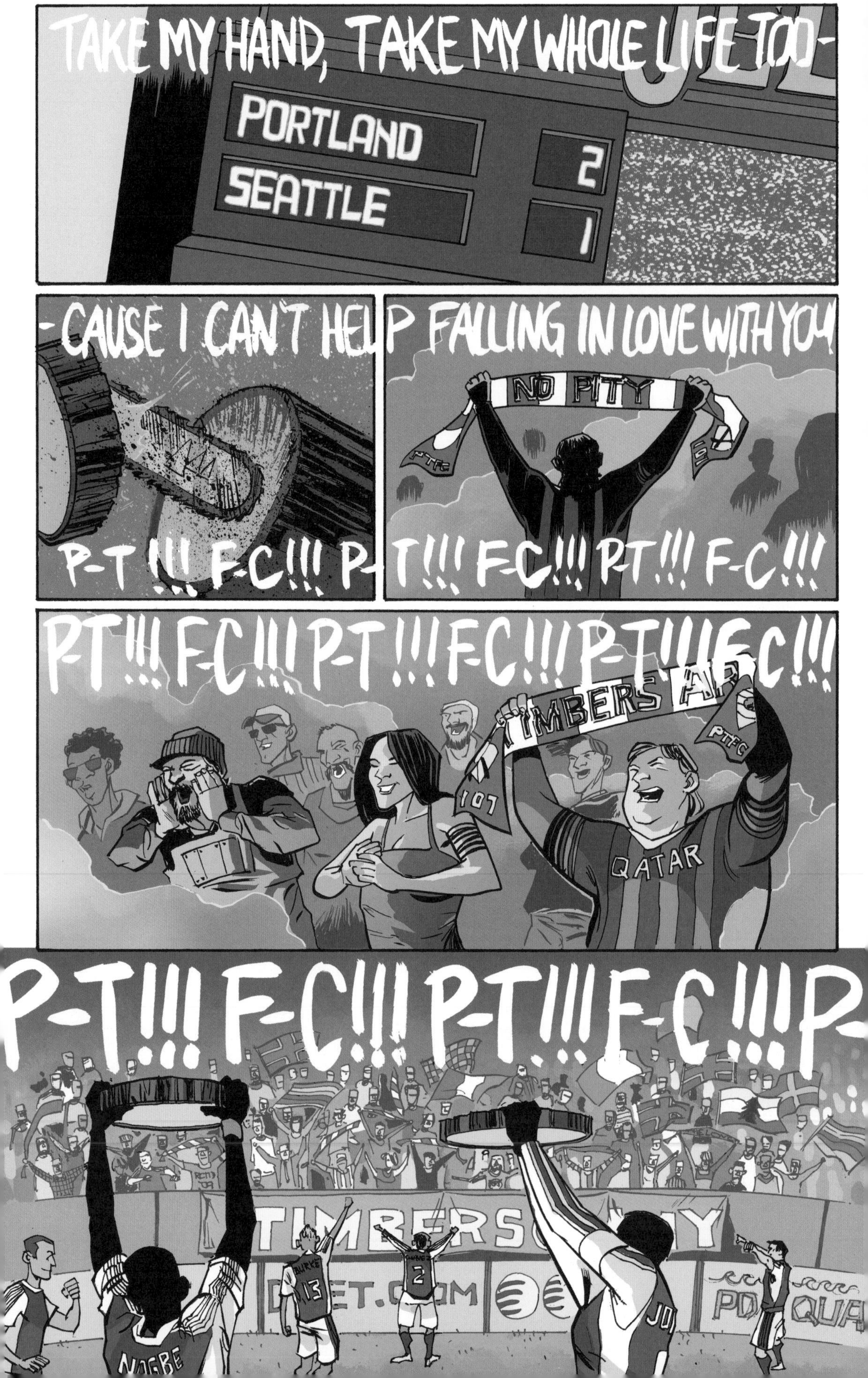
TAKE MY HAND, TAKE MY WHOLE LIFE TOO-
PORTLAND 2
SEATTLE 1
-CAUSE I CAN'T HELP FALLING IN LOVE WITH YOU!
NO PITY
PTFC
P-T!!! F-C!!! P-T!!! F-C!!! P-T!!! F-C!!!
P-T!!! F-C!!! P-T!!! F-C!!! P-T!!! F-C!!!
TIMBERS AR
PTFC
107
QATAR
P-T!!! F-C!!! P-T!!! F-C!!! P-
TIMBERS
BURKE
13
2
NAGBE

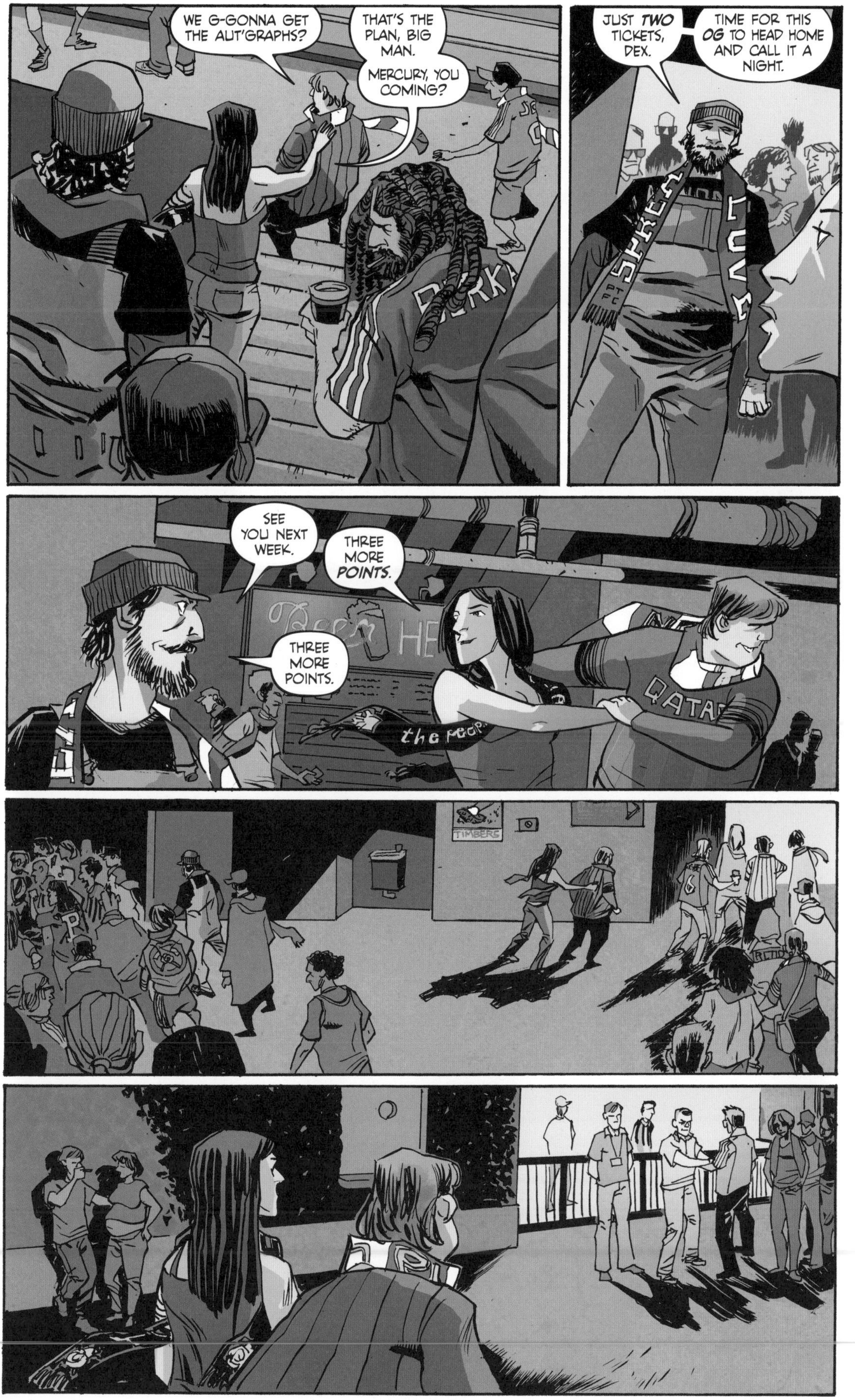
WE G-GONNA GET THE AUT'GRAPHS?
THAT'S THE PLAN, BIG MAN.
MERCURY, YOU COMING?
JUST TWO TICKETS, DEX.
TIME FOR THIS OG TO HEAD HOME AND CALL IT A NIGHT.
SEE YOU NEXT WEEK.
THREE MORE POINTS.
THREE MORE POINTS.
TIMBERS

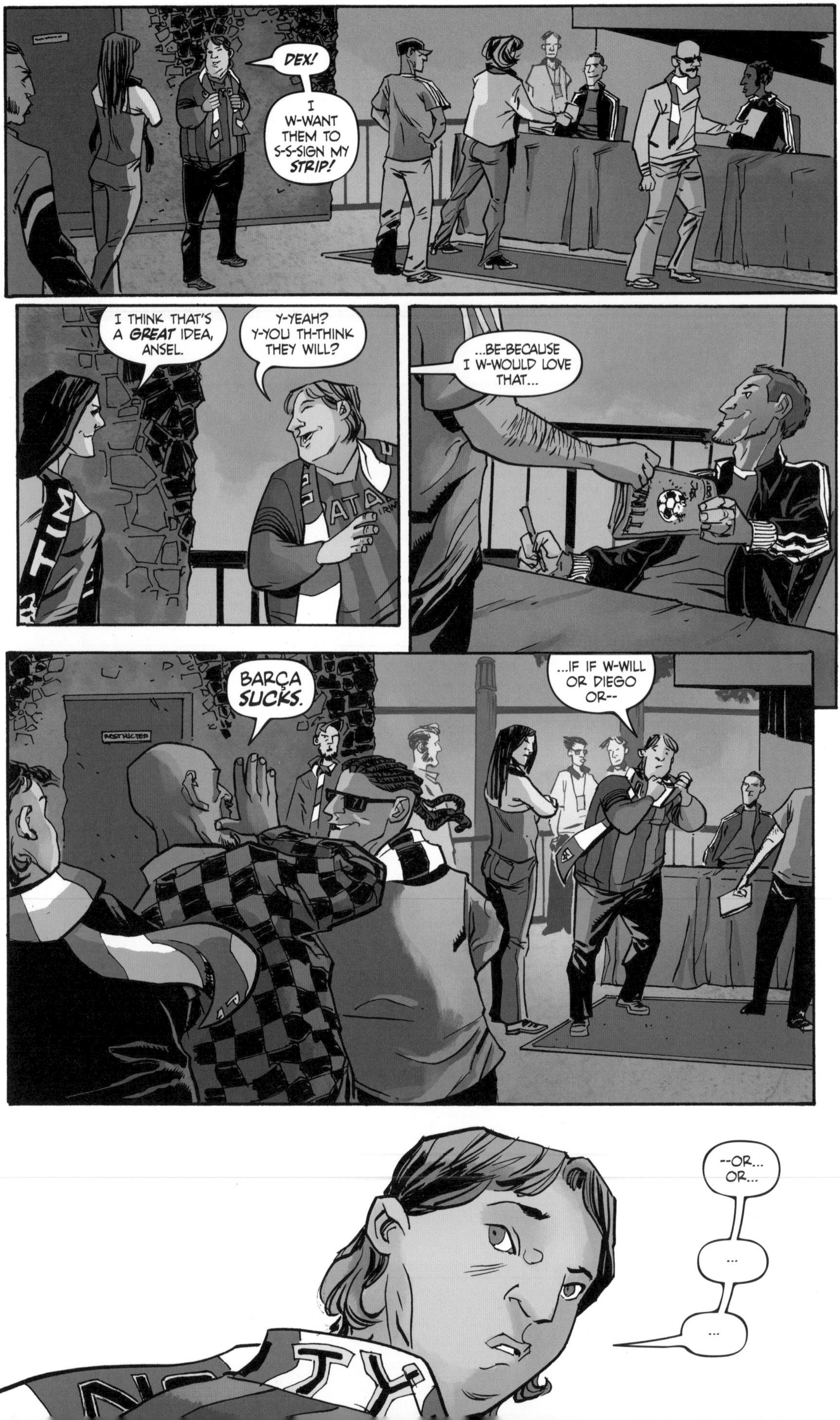
DEX!
I W-WANT THEM TO S-S-SIGN MY STRIP!
I THINK THAT'S A GREAT IDEA, ANSEL.
Y-YEAH? Y-YOU TH-THINK THEY WILL?
...BE-BECAUSE I W-WOULD LOVE THAT...
RESTRICTED
BARÇA SUCKS.
...IF IF W-WILL OR DIEGO OR--
--OR... OR...
...
...

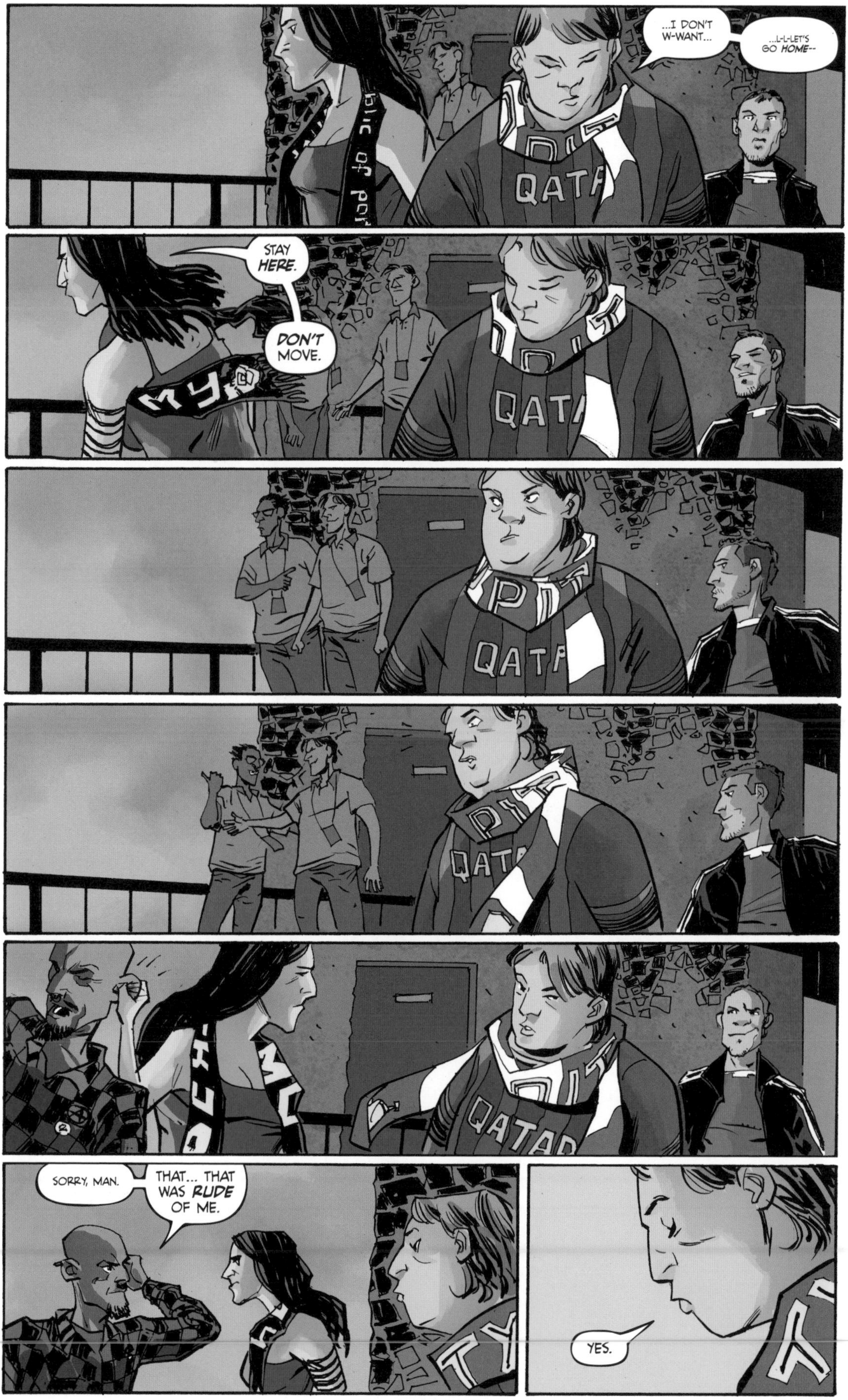
...I DON'T W-WANT...
...L-L-LET'S GO HOME--
STAY HERE.
DON'T MOVE.
QATAR
SORRY, MAN.
THAT... THAT WAS RUDE OF ME.
YES.

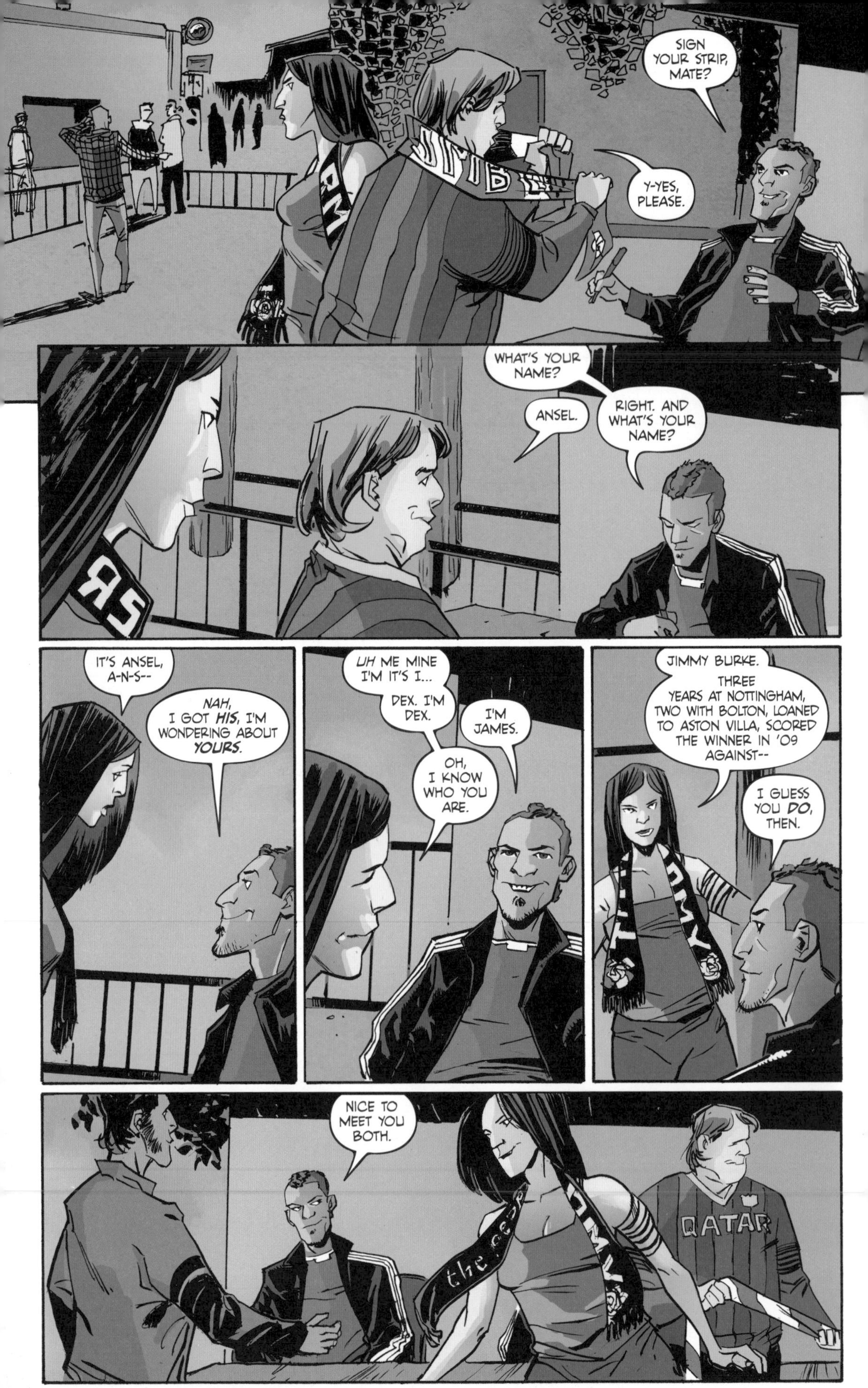
SIGN YOUR STRIP, MATE?
Y-YES, PLEASE.
WHAT'S YOUR NAME?
ANSEL.
RIGHT. AND WHAT'S YOUR NAME?
IT'S ANSEL, A-N-S--
NAH, I GOT HIS, I'M WONDERING ABOUT YOURS.
UH ME MINE I'M IT'S I...
DEX. I'M DEX.
I'M JAMES.
OH, I KNOW WHO YOU ARE.
JIMMY BURKE.
THREE YEARS AT NOTTINGHAM, TWO WITH BOLTON, LOANED TO ASTON VILLA, SCORED THE WINNER IN '09 AGAINST--
I GUESS YOU DO, THEN.
NICE TO MEET YOU BOTH.
QATAR

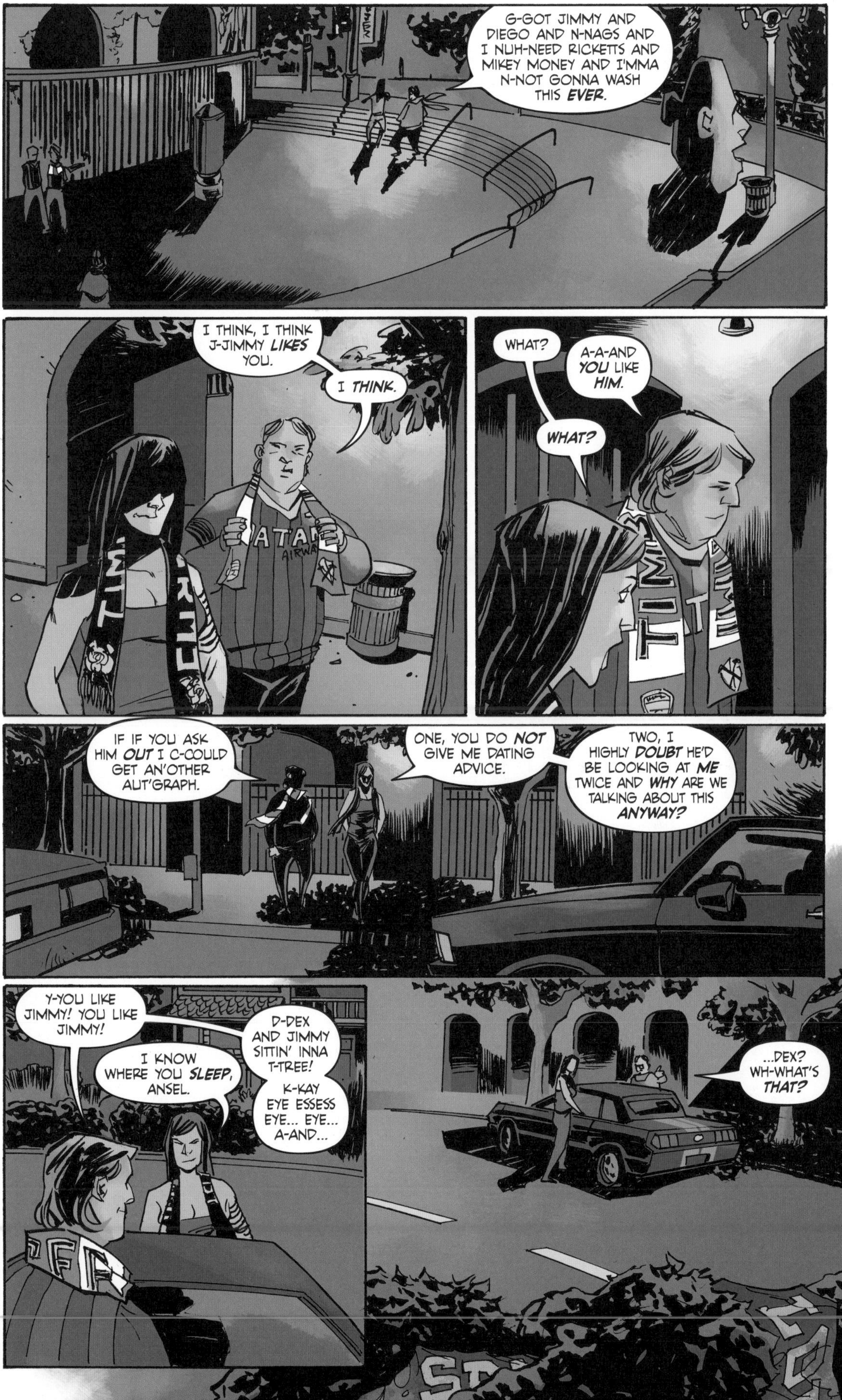
G-GOT JIMMY AND DIEGO AND N-NAGS AND I NUH-NEED RICKETTS AND MIKEY MONEY AND I'MMA N-NOT GONNA WASH THIS EVER.
I THINK, I THINK J-JIMMY LIKES YOU.
I THINK.
WHAT?
A-A-AND YOU LIKE HIM.
WHAT?
IF IF YOU ASK HIM OUT I C-COULD GET AN'OTHER AUT'GRAPH.
ONE, YOU DO NOT GIVE ME DATING ADVICE.
TWO, I HIGHLY DOUBT HE'D BE LOOKING AT ME TWICE AND WHY ARE WE TALKING ABOUT THIS ANYWAY?
Y-YOU LIKE JIMMY! YOU LIKE JIMMY!
D-DEX AND JIMMY SITTIN' INNA T-TREE!
I KNOW WHERE YOU SLEEP, ANSEL.
K-KAY EYE ESSESS EYE... EYE... A-AND...
...DEX? WH-WHAT'S THAT?

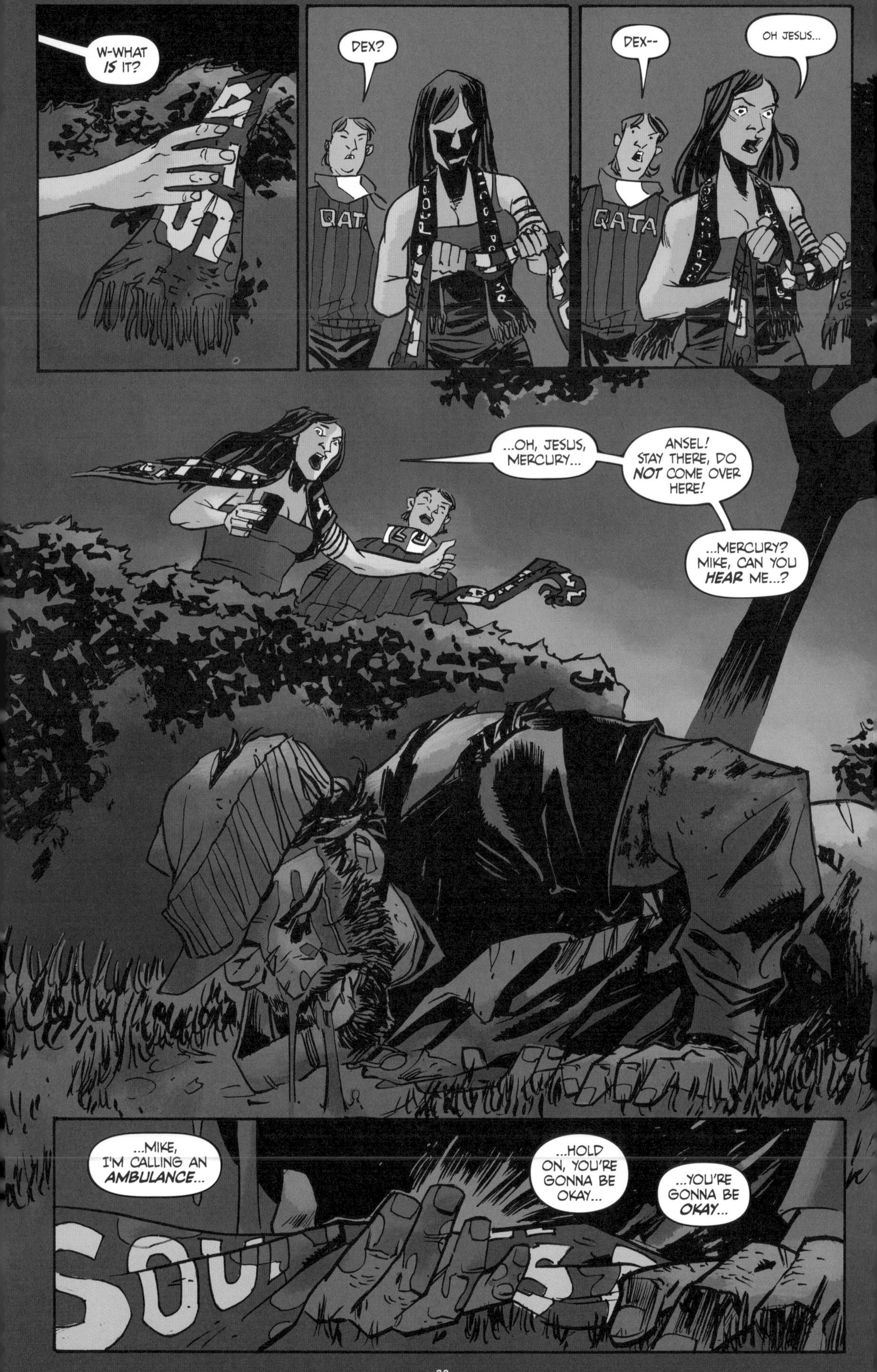
W-WHAT IS IT?
DEX?
DEX--
OH JESUS...
...OH, JESUS, MERCURY...
ANSEL! STAY THERE, DO NOT COME OVER HERE!
...MERCURY? MIKE, CAN YOU HEAR ME...?
...MIKE, I'M CALLING AN AMBULANCE...
...HOLD ON, YOU'RE GONNA BE OKAY...
...YOU'RE GONNA BE OKAY...

Chapter Two

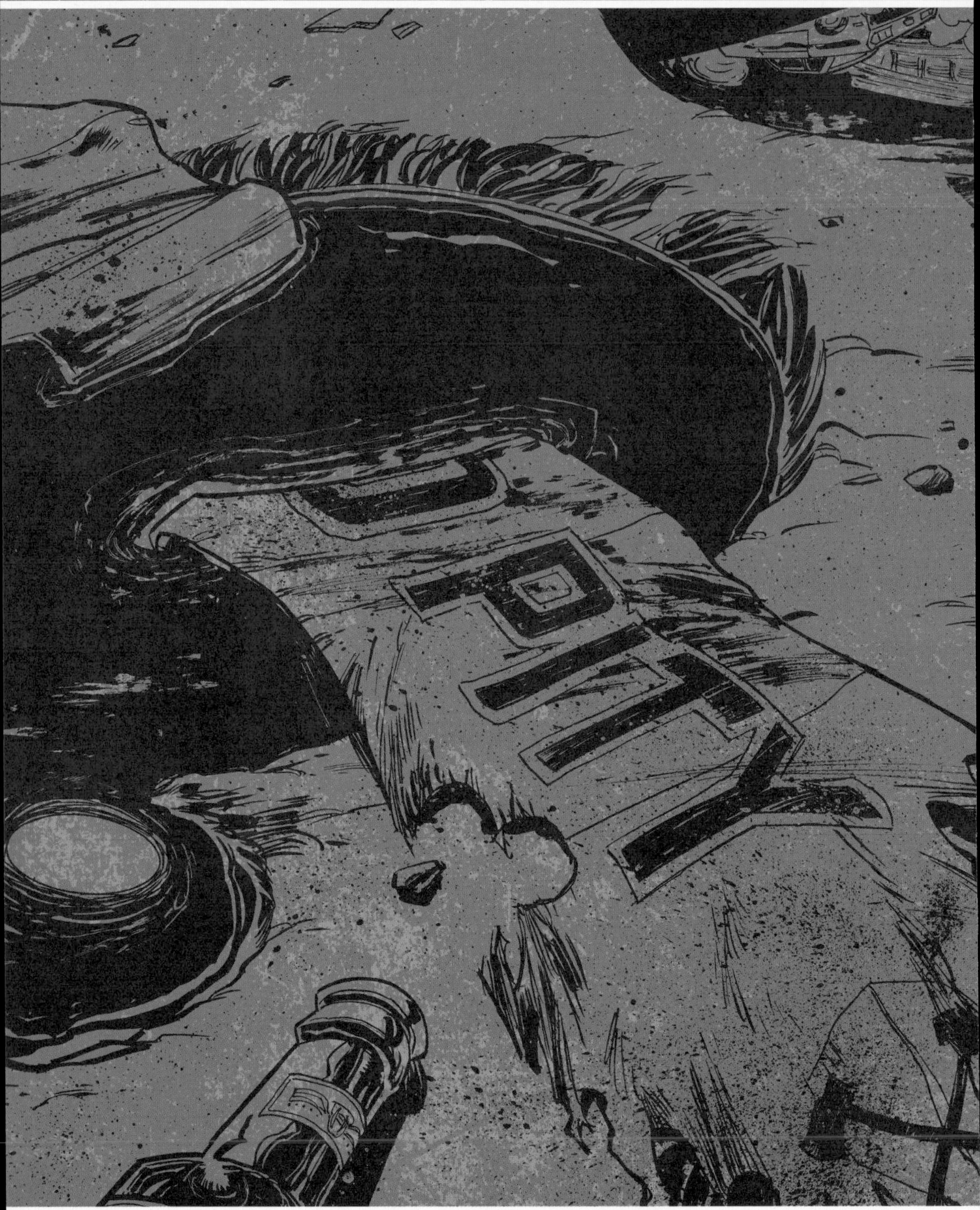
PITY

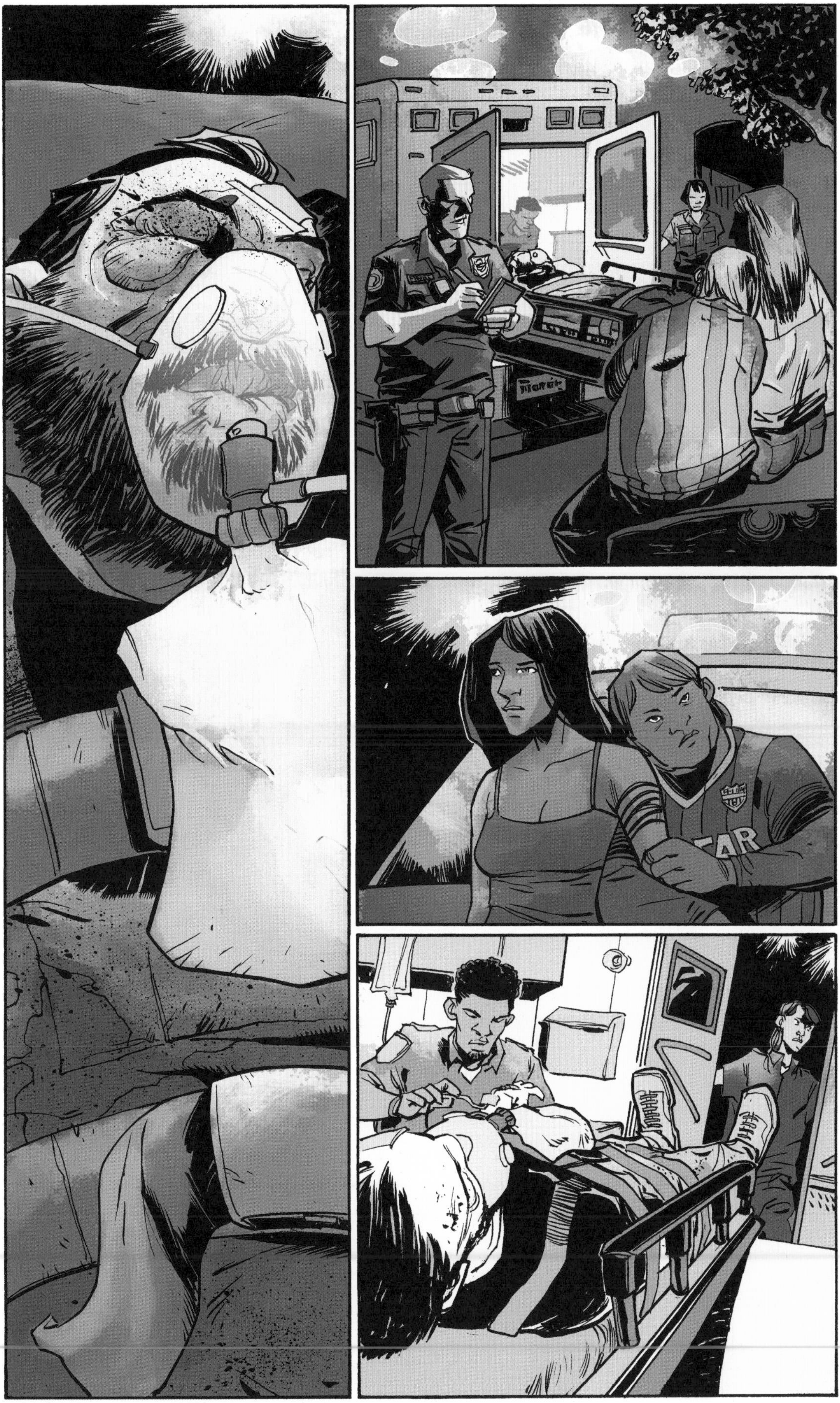

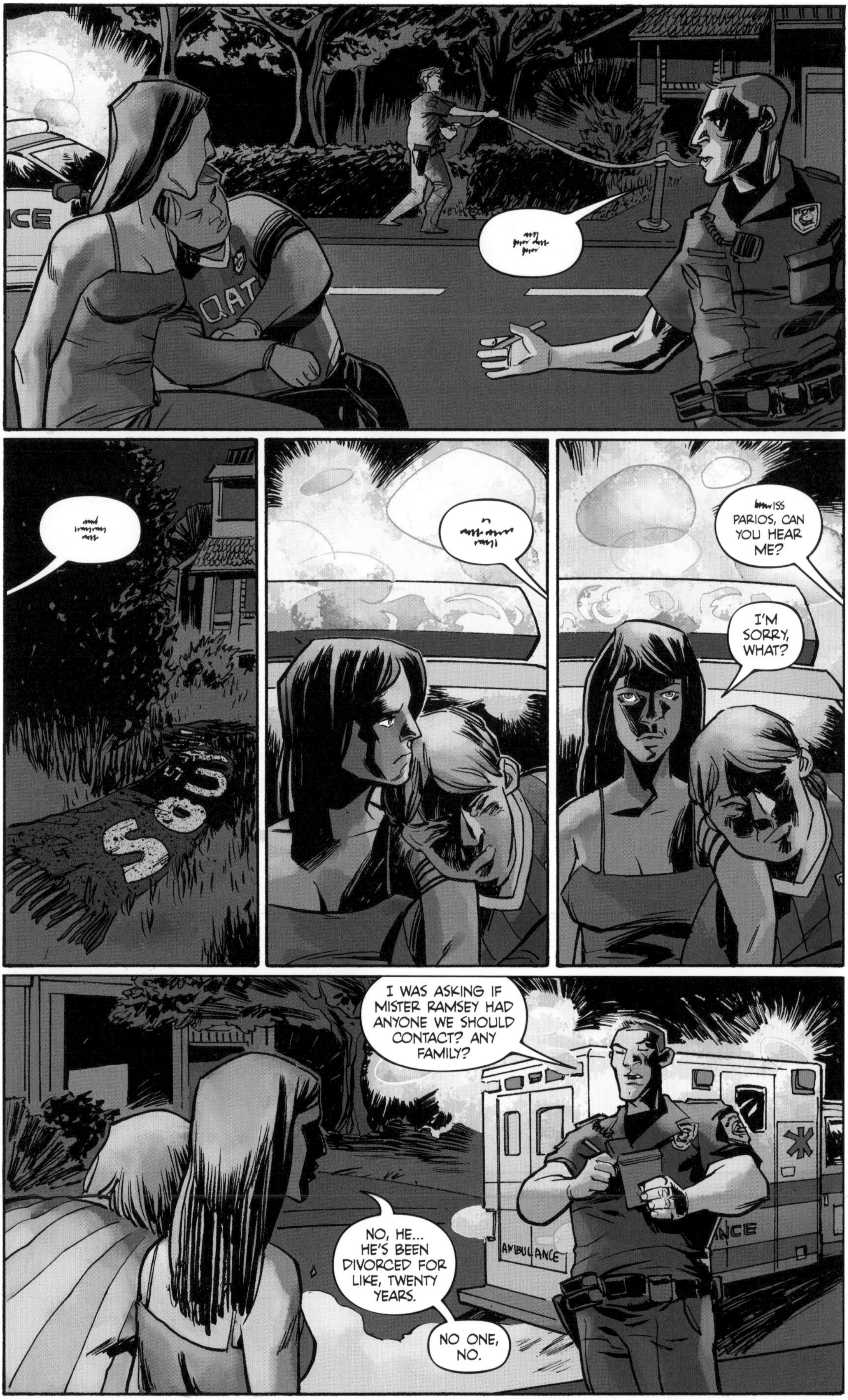
ISS PARIOS, CAN YOU HEAR ME?
I'M SORRY, WHAT?
I WAS ASKING IF MISTER RAMSEY HAD ANYONE WE SHOULD CONTACT? ANY FAMILY?
AMBULANCE
NO, HE... HE'S BEEN DIVORCED FOR LIKE, TWENTY YEARS.
NO ONE, NO.

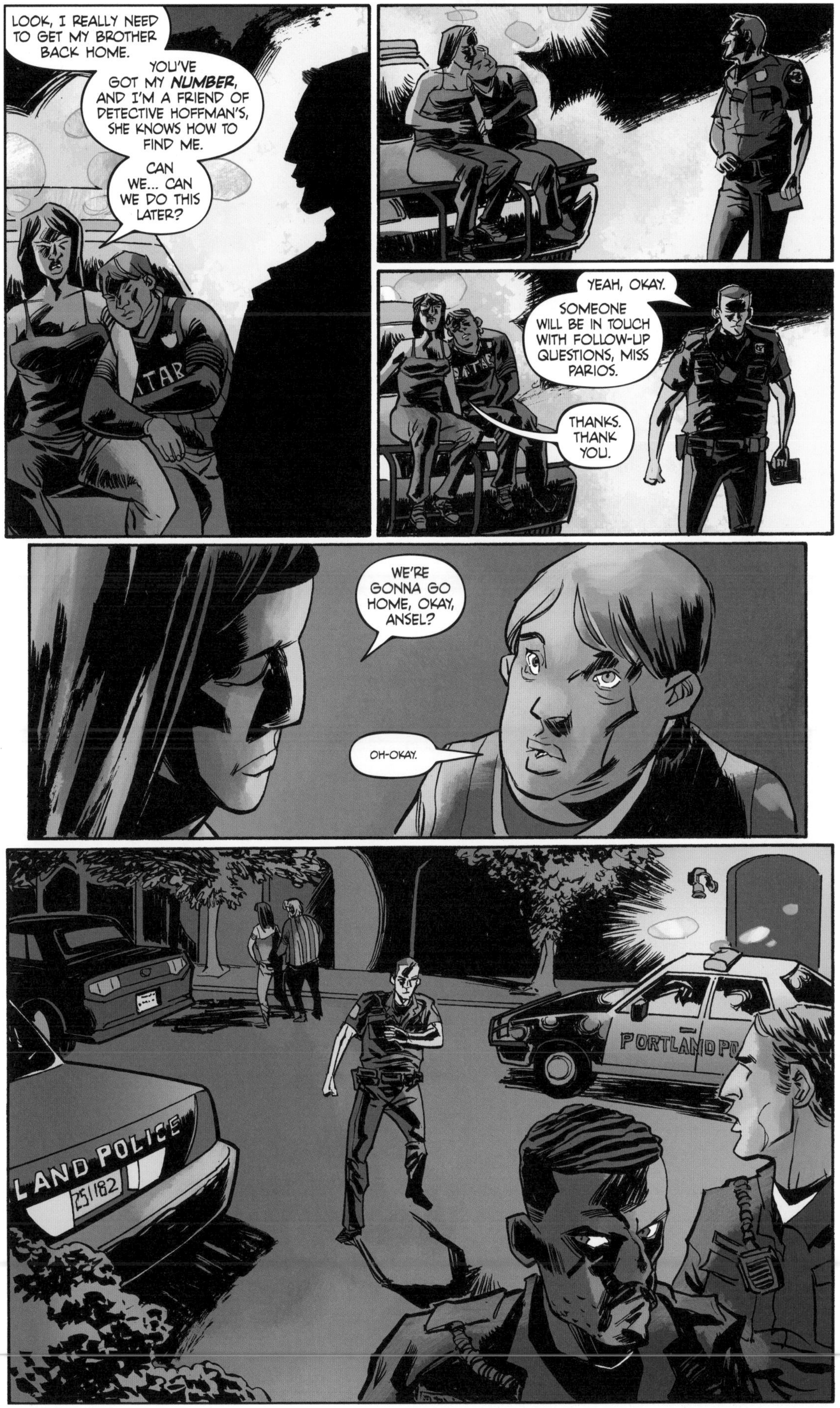
LOOK, I REALLY NEED TO GET MY BROTHER BACK HOME.
YOU'VE GOT MY NUMBER, AND I'M A FRIEND OF DETECTIVE HOFFMAN'S, SHE KNOWS HOW TO FIND ME.
CAN WE... CAN WE DO THIS LATER?
YEAH, OKAY.
SOMEONE WILL BE IN TOUCH WITH FOLLOW-UP QUESTIONS, MISS PARIOS.
THANKS. THANK YOU.
WE'RE GONNA GO HOME, OKAY, ANSEL?
OH-OKAY.
PORTLAND PO
LAND POLICE
251182

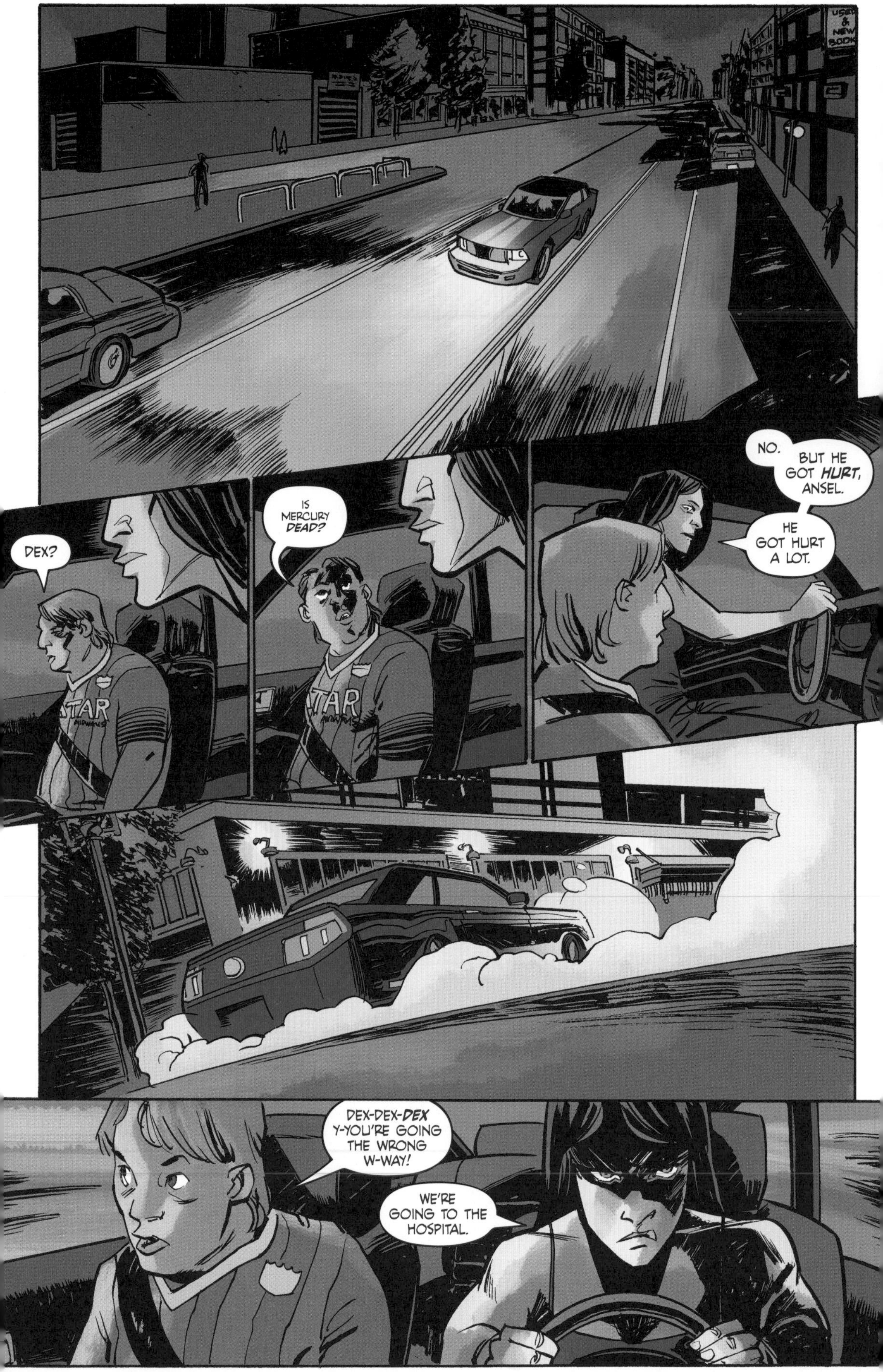

USED & NEW BOOKS
DEX?
IS MERCURY DEAD?
NO.
BUT HE GOT HURT, ANSEL.
HE GOT HURT A LOT.
DEX-DEX-DEX Y-YOU'RE GOING THE WRONG W-WAY!
WE'RE GOING TO THE HOSPITAL.

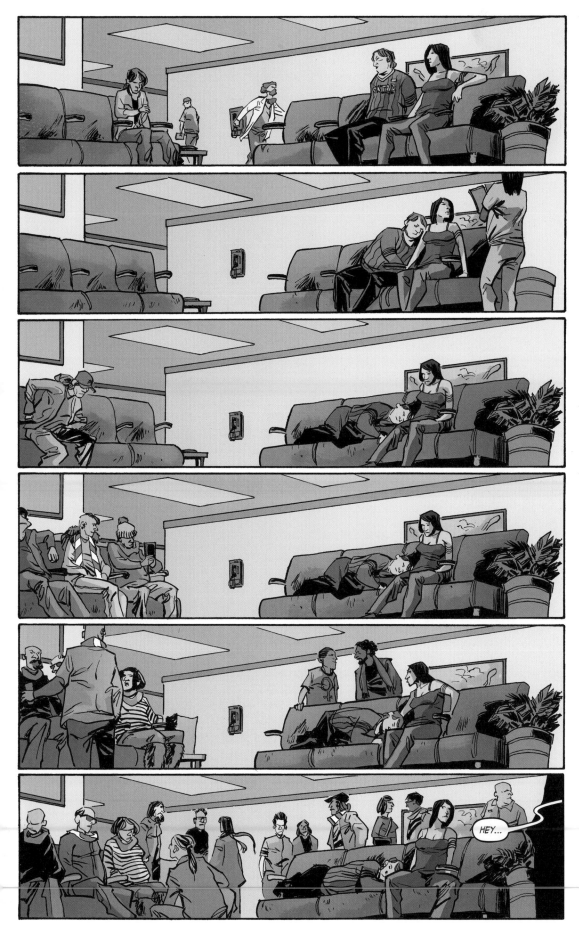

HEY...

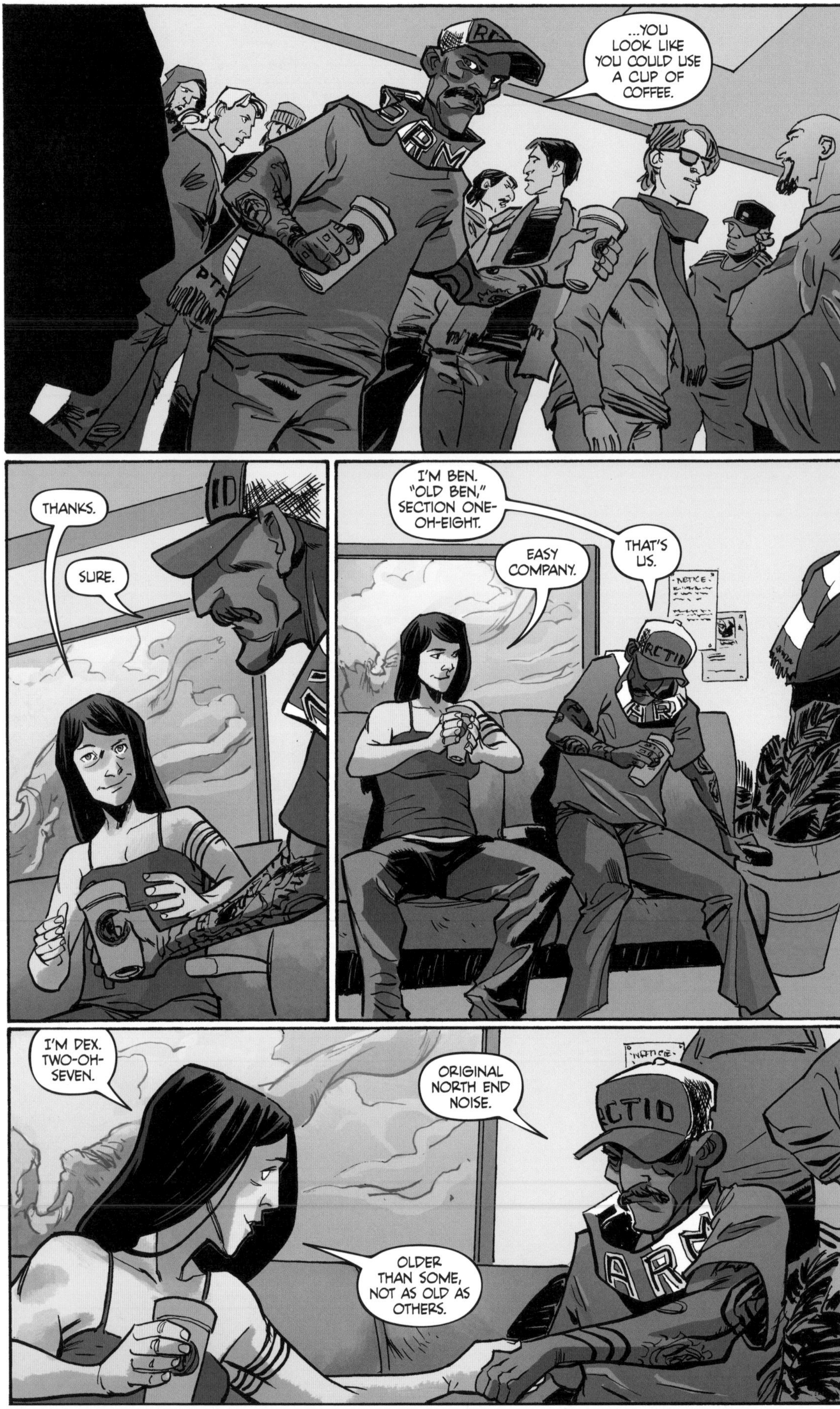
...YOU LOOK LIKE YOU COULD USE A CUP OF COFFEE.
THANKS.
SURE.
I'M BEN. "OLD BEN," SECTION ONE-OH-EIGHT.
EASY COMPANY.
THAT'S US.
I'M DEX. TWO-OH-SEVEN.
ORIGINAL NORTH END NOISE.
OLDER THAN SOME, NOT AS OLD AS OTHERS.

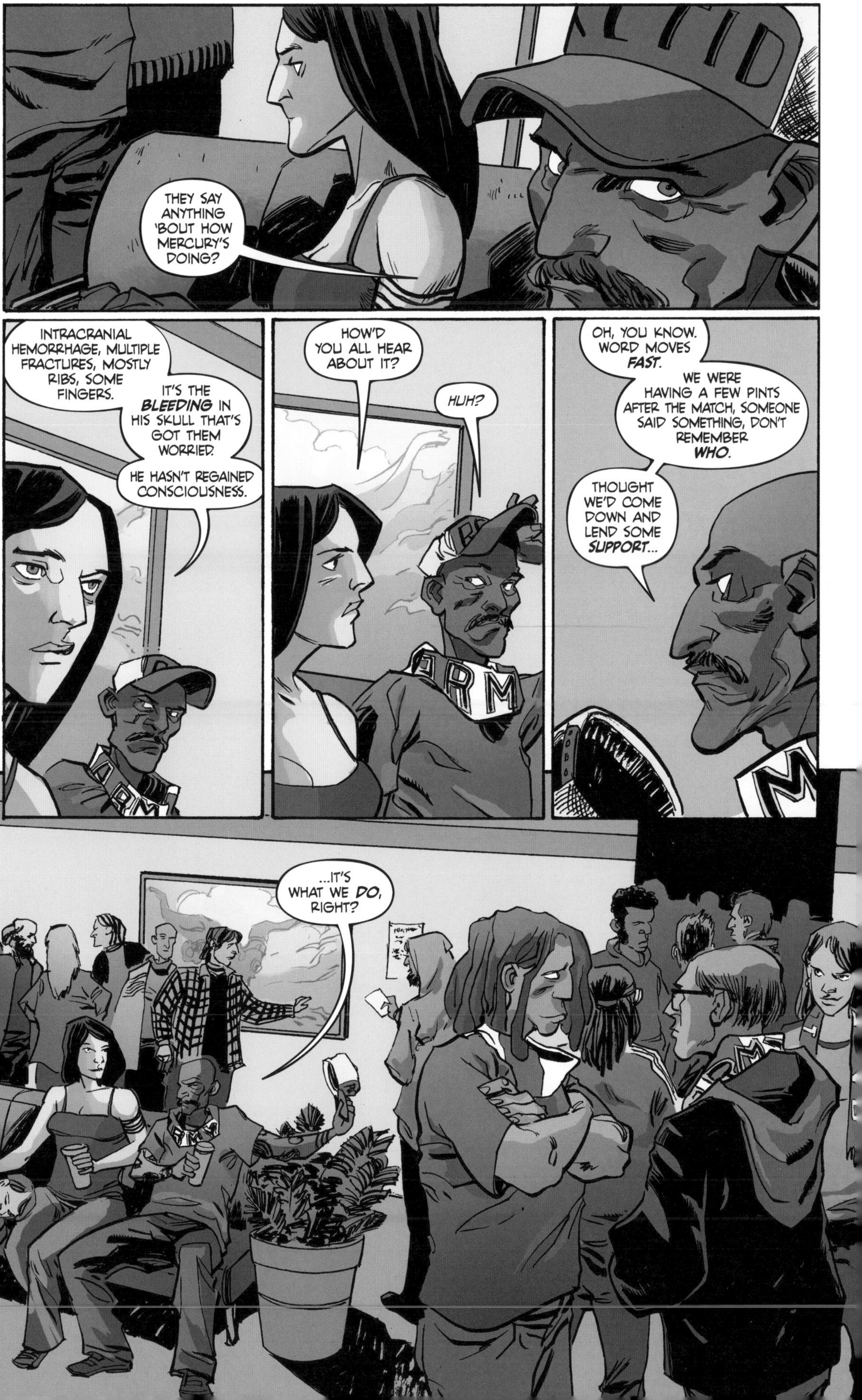
THEY SAY ANYTHING 'BOUT HOW MERCURY'S DOING?
INTRACRANIAL HEMORRHAGE, MULTIPLE FRACTURES, MOSTLY RIBS, SOME FINGERS.
IT'S THE BLEEDING IN HIS SKULL THAT'S GOT THEM WORRIED.
HE HASN'T REGAINED CONSCIOUSNESS.
HOW'D YOU ALL HEAR ABOUT IT?
HUH?
OH, YOU KNOW. WORD MOVES FAST.
WE WERE HAVING A FEW PINTS AFTER THE MATCH, SOMEONE SAID SOMETHING, DON'T REMEMBER WHO.
THOUGHT WE'D COME DOWN AND LEND SOME SUPPORT...
...IT'S WHAT WE DO, RIGHT?

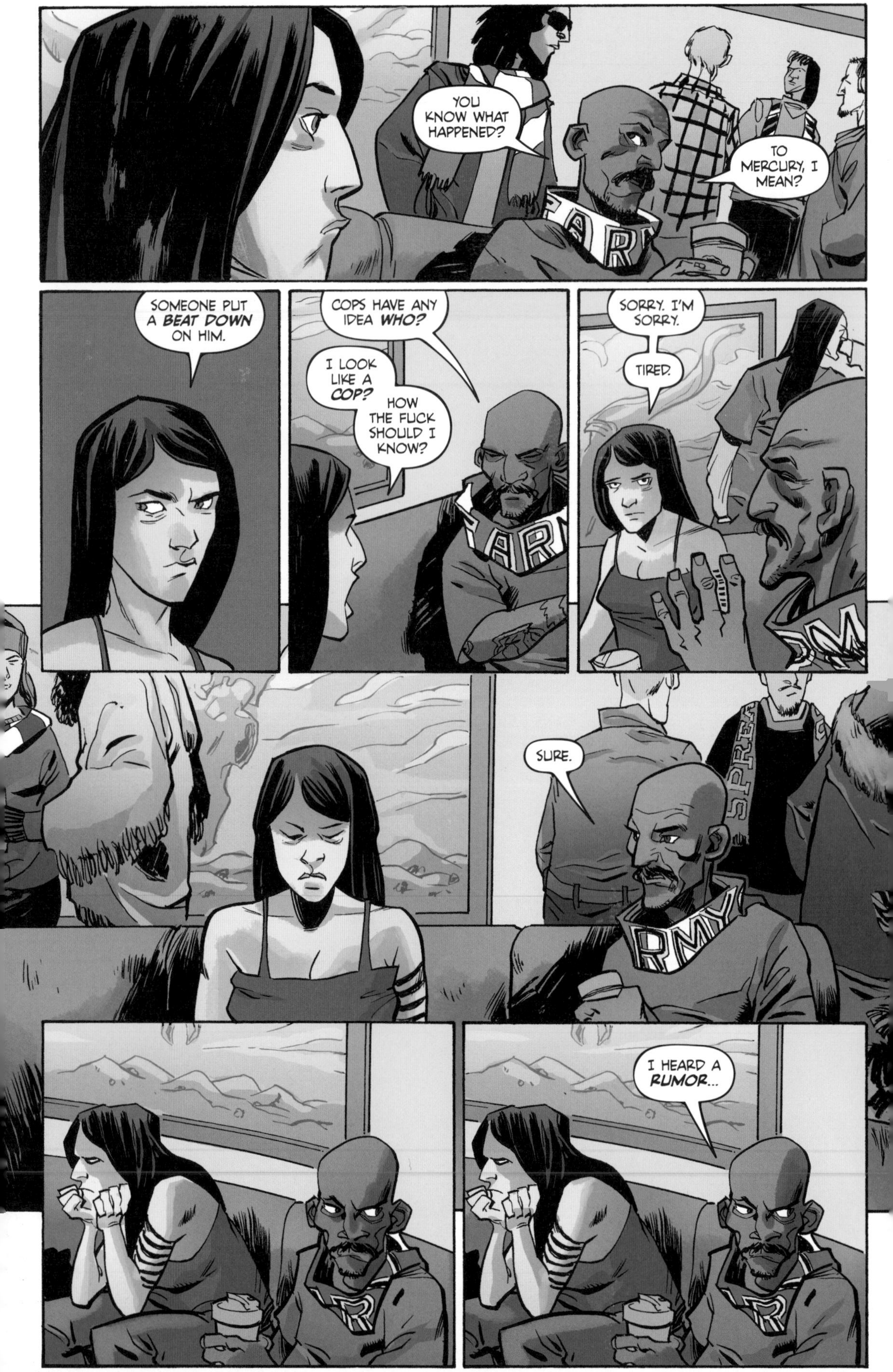

YOU KNOW WHAT HAPPENED?
TO MERCURY, I MEAN?
SOMEONE PUT A **BEAT DOWN** ON HIM.
COPS HAVE ANY IDEA **WHO?**
I LOOK LIKE A **COP?**
HOW THE FUCK SHOULD I KNOW?
SORRY. I'M SORRY.
TIRED.
SURE.
I HEARD A **RUMOR...**

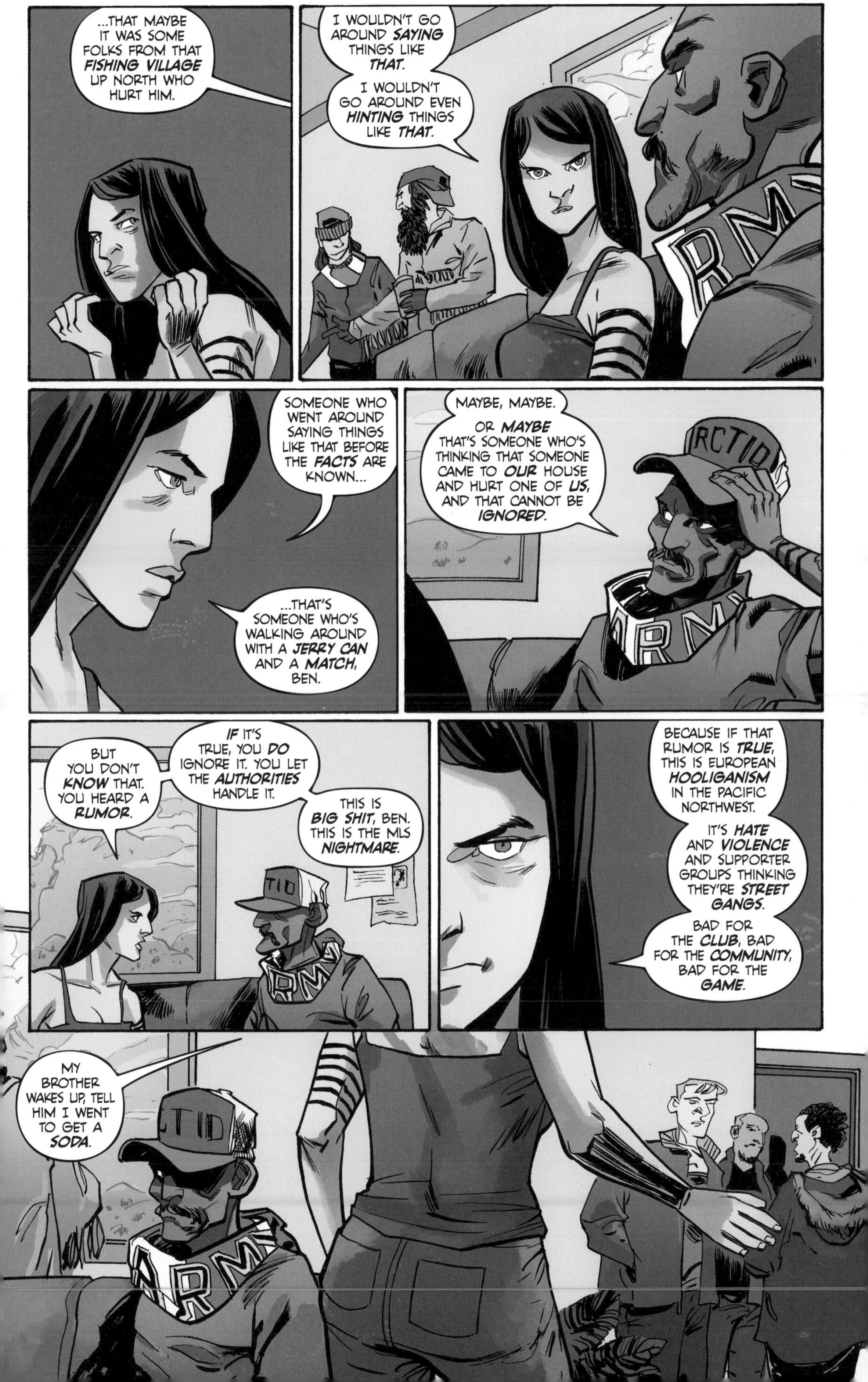
...THAT MAYBE IT WAS SOME FOLKS FROM THAT FISHING VILLAGE UP NORTH WHO HURT HIM.
I WOULDN'T GO AROUND SAYING THINGS LIKE THAT.
I WOULDN'T GO AROUND EVEN HINTING THINGS LIKE THAT.
SOMEONE WHO WENT AROUND SAYING THINGS LIKE THAT BEFORE THE FACTS ARE KNOWN...
...THAT'S SOMEONE WHO'S WALKING AROUND WITH A JERRY CAN AND A MATCH, BEN.
MAYBE, MAYBE.
OR MAYBE THAT'S SOMEONE WHO'S THINKING THAT SOMEONE CAME TO OUR HOUSE AND HURT ONE OF US, AND THAT CANNOT BE IGNORED.
BUT YOU DON'T KNOW THAT. YOU HEARD A RUMOR.
IF IT'S TRUE, YOU DO IGNORE IT. YOU LET THE AUTHORITIES HANDLE IT.
THIS IS BIG SHIT, BEN. THIS IS THE MLS NIGHTMARE.
BECAUSE IF THAT RUMOR IS TRUE, THIS IS EUROPEAN HOOLIGANISM IN THE PACIFIC NORTHWEST.
IT'S HATE AND VIOLENCE AND SUPPORTER GROUPS THINKING THEY'RE STREET GANGS.
BAD FOR THE CLUB, BAD FOR THE COMMUNITY, BAD FOR THE GAME.
MY BROTHER WAKES UP, TELL HIM I WENT TO GET A SODA.

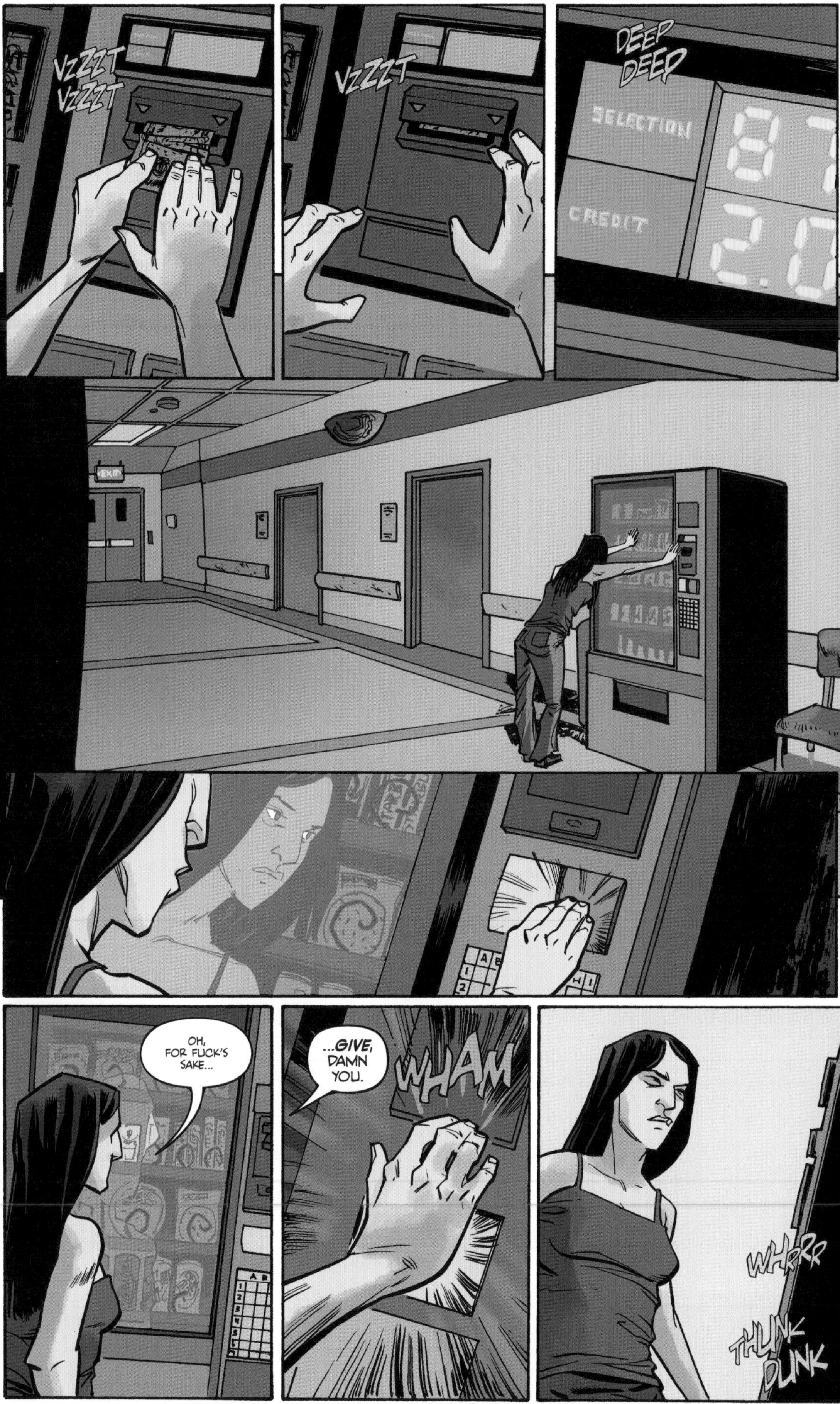
VZZZT
VZZZT
VZZZT
DEEP
DEEP
SELECTION
CREDIT
EXIT
OH, FOR FUCK'S SAKE...
...GIVE, DAMN YOU.
WHAM
WHRRR
THUNK
DUNK

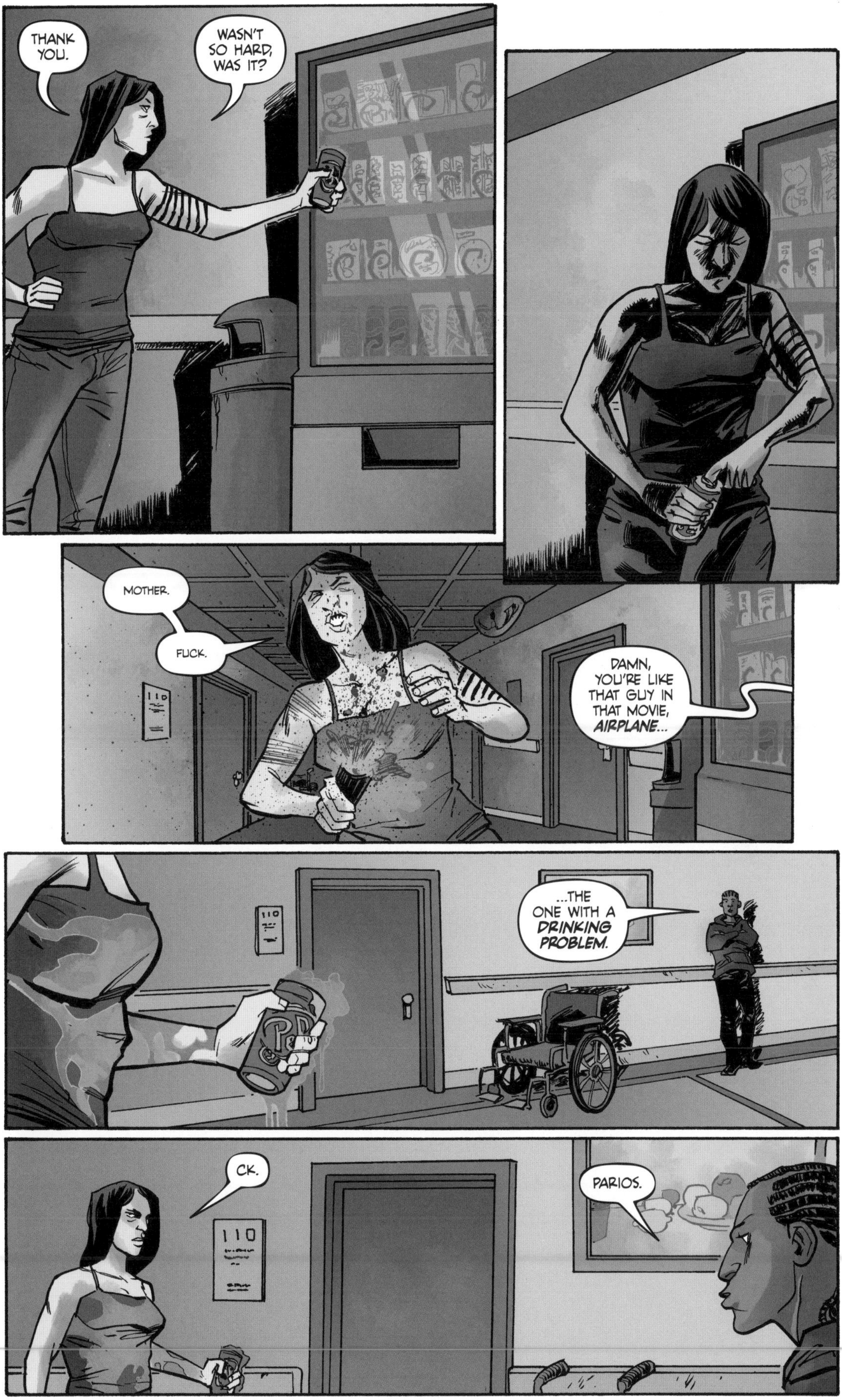
THANK YOU.
WASN'T SO HARD, WAS IT?
MOTHER.
FUCK.
DAMN, YOU'RE LIKE THAT GUY IN THAT MOVIE, *AIRPLANE*...
...THE ONE WITH A *DRINKING PROBLEM*.
CK.
PARIOS.

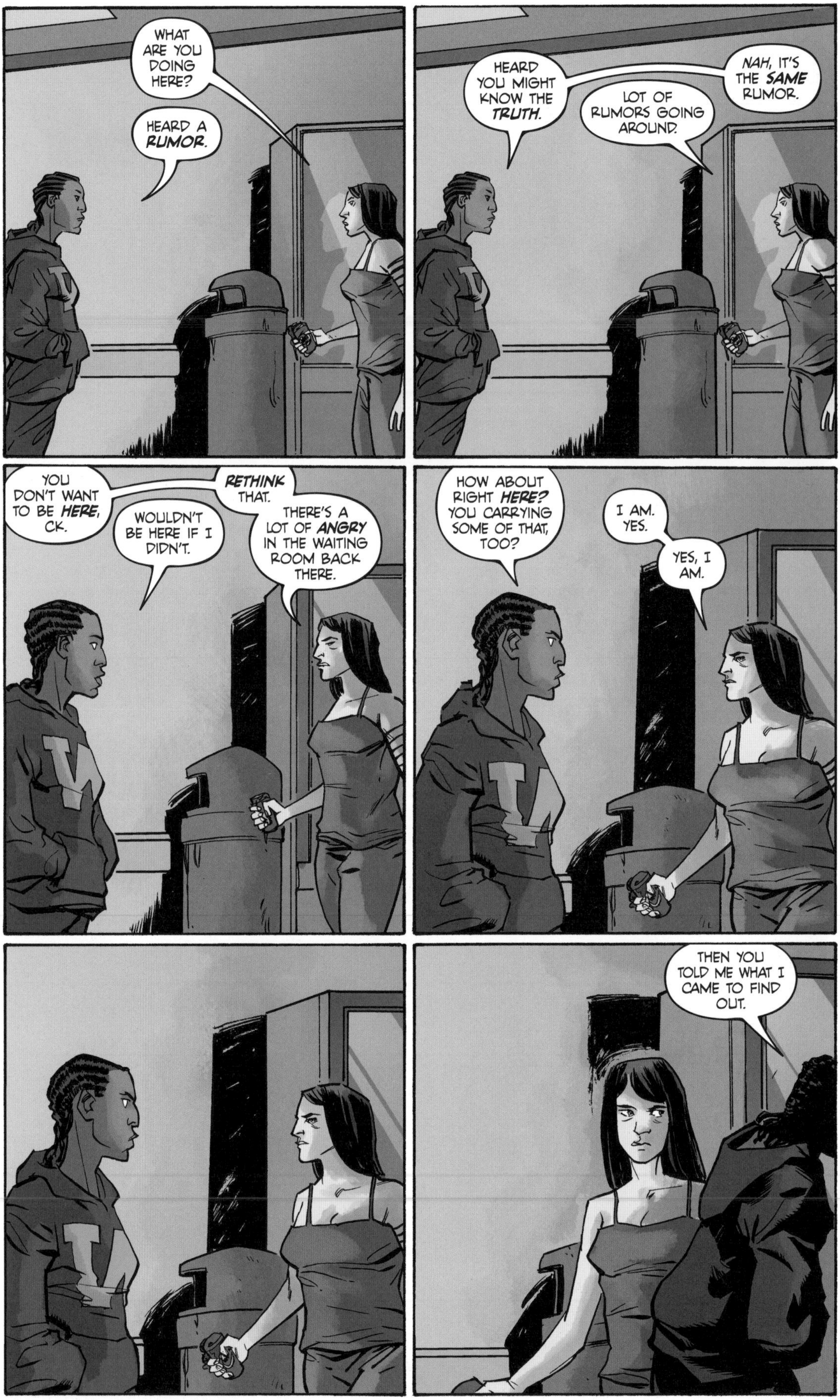
WHAT ARE YOU DOING HERE?
HEARD A RUMOR.
HEARD YOU MIGHT KNOW THE TRUTH.
LOT OF RUMORS GOING AROUND.
NAH, IT'S THE SAME RUMOR.
YOU DON'T WANT TO BE HERE, CK.
WOULDN'T BE HERE IF I DIDN'T.
RETHINK THAT.
THERE'S A LOT OF ANGRY IN THE WAITING ROOM BACK THERE.
HOW ABOUT RIGHT HERE? YOU CARRYING SOME OF THAT, TOO?
I AM. YES.
YES, I AM.
THEN YOU TOLD ME WHAT I CAME TO FIND OUT.

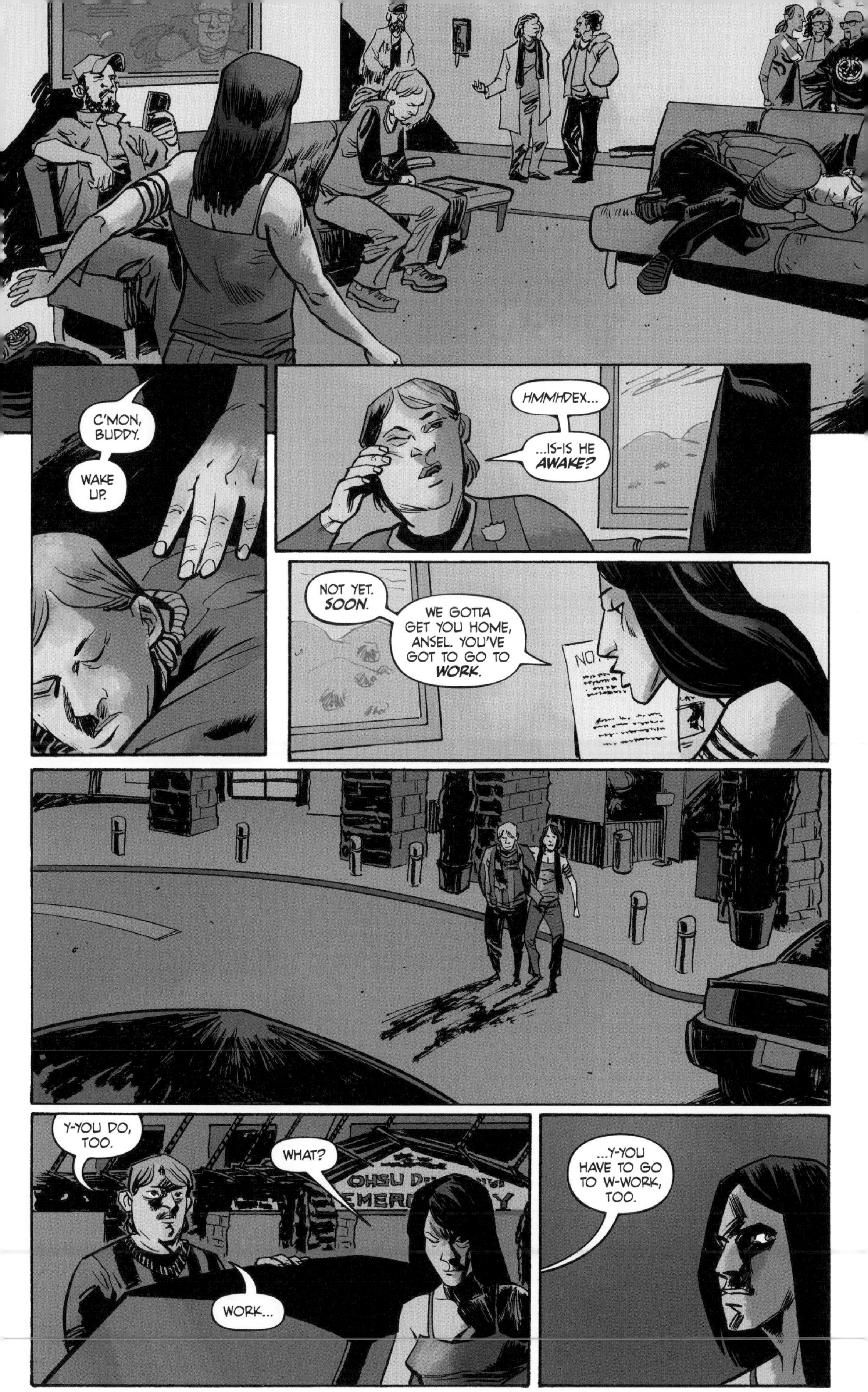
C'MON, BUDDY.
WAKE UP.
HMMHDEX...
...IS-IS HE AWAKE?
NOT YET. SOON.
WE GOTTA GET YOU HOME, ANSEL. YOU'VE GOT TO GO TO WORK.
Y-YOU DO, TOO.
WHAT?
WORK...
...Y-YOU HAVE TO GO TO W-WORK, TOO.

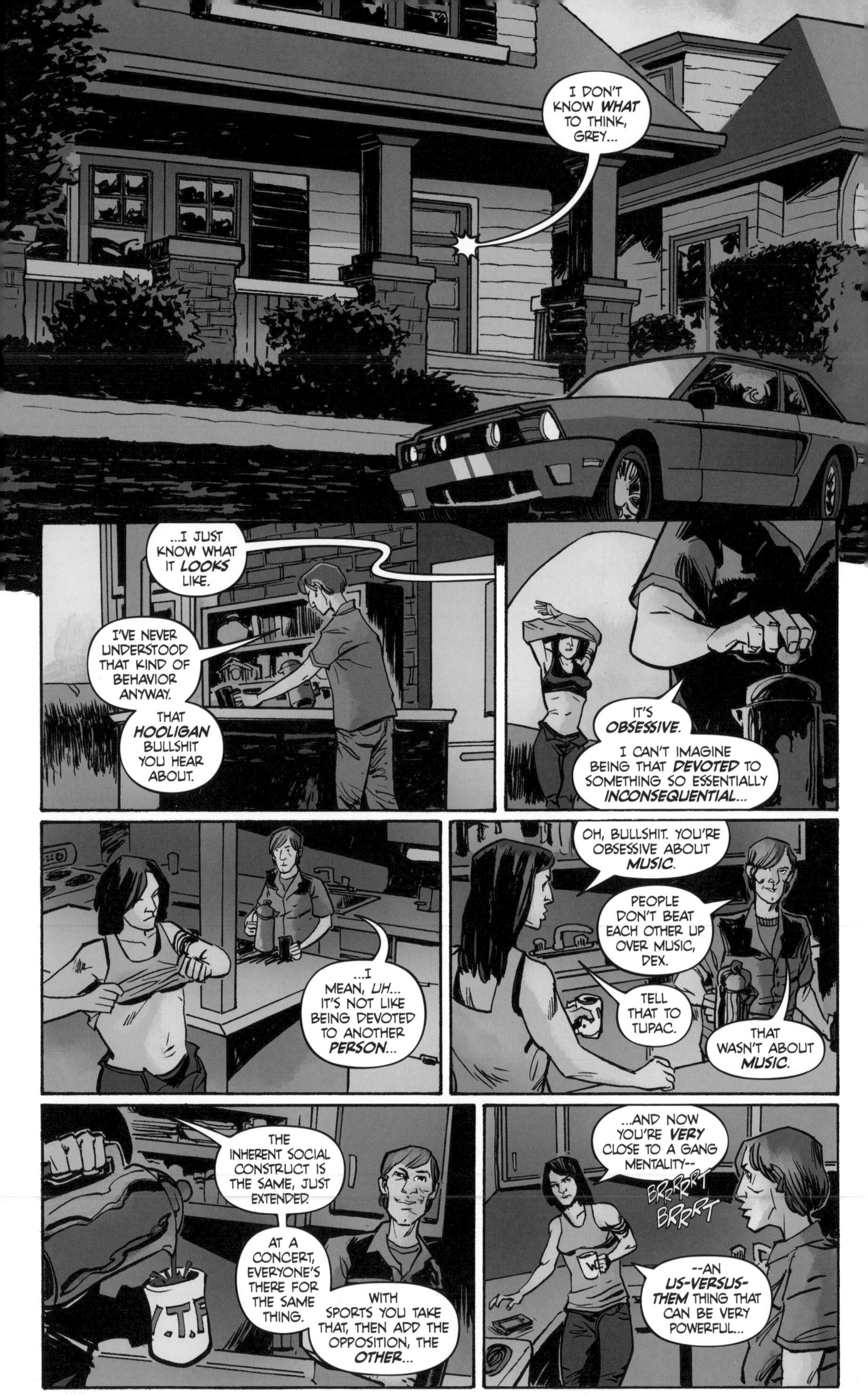
I DON'T KNOW WHAT TO THINK, GREY...
...I JUST KNOW WHAT IT LOOKS LIKE.
I'VE NEVER UNDERSTOOD THAT KIND OF BEHAVIOR ANYWAY.
THAT HOOLIGAN BULLSHIT YOU HEAR ABOUT.
IT'S OBSESSIVE.
I CAN'T IMAGINE BEING THAT DEVOTED TO SOMETHING SO ESSENTIALLY INCONSEQUENTIAL...
...I MEAN, UH... IT'S NOT LIKE BEING DEVOTED TO ANOTHER PERSON...
OH, BULLSHIT. YOU'RE OBSESSIVE ABOUT MUSIC.
PEOPLE DON'T BEAT EACH OTHER UP OVER MUSIC, DEX.
TELL THAT TO TUPAC.
THAT WASN'T ABOUT MUSIC.
THE INHERENT SOCIAL CONSTRUCT IS THE SAME, JUST EXTENDED.
AT A CONCERT, EVERYONE'S THERE FOR THE SAME THING.
WITH SPORTS YOU TAKE THAT, THEN ADD THE OPPOSITION, THE OTHER...
...AND NOW YOU'RE VERY CLOSE TO A GANG MENTALITY--
BRRRRRT
BRRRRT
--AN US-VERSUS-THEM THING THAT CAN BE VERY POWERFUL...

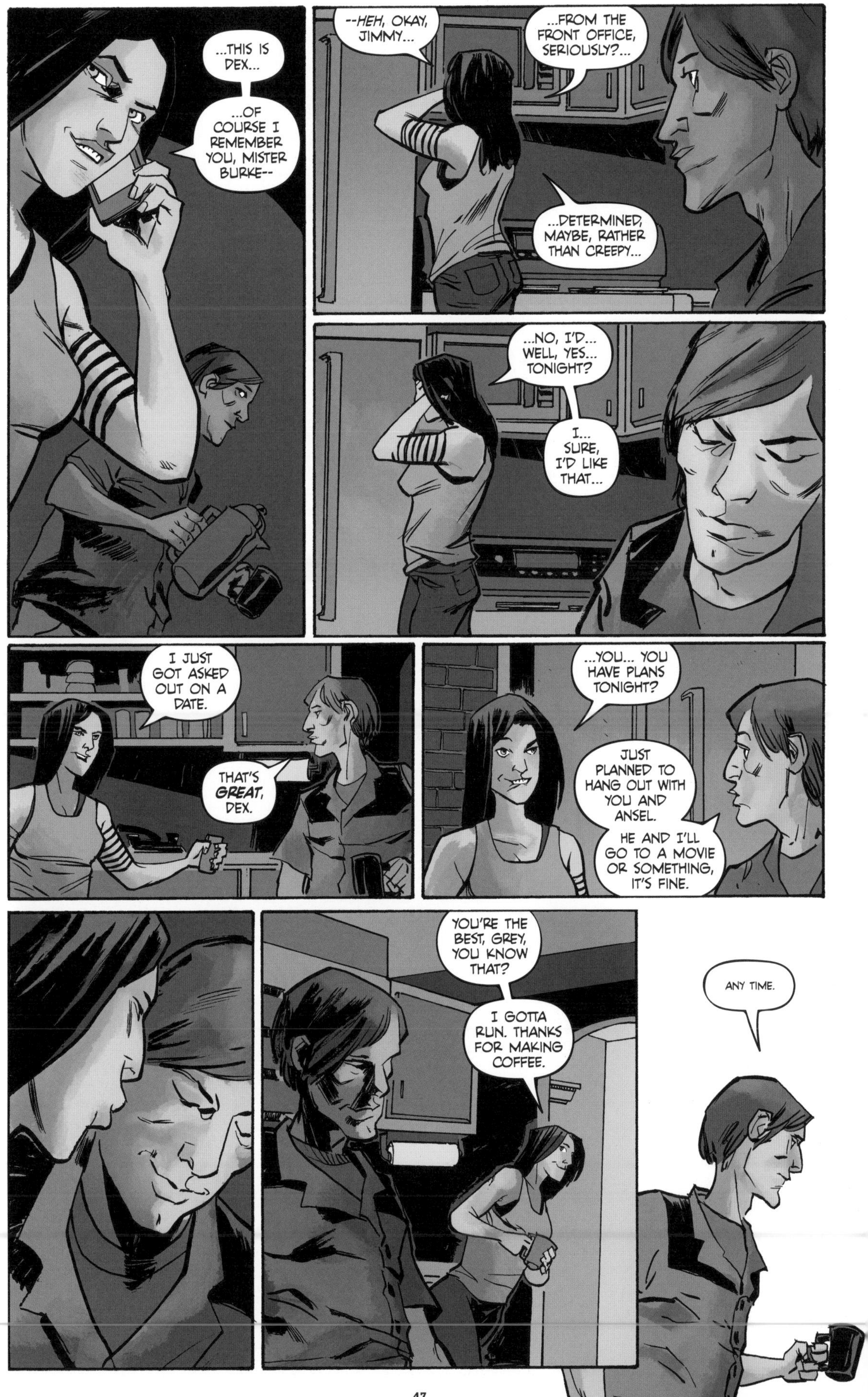
...THIS IS DEX...
...OF COURSE I REMEMBER YOU, MISTER BURKE--
--HEH, OKAY, JIMMY...
...FROM THE FRONT OFFICE, SERIOUSLY?...
...DETERMINED, MAYBE, RATHER THAN CREEPY...
...NO, I'D... WELL, YES... TONIGHT?
I... SURE, I'D LIKE THAT...
I JUST GOT ASKED OUT ON A DATE.
THAT'S GREAT, DEX.
...YOU... YOU HAVE PLANS TONIGHT?
JUST PLANNED TO HANG OUT WITH YOU AND ANSEL.
HE AND I'LL GO TO A MOVIE OR SOMETHING, IT'S FINE.
YOU'RE THE BEST, GREY, YOU KNOW THAT?
I GOTTA RUN. THANKS FOR MAKING COFFEE.
ANY TIME.

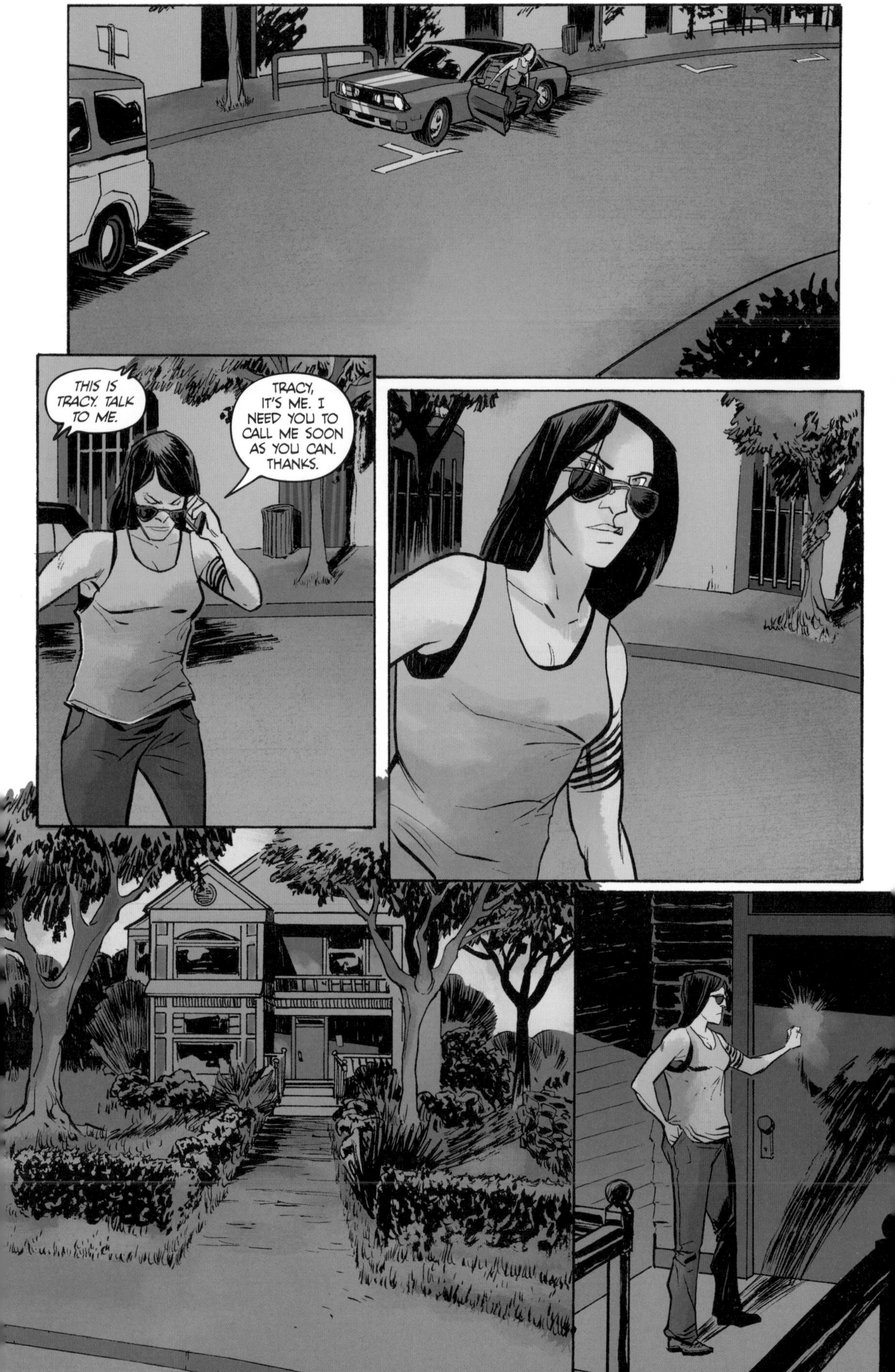
THIS IS TRACY. TALK TO ME.
TRACY, IT'S ME. I NEED YOU TO CALL ME SOON AS YOU CAN. THANKS.

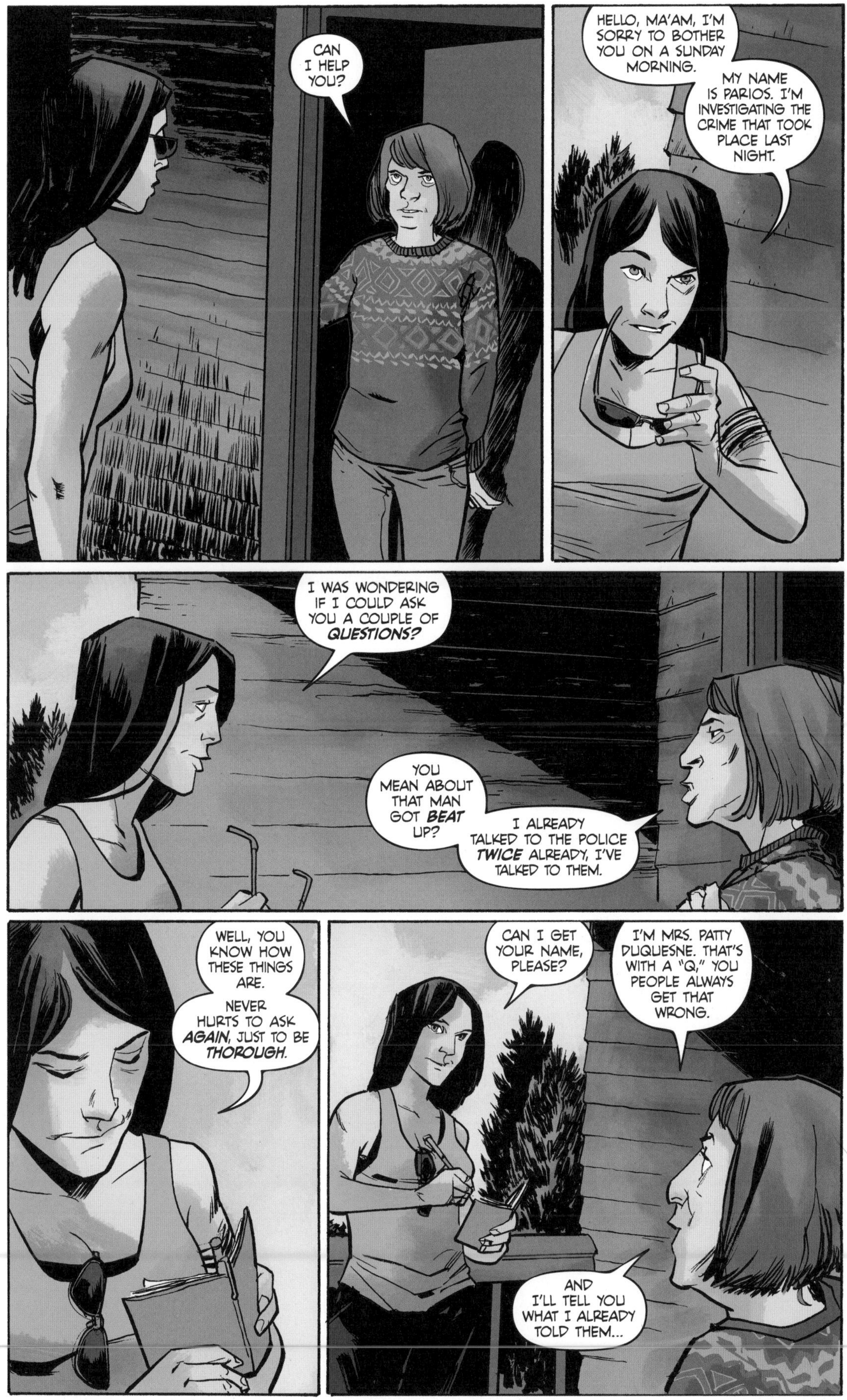
CAN I HELP YOU?
HELLO, MA'AM, I'M SORRY TO BOTHER YOU ON A SUNDAY MORNING.
MY NAME IS PARIOS. I'M INVESTIGATING THE CRIME THAT TOOK PLACE LAST NIGHT.
I WAS WONDERING IF I COULD ASK YOU A COUPLE OF QUESTIONS?
YOU MEAN ABOUT THAT MAN GOT BEAT UP?
I ALREADY TALKED TO THE POLICE TWICE ALREADY, I'VE TALKED TO THEM.
WELL, YOU KNOW HOW THESE THINGS ARE.
NEVER HURTS TO ASK AGAIN, JUST TO BE THOROUGH.
CAN I GET YOUR NAME, PLEASE?
I'M MRS. PATTY DUQUESNE. THAT'S WITH A "Q," YOU PEOPLE ALWAYS GET THAT WRONG.
AND I'LL TELL YOU WHAT I ALREADY TOLD THEM...

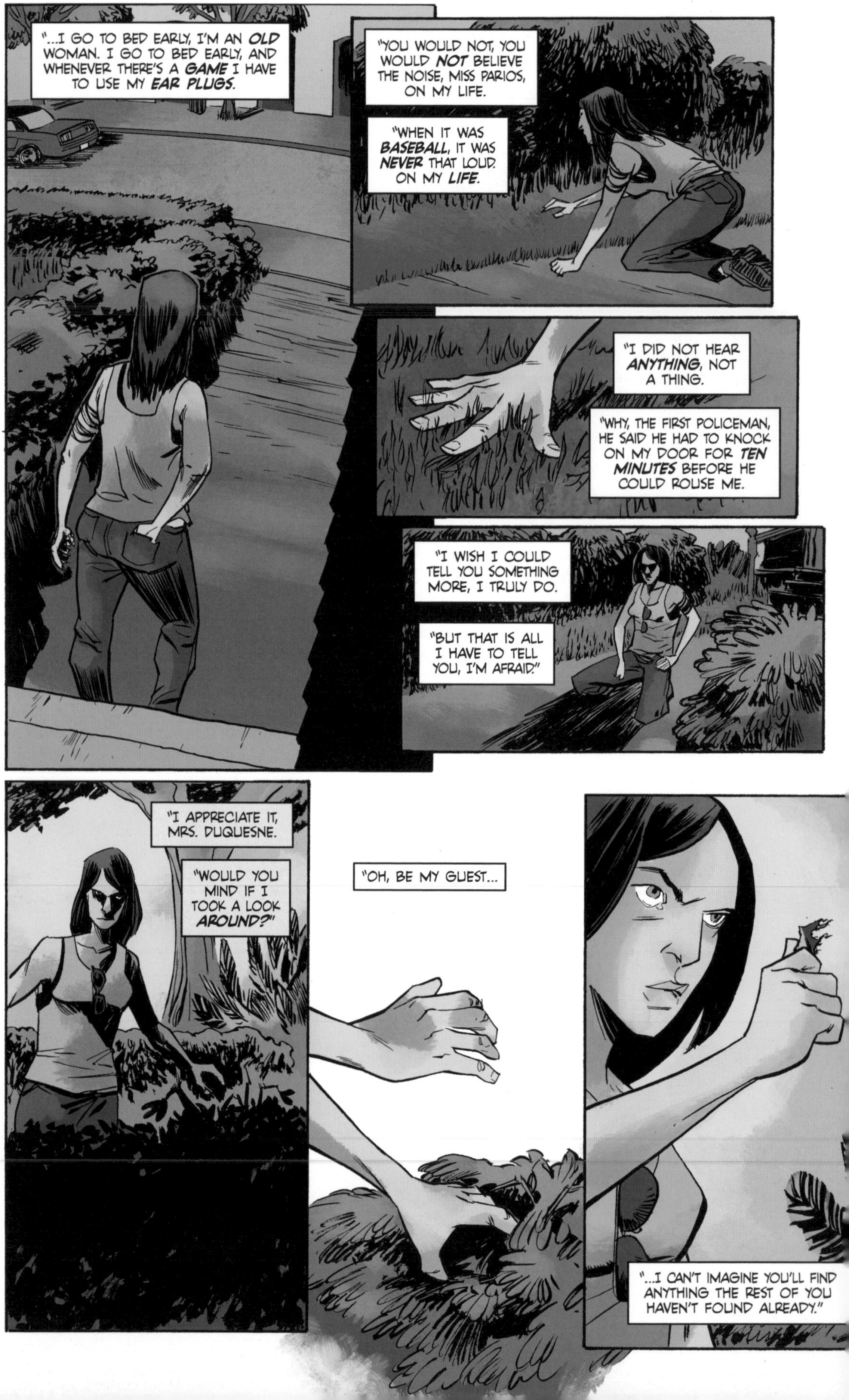
"...I GO TO BED EARLY, I'M AN OLD WOMAN. I GO TO BED EARLY, AND WHENEVER THERE'S A GAME I HAVE TO USE MY EAR PLUGS.
"YOU WOULD NOT, YOU WOULD NOT BELIEVE THE NOISE, MISS PARIOS, ON MY LIFE.
"WHEN IT WAS BASEBALL, IT WAS NEVER THAT LOUD. ON MY LIFE.
"I DID NOT HEAR ANYTHING, NOT A THING.
"WHY, THE FIRST POLICEMAN, HE SAID HE HAD TO KNOCK ON MY DOOR FOR TEN MINUTES BEFORE HE COULD ROUSE ME.
"I WISH I COULD TELL YOU SOMETHING MORE, I TRULY DO.
"BUT THAT IS ALL I HAVE TO TELL YOU, I'M AFRAID."
"I APPRECIATE IT, MRS. DUQUESNE.
"WOULD YOU MIND IF I TOOK A LOOK AROUND?"
"OH, BE MY GUEST...
"...I CAN'T IMAGINE YOU'LL FIND ANYTHING THE REST OF YOU HAVEN'T FOUND ALREADY."

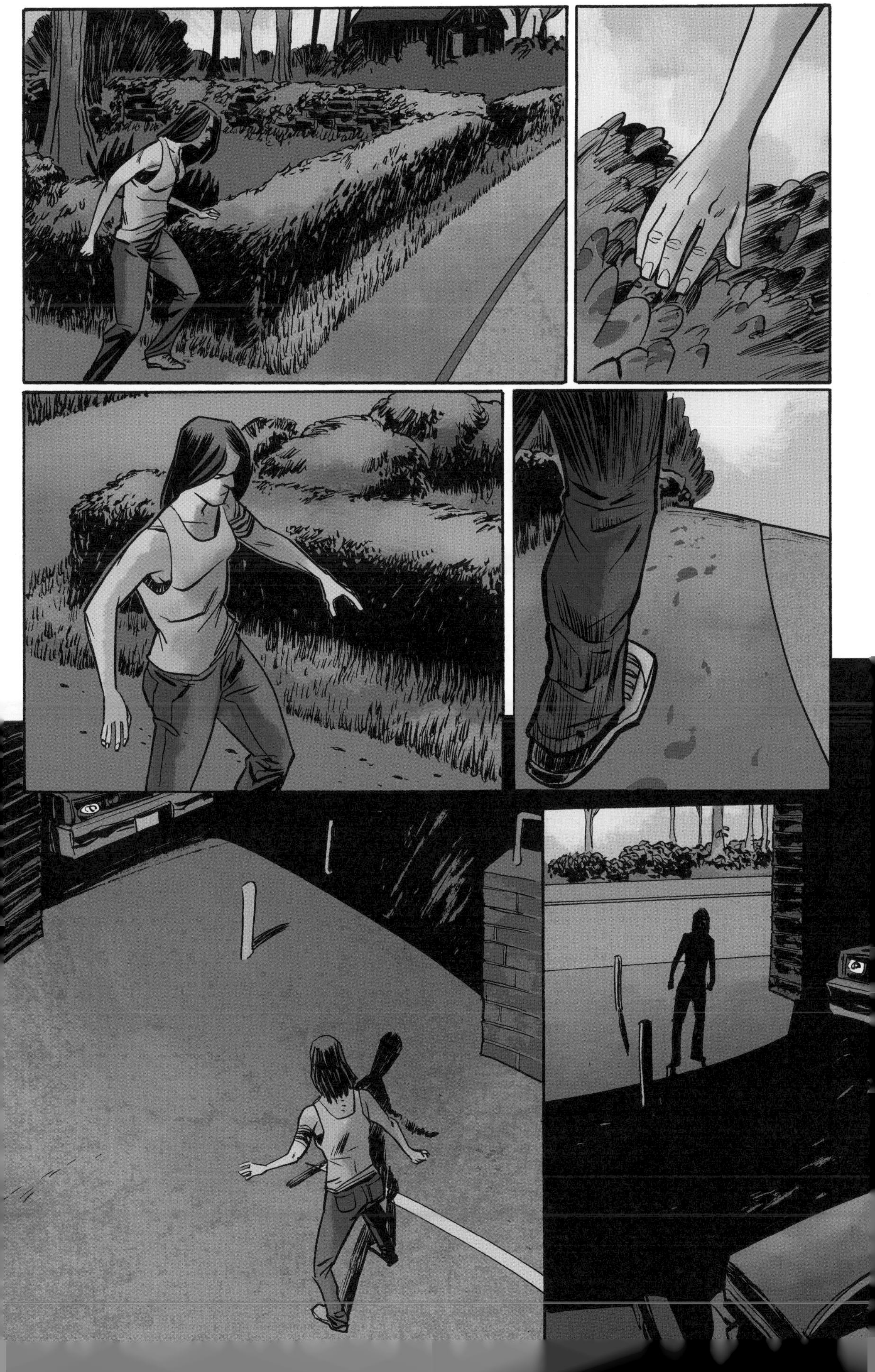

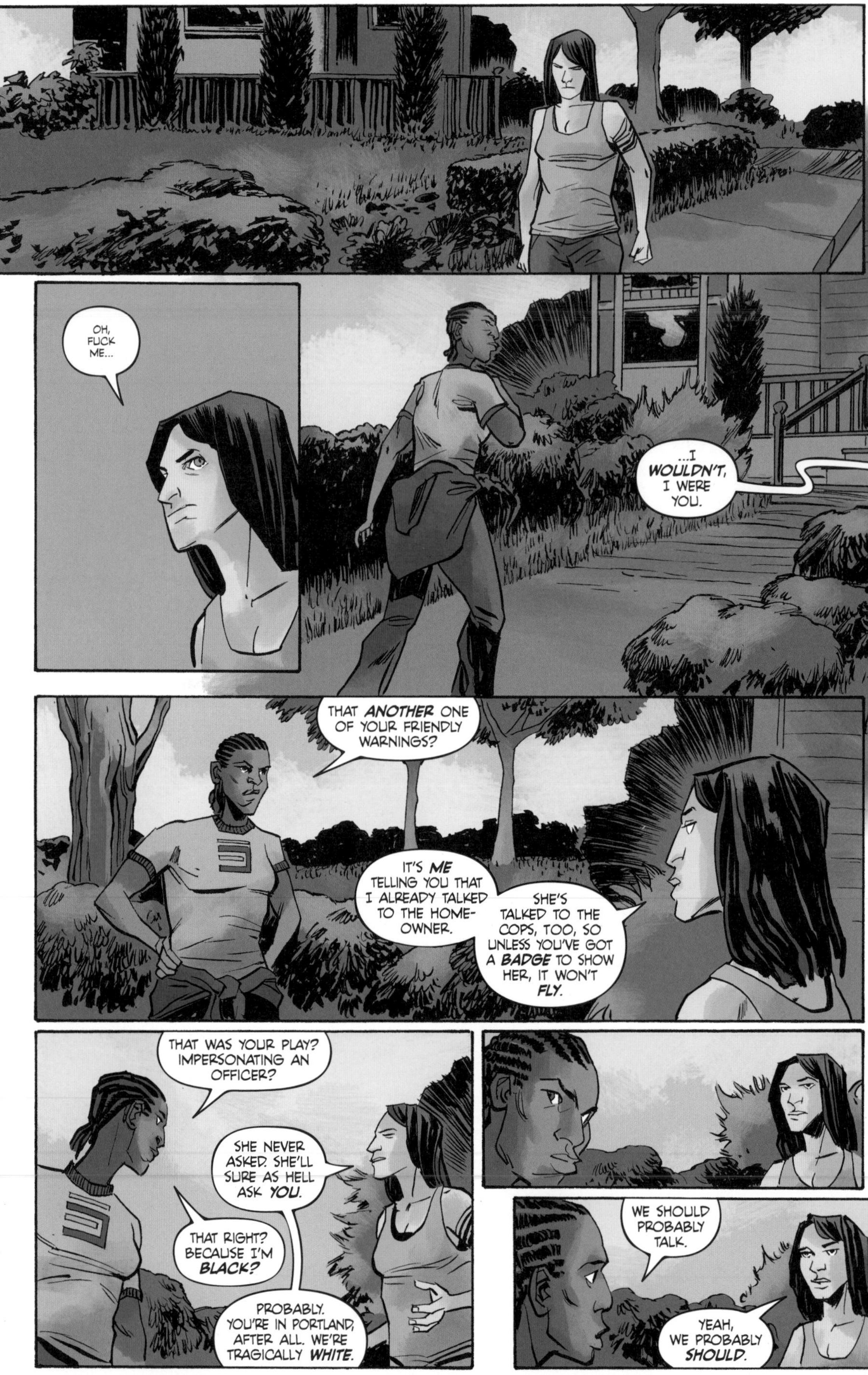
OH, FUCK ME...
...I WOULDN'T, I WERE YOU.
THAT ANOTHER ONE OF YOUR FRIENDLY WARNINGS?
IT'S ME TELLING YOU THAT I ALREADY TALKED TO THE HOME-OWNER.
SHE'S TALKED TO THE COPS, TOO, SO UNLESS YOU'VE GOT A BADGE TO SHOW HER, IT WON'T FLY.
THAT WAS YOUR PLAY? IMPERSONATING AN OFFICER?
SHE NEVER ASKED. SHE'LL SURE AS HELL ASK YOU.
THAT RIGHT? BECAUSE I'M BLACK?
PROBABLY. YOU'RE IN PORTLAND, AFTER ALL. WE'RE TRAGICALLY WHITE.
WE SHOULD PROBABLY TALK.
YEAH, WE PROBABLY SHOULD.

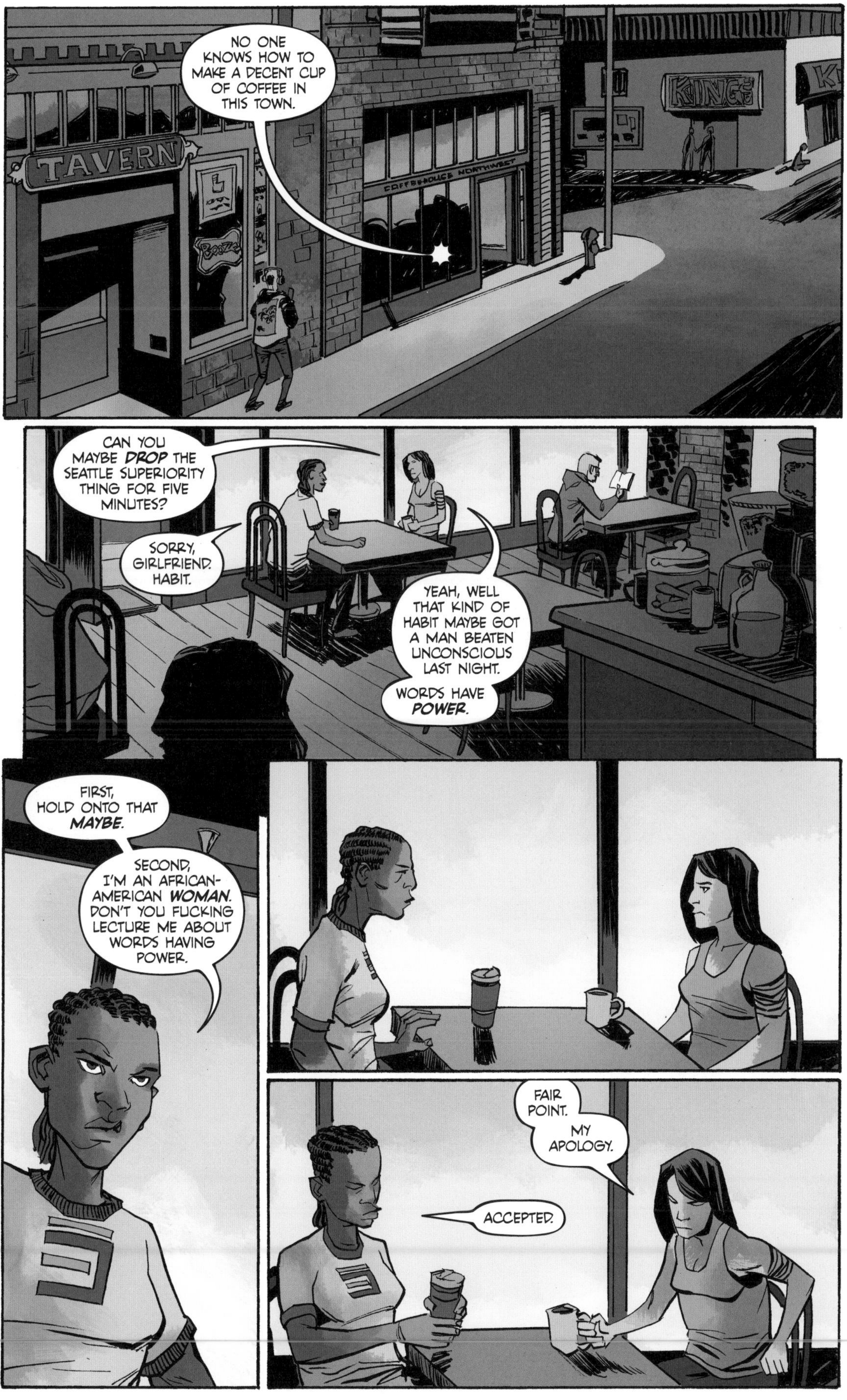
NO ONE KNOWS HOW TO MAKE A DECENT CUP OF COFFEE IN THIS TOWN.
TAVERN
COFFEEHOUSE NORTHWEST
CAN YOU MAYBE DROP THE SEATTLE SUPERIORITY THING FOR FIVE MINUTES?
SORRY, GIRLFRIEND. HABIT.
YEAH, WELL THAT KIND OF HABIT MAYBE GOT A MAN BEATEN UNCONSCIOUS LAST NIGHT.
WORDS HAVE POWER.
FIRST, HOLD ONTO THAT MAYBE.
SECOND, I'M AN AFRICAN-AMERICAN WOMAN. DON'T YOU FUCKING LECTURE ME ABOUT WORDS HAVING POWER.
FAIR POINT.
MY APOLOGY.
ACCEPTED.

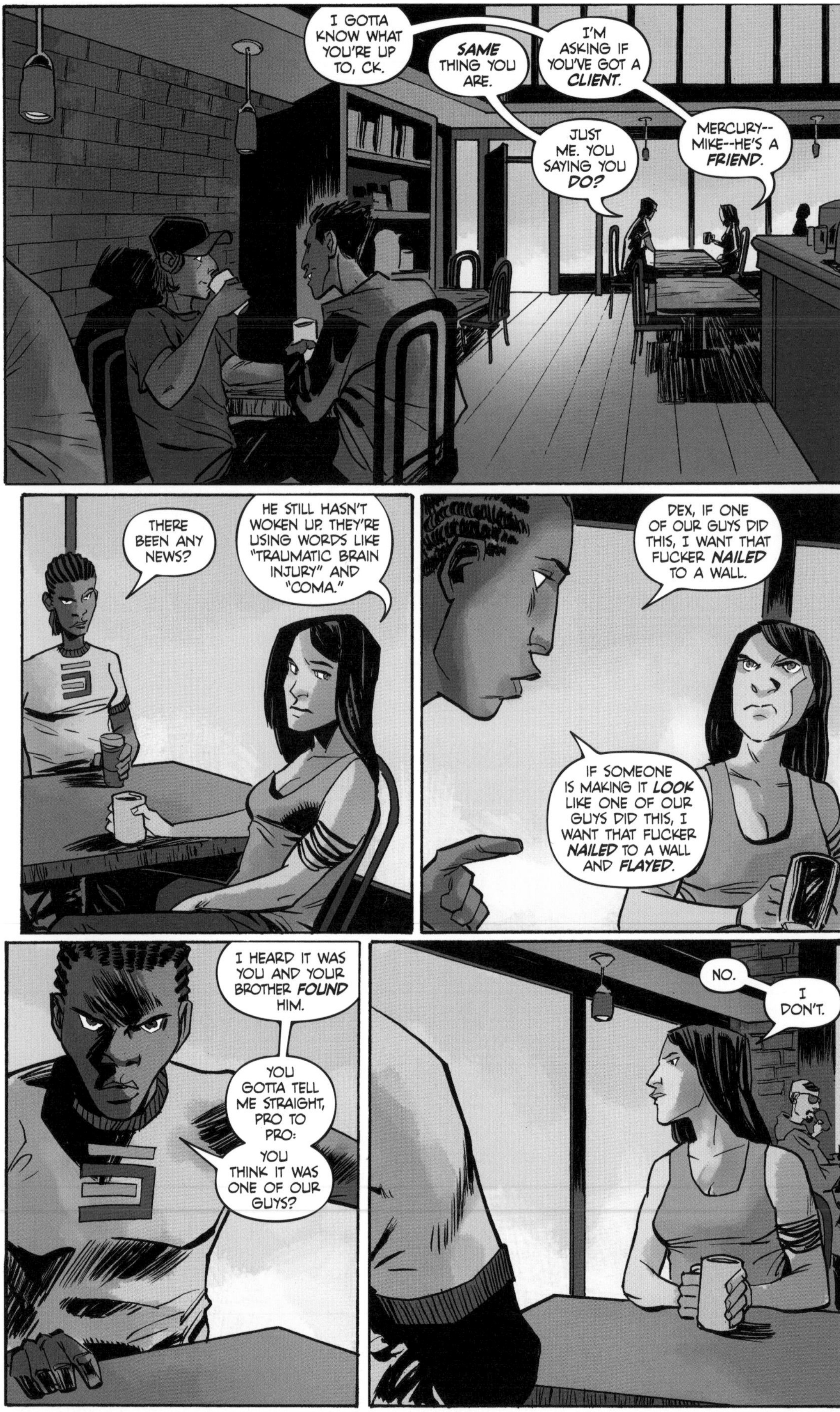
I GOTTA KNOW WHAT YOU'RE UP TO, CK.
SAME THING YOU ARE.
I'M ASKING IF YOU'VE GOT A CLIENT.
JUST ME. YOU SAYING YOU DO?
MERCURY--MIKE--HE'S A FRIEND.
THERE BEEN ANY NEWS?
HE STILL HASN'T WOKEN UP. THEY'RE USING WORDS LIKE "TRAUMATIC BRAIN INJURY" AND "COMA."
DEX, IF ONE OF OUR GUYS DID THIS, I WANT THAT FUCKER NAILED TO A WALL.
IF SOMEONE IS MAKING IT LOOK LIKE ONE OF OUR GUYS DID THIS, I WANT THAT FUCKER NAILED TO A WALL AND FLAYED.
I HEARD IT WAS YOU AND YOUR BROTHER FOUND HIM.
YOU GOTTA TELL ME STRAIGHT, PRO TO PRO:
YOU THINK IT WAS ONE OF OUR GUYS?
NO.
I DON'T.

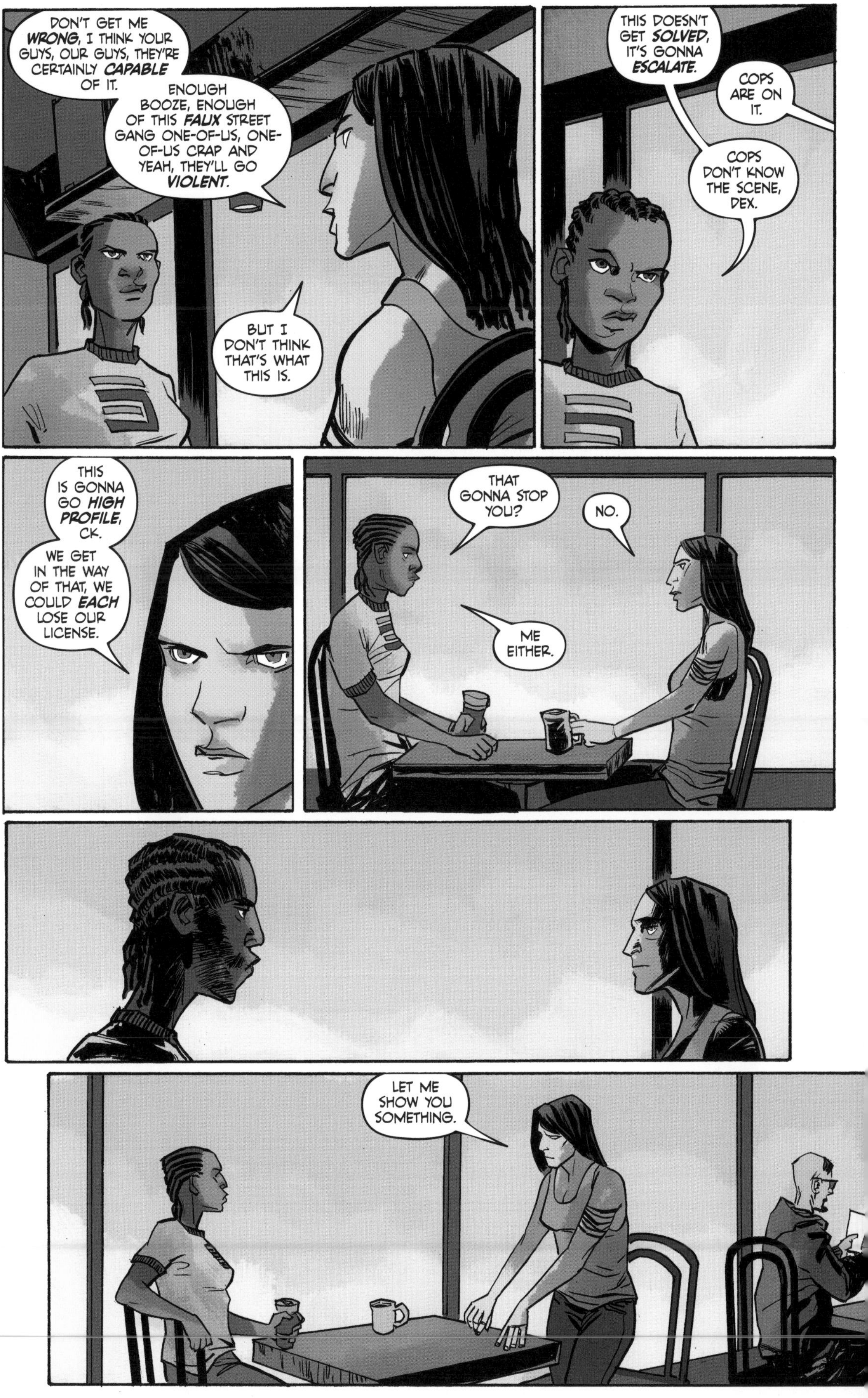
DON'T GET ME WRONG, I THINK YOUR GUYS, OUR GUYS, THEY'RE CERTAINLY CAPABLE OF IT.
ENOUGH BOOZE, ENOUGH OF THIS FAUX STREET GANG ONE-OF-US, ONE-OF-US CRAP AND YEAH, THEY'LL GO VIOLENT.
BUT I DON'T THINK THAT'S WHAT THIS IS.
THIS DOESN'T GET SOLVED, IT'S GONNA ESCALATE.
COPS ARE ON IT.
COPS DON'T KNOW THE SCENE, DEX.
THIS IS GONNA GO HIGH PROFILE, CK.
WE GET IN THE WAY OF THAT, WE COULD EACH LOSE OUR LICENSE.
THAT GONNA STOP YOU?
NO.
ME EITHER.
LET ME SHOW YOU SOMETHING.

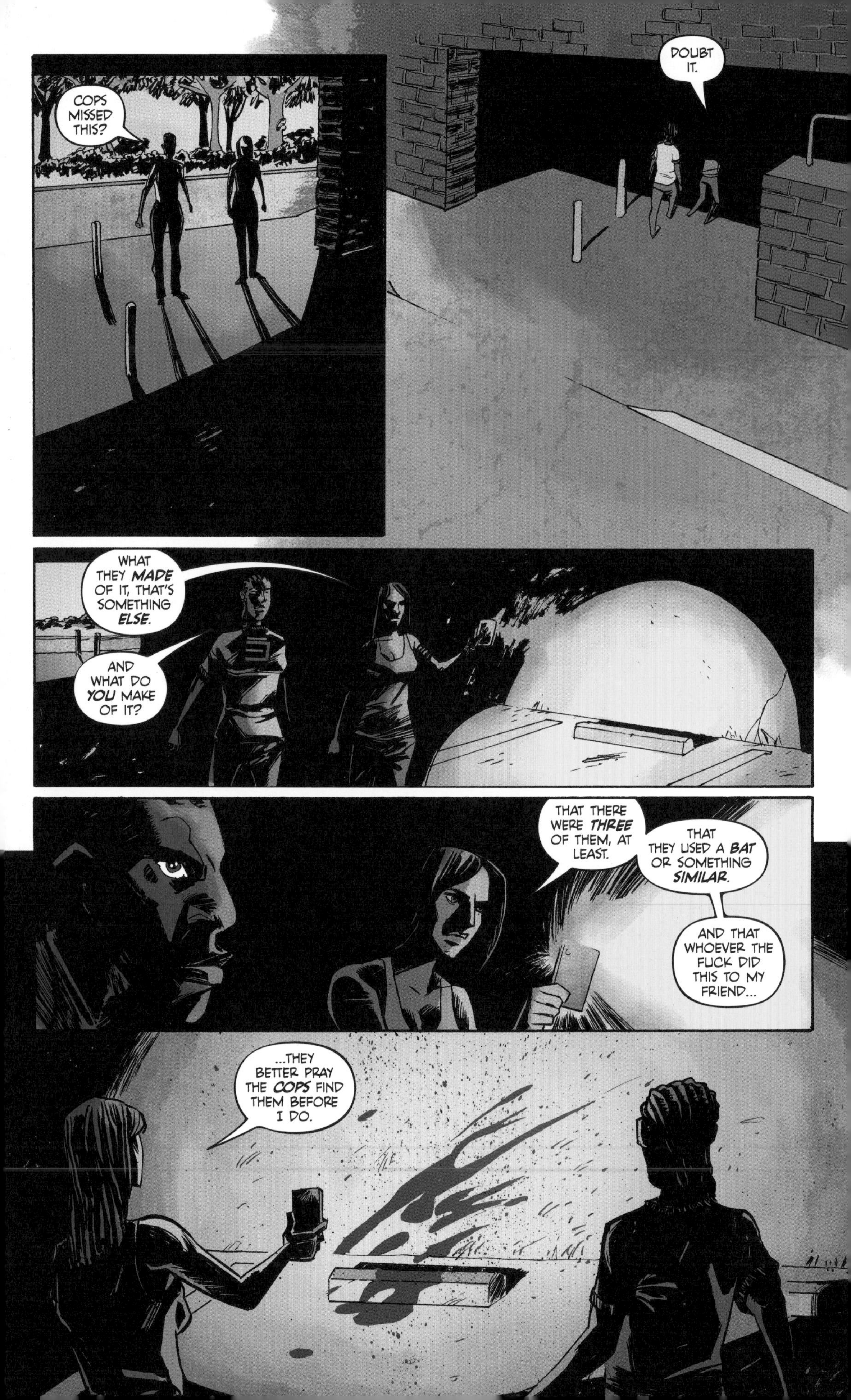
COPS MISSED THIS?
DOUBT IT.
WHAT THEY MADE OF IT, THAT'S SOMETHING ELSE.
AND WHAT DO YOU MAKE OF IT?
THAT THERE WERE THREE OF THEM, AT LEAST.
THAT THEY USED A BAT OR SOMETHING SIMILAR.
AND THAT WHOEVER THE FUCK DID THIS TO MY FRIEND...
...THEY BETTER PRAY THE COPS FIND THEM BEFORE I DO.

Chapter Three

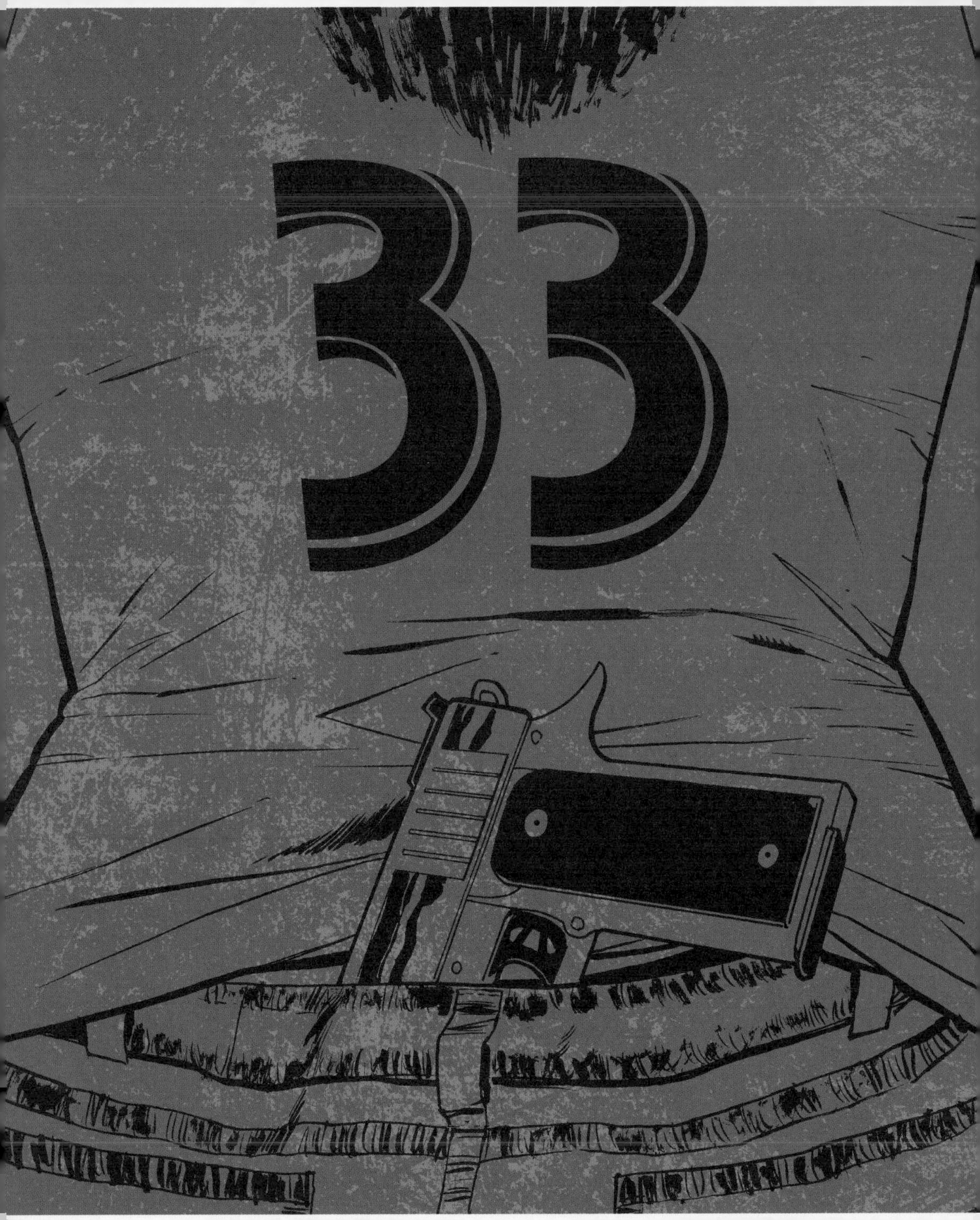
33

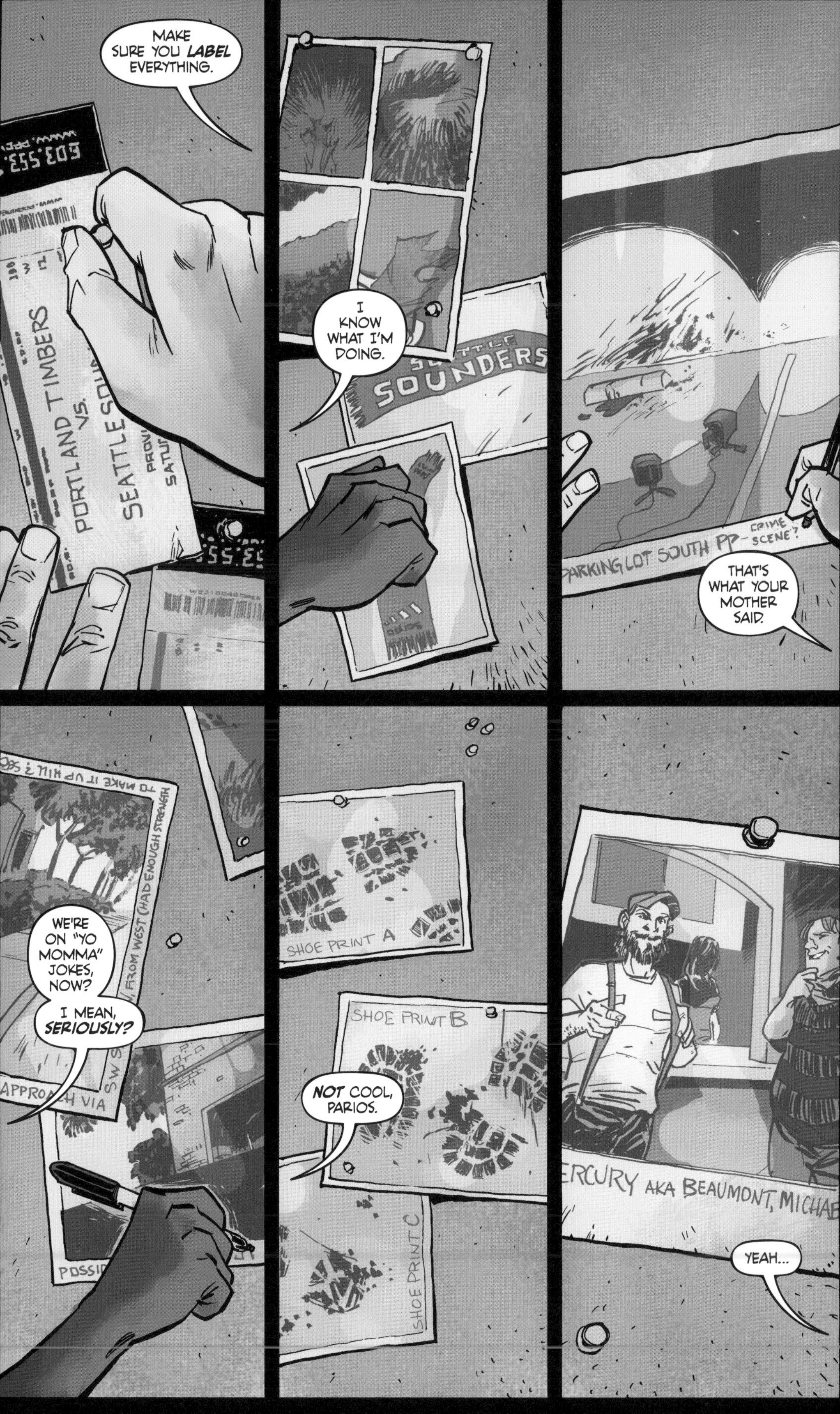
MAKE SURE YOU ***LABEL*** EVERYTHING.
PORTLAND TIMBERS VS.
I KNOW WHAT I'M DOING.
SOUNDERS
THAT'S WHAT YOUR MOTHER SAID.
WE'RE ON "YO MOMMA" JOKES, NOW?
I MEAN, ***SERIOUSLY?***
SHOE PRINT A
SHOE PRINT B
NOT COOL, PARIOS.
SHOE PRINT C
AKA BEAUMONT,
YEAH...

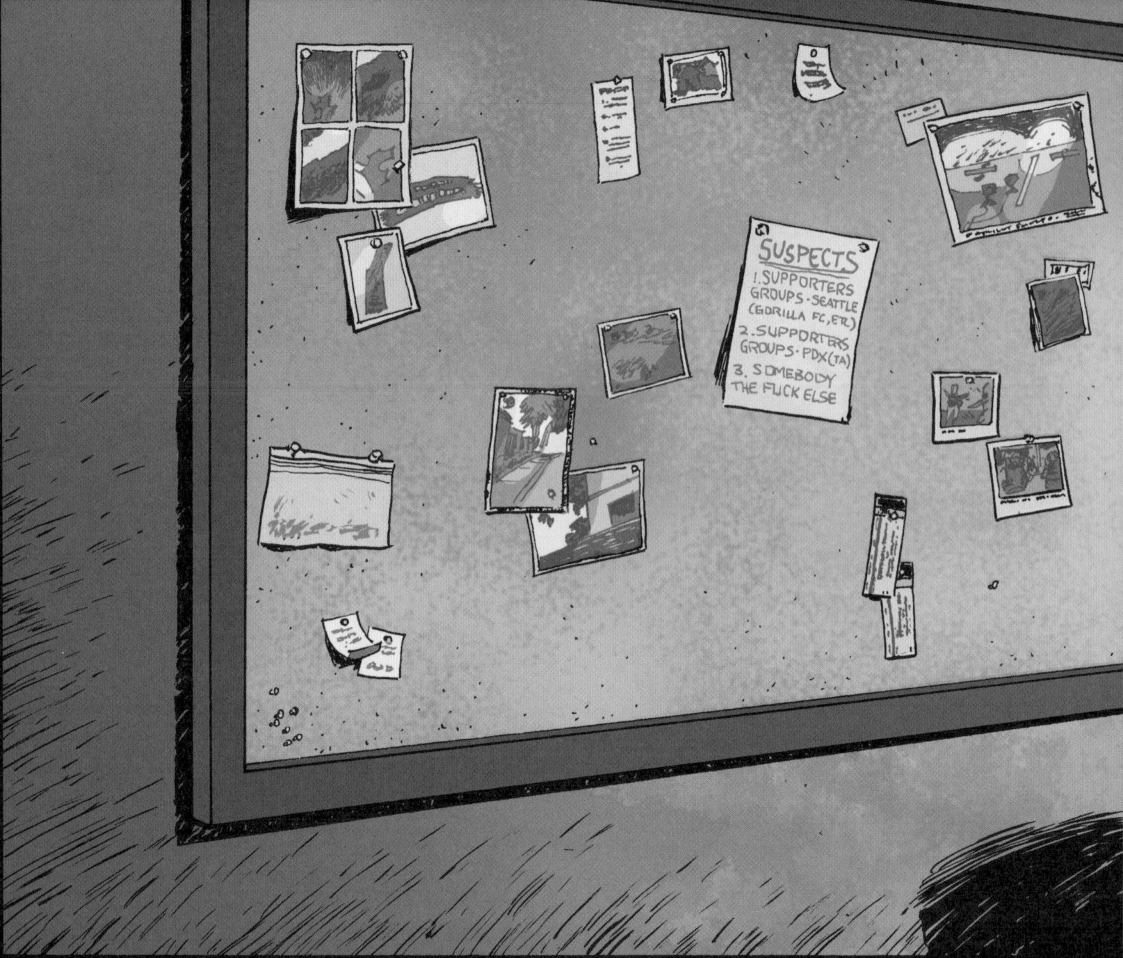
SUSPECTS
1. SUPPORTERS GROUPS - SEATTLE (GORILLA FC, ETC)
2. SUPPORTERS GROUPS - PDX (TA)
3. SOMEBODY THE FUCK ELSE

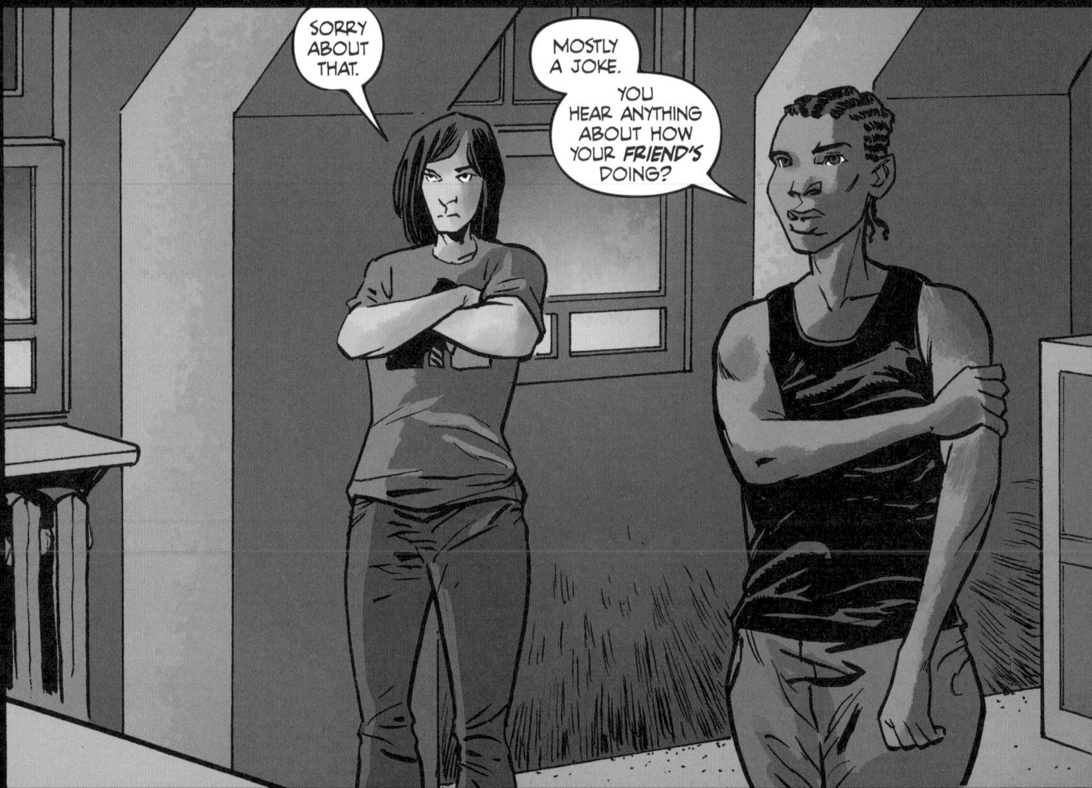
SORRY ABOUT THAT.
MOSTLY A JOKE.
YOU HEAR ANYTHING ABOUT HOW YOUR *FRIEND'S* DOING?

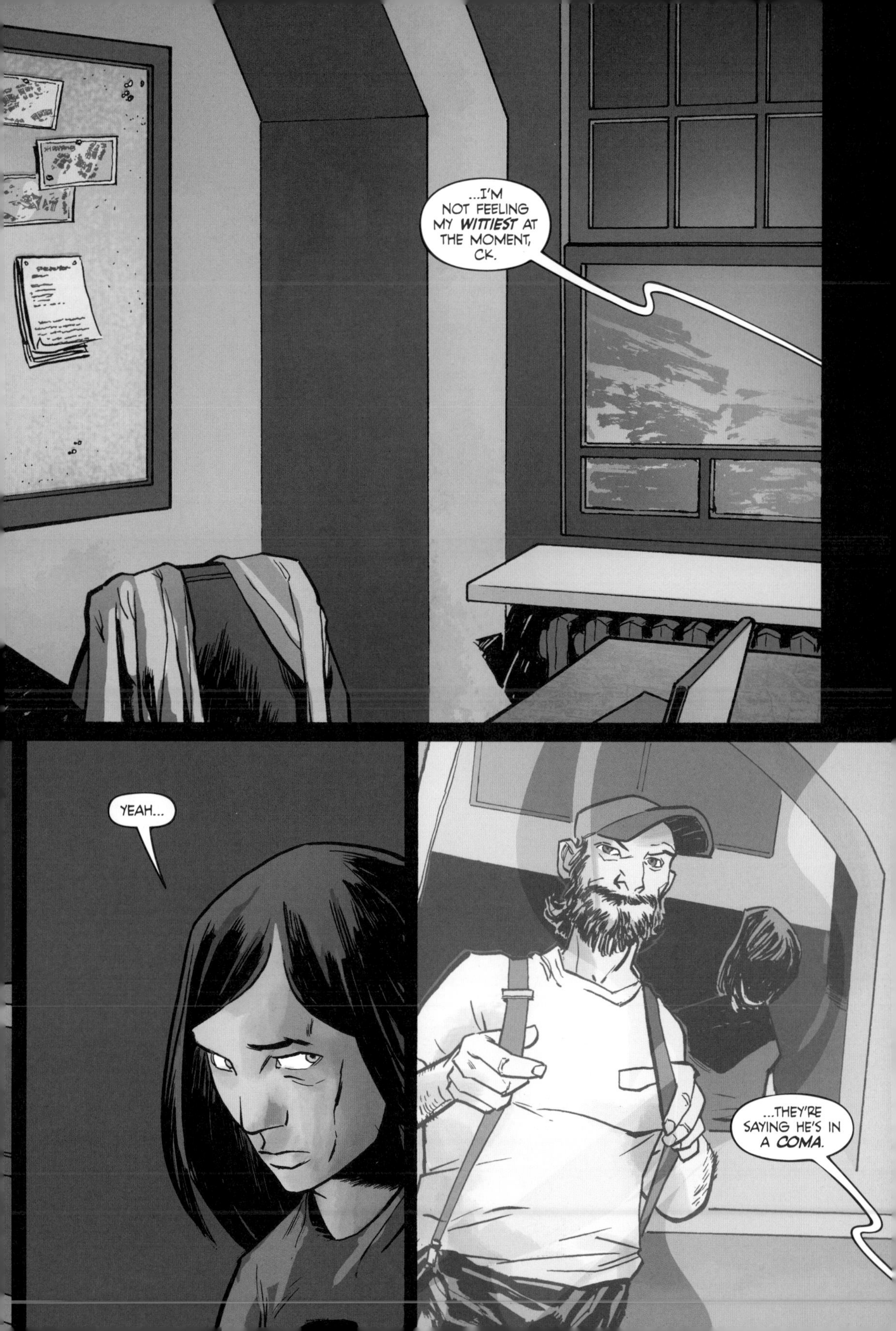
...I'M NOT FEELING MY *WITTIEST* AT THE MOMENT, CK.
YEAH...
...THEY'RE SAYING HE'S IN A *COMA*.

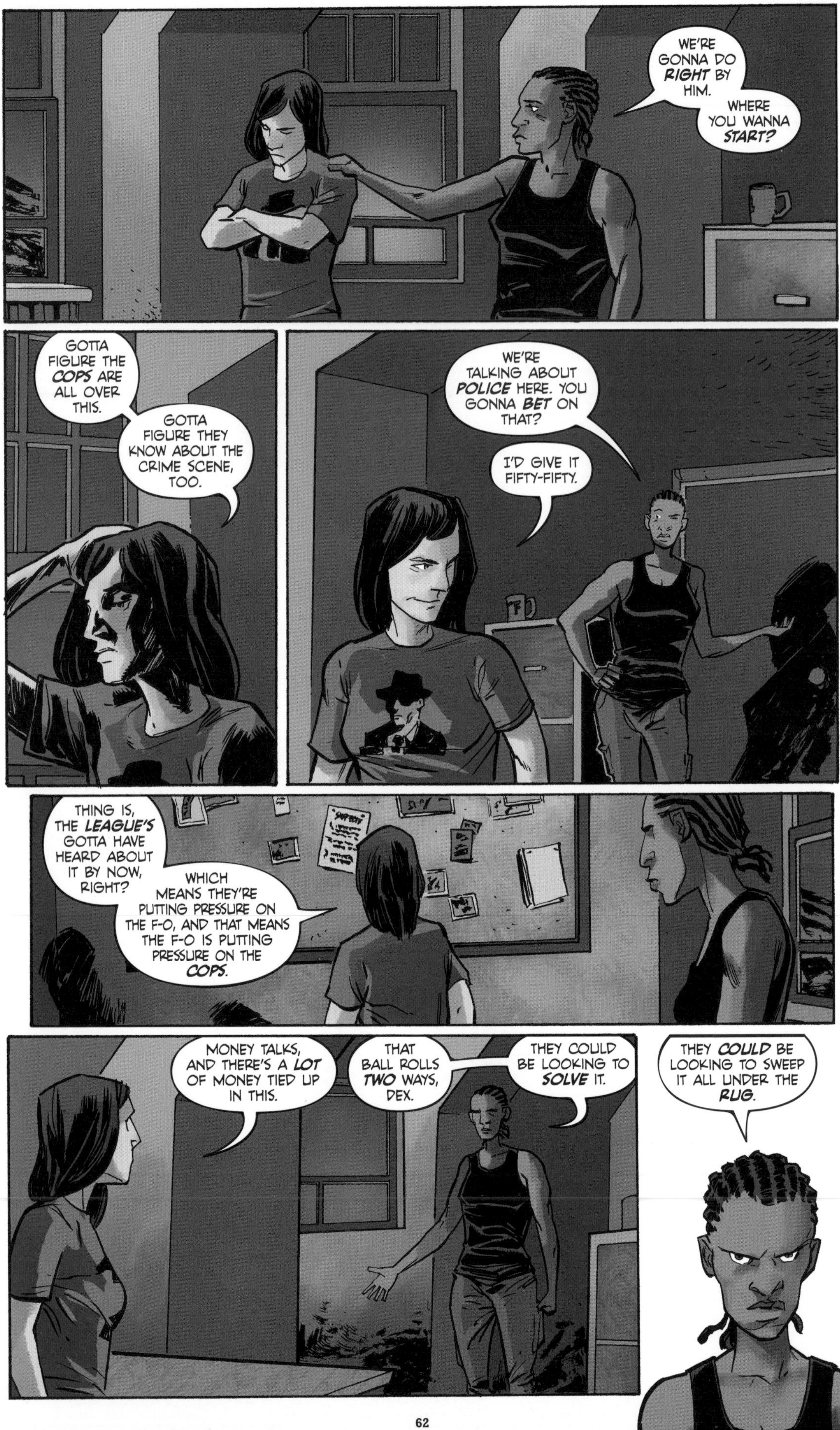
WE'RE GONNA DO RIGHT BY HIM.
WHERE YOU WANNA START?
GOTTA FIGURE THE COPS ARE ALL OVER THIS.
GOTTA FIGURE THEY KNOW ABOUT THE CRIME SCENE, TOO.
WE'RE TALKING ABOUT POLICE HERE. YOU GONNA BET ON THAT?
I'D GIVE IT FIFTY-FIFTY.
THING IS, THE LEAGUE'S GOTTA HAVE HEARD ABOUT IT BY NOW, RIGHT?
WHICH MEANS THEY'RE PUTTING PRESSURE ON THE F-O, AND THAT MEANS THE F-O IS PUTTING PRESSURE ON THE COPS.
MONEY TALKS, AND THERE'S A LOT OF MONEY TIED UP IN THIS.
THAT BALL ROLLS TWO WAYS, DEX.
THEY COULD BE LOOKING TO SOLVE IT.
THEY COULD BE LOOKING TO SWEEP IT ALL UNDER THE RUG.

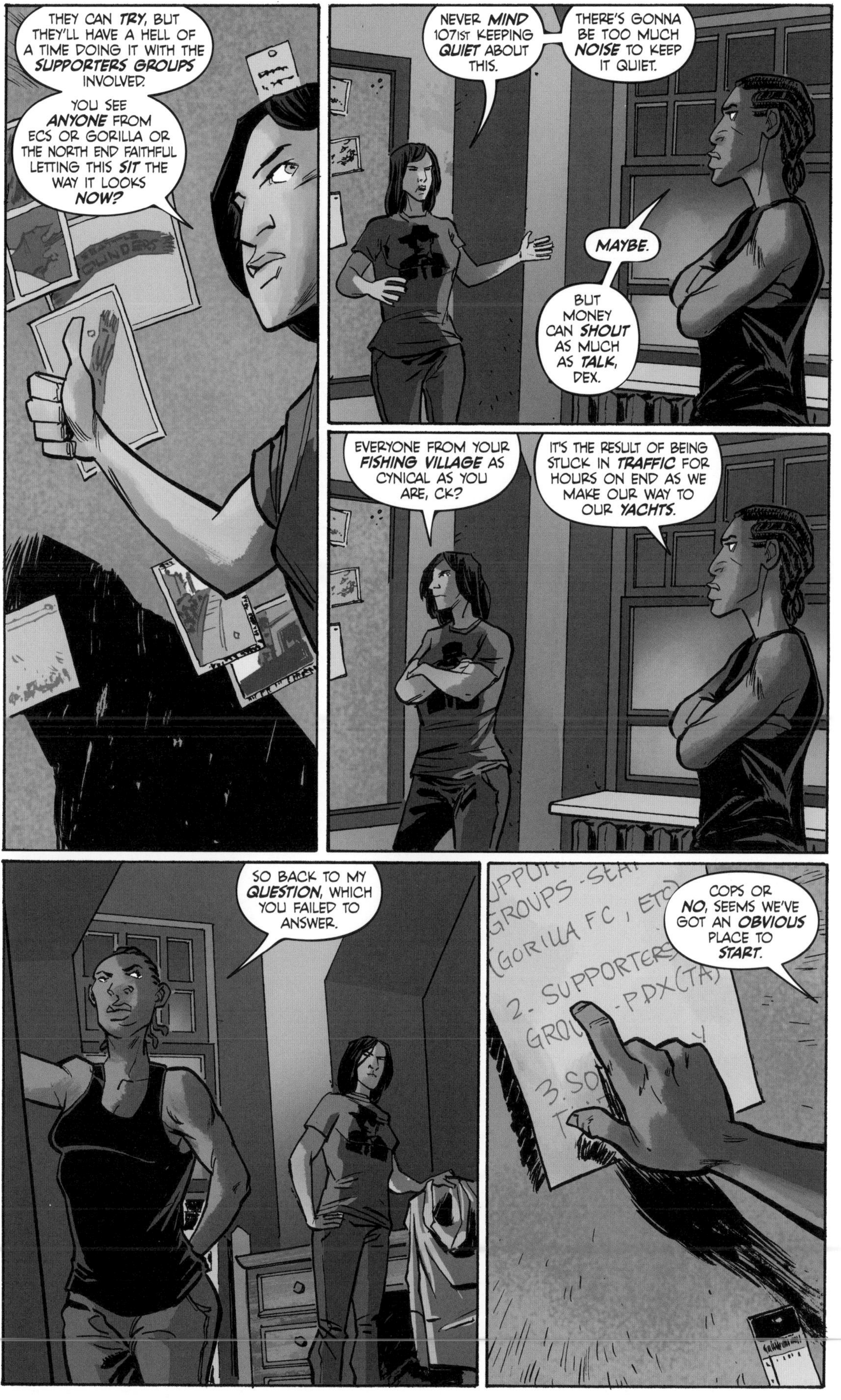

THEY CAN *TRY*, BUT THEY'LL HAVE A HELL OF A TIME DOING IT WITH THE *SUPPORTERS GROUPS* INVOLVED.
YOU SEE *ANYONE* FROM ECS OR GORILLA OR THE NORTH END FAITHFUL LETTING THIS *SIT* THE WAY IT LOOKS *NOW?*
NEVER *MIND* 107IST KEEPING *QUIET* ABOUT THIS.
THERE'S GONNA BE TOO MUCH *NOISE* TO KEEP IT QUIET.
MAYBE.
BUT MONEY CAN *SHOUT* AS MUCH AS *TALK*, DEX.
EVERYONE FROM YOUR *FISHING VILLAGE* AS CYNICAL AS YOU ARE, CK?
IT'S THE RESULT OF BEING STUCK IN *TRAFFIC* FOR HOURS ON END AS WE MAKE OUR WAY TO OUR *YACHTS*.
SO BACK TO MY *QUESTION*, WHICH YOU FAILED TO ANSWER.
COPS OR *NO*, SEEMS WE'VE GOT AN *OBVIOUS* PLACE TO *START*.

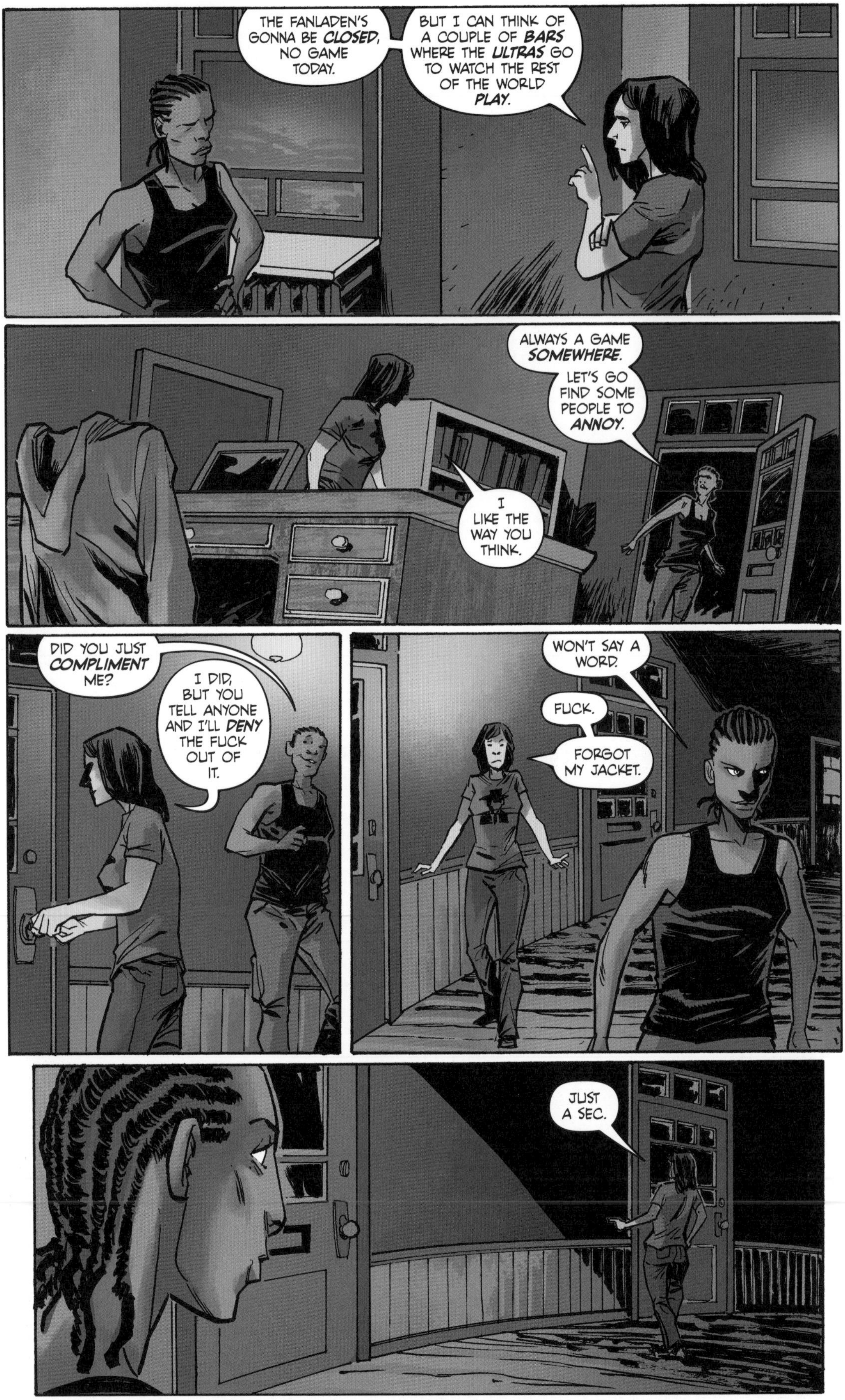
THE FANLADEN'S GONNA BE CLOSED, NO GAME TODAY.
BUT I CAN THINK OF A COUPLE OF BARS WHERE THE ULTRAS GO TO WATCH THE REST OF THE WORLD PLAY.
ALWAYS A GAME SOMEWHERE.
LET'S GO FIND SOME PEOPLE TO ANNOY.
I LIKE THE WAY YOU THINK.
DID YOU JUST COMPLIMENT ME?
I DID, BUT YOU TELL ANYONE AND I'LL DENY THE FUCK OUT OF IT.
WON'T SAY A WORD.
FUCK.
FORGOT MY JACKET.
JUST A SEC.

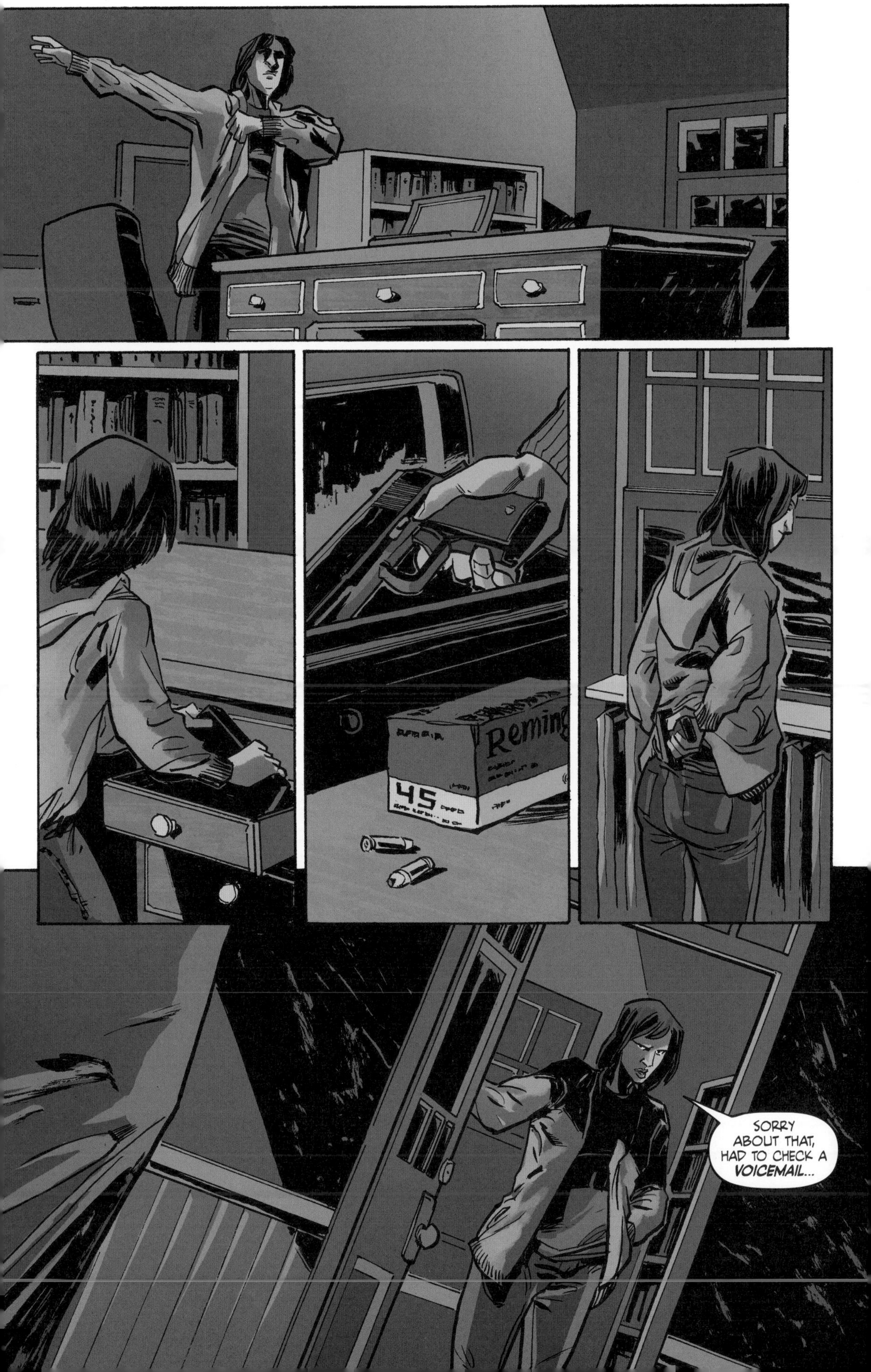
SORRY ABOUT THAT, HAD TO CHECK A VOICEMAIL...

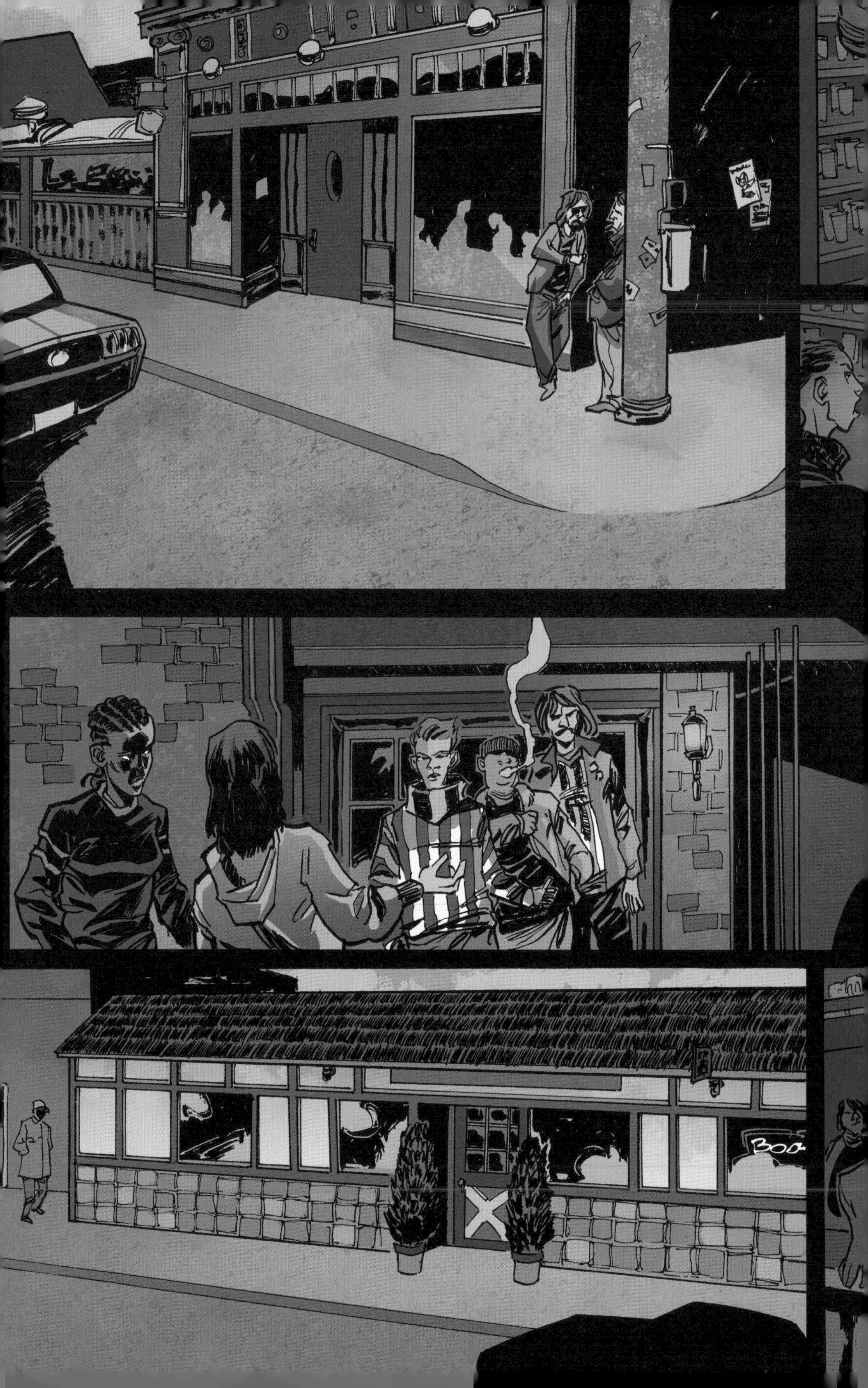

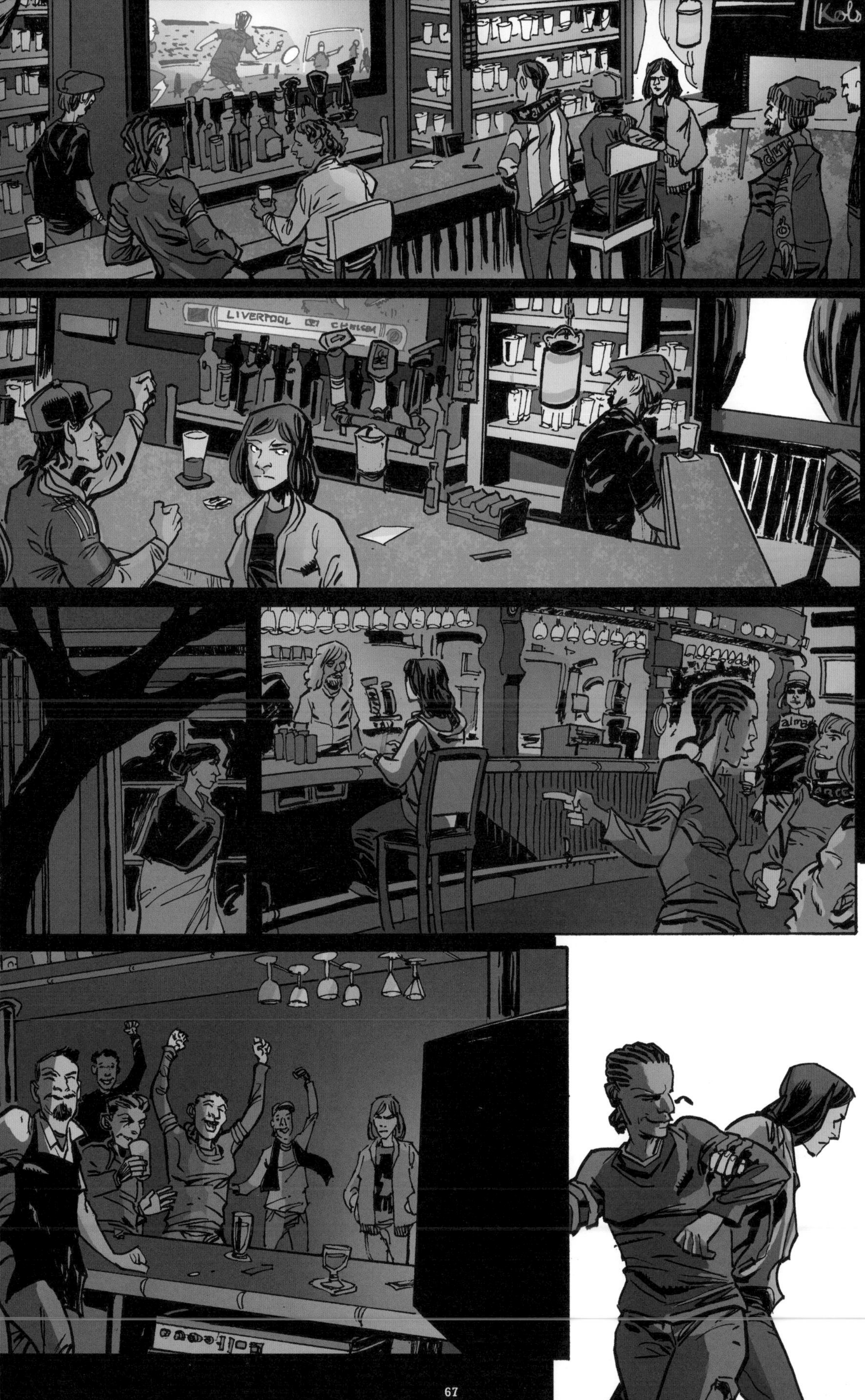
Kols
LIVERPOOL

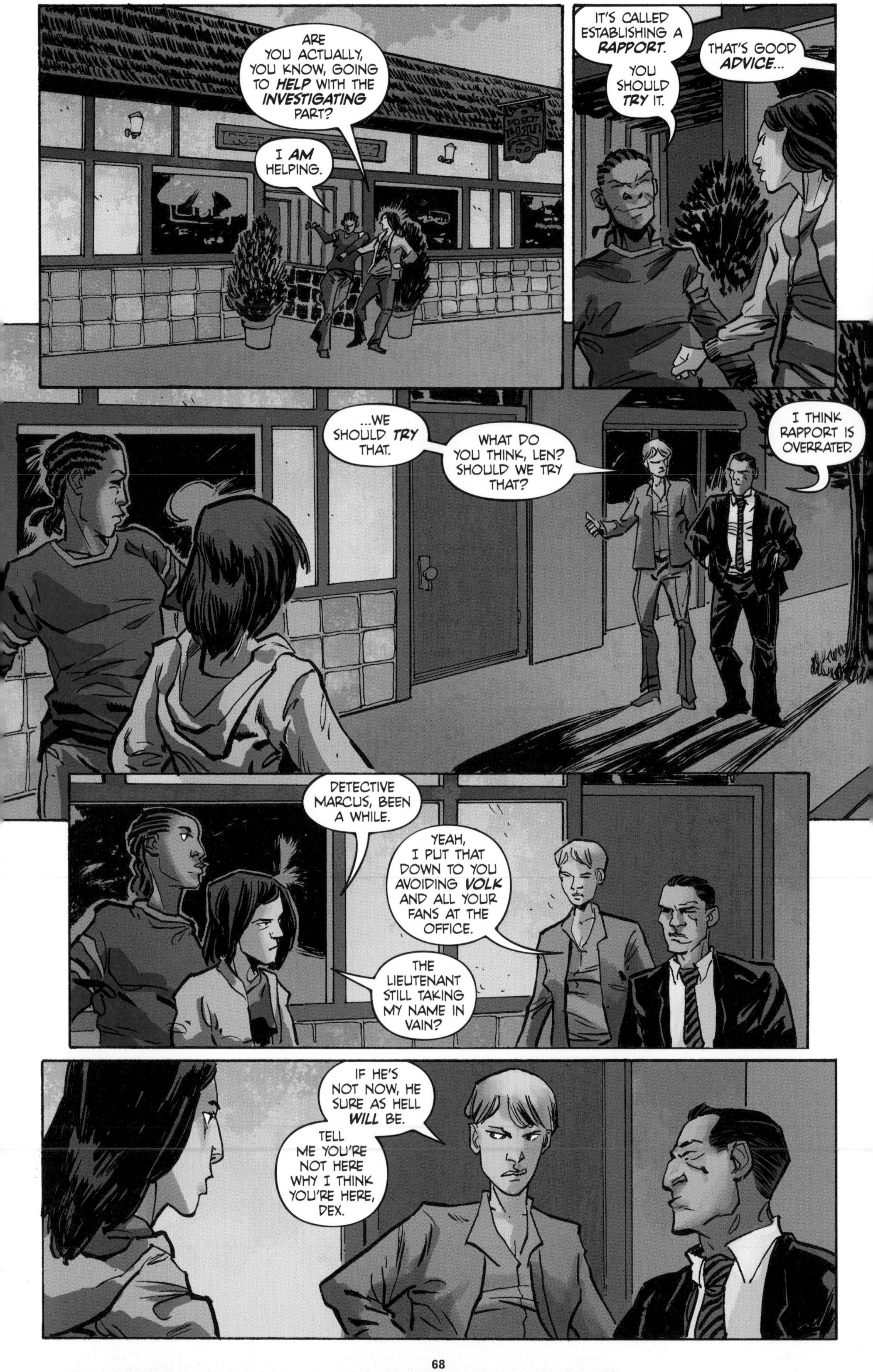
ARE YOU ACTUALLY, YOU KNOW, GOING TO HELP WITH THE INVESTIGATING PART?
I AM HELPING.
IT'S CALLED ESTABLISHING A RAPPORT.
YOU SHOULD TRY IT.
THAT'S GOOD ADVICE...
...WE SHOULD TRY THAT.
WHAT DO YOU THINK, LEN? SHOULD WE TRY THAT?
I THINK RAPPORT IS OVERRATED.
DETECTIVE MARCUS, BEEN A WHILE.
YEAH, I PUT THAT DOWN TO YOU AVOIDING VOLK AND ALL YOUR FANS AT THE OFFICE.
THE LIEUTENANT STILL TAKING MY NAME IN VAIN?
IF HE'S NOT NOW, HE SURE AS HELL WILL BE.
TELL ME YOU'RE NOT HERE WHY I THINK YOU'RE HERE, DEX.

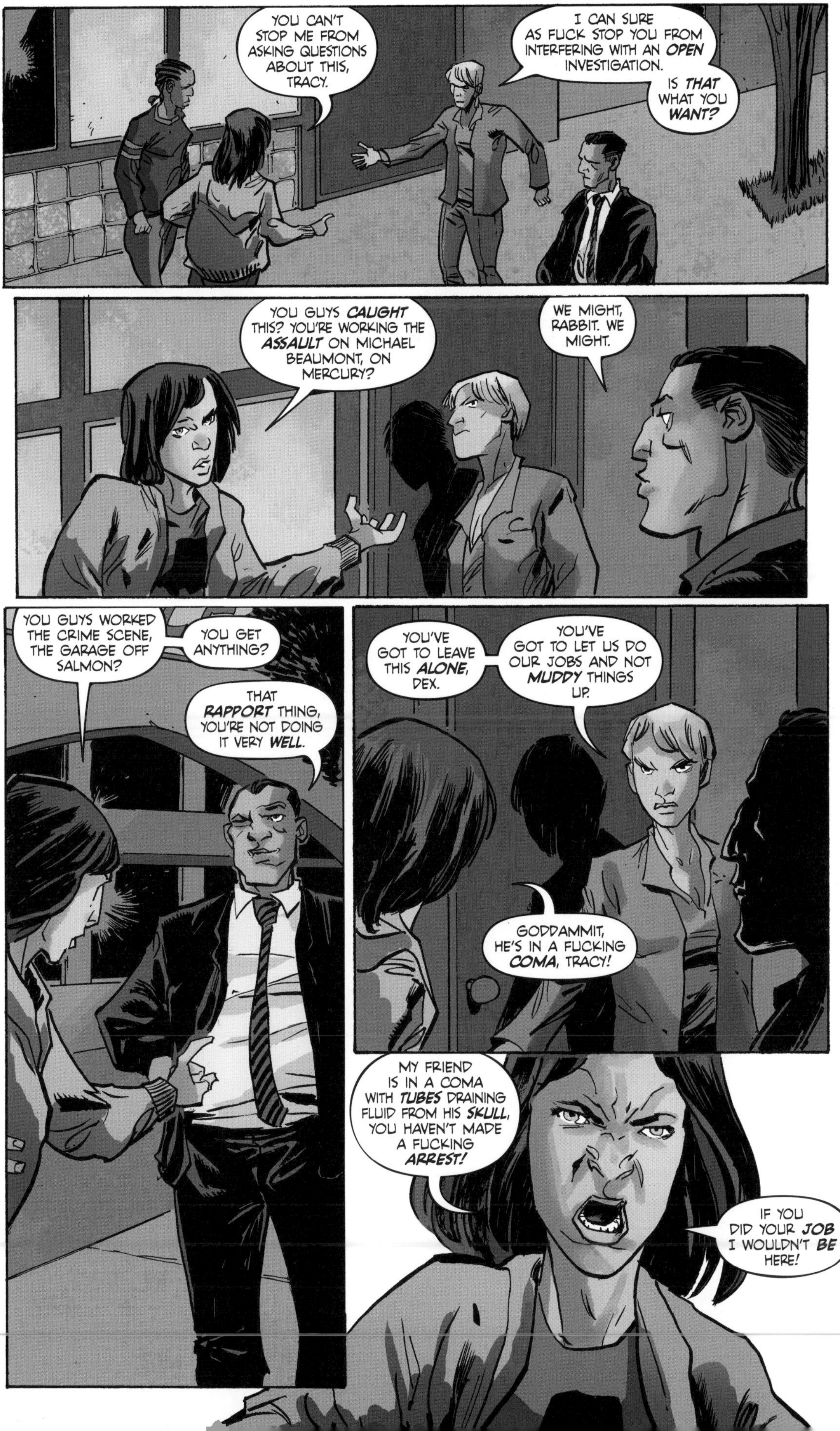
YOU CAN'T STOP ME FROM ASKING QUESTIONS ABOUT THIS, TRACY.
I CAN SURE AS FUCK STOP YOU FROM INTERFERING WITH AN OPEN INVESTIGATION.
IS THAT WHAT YOU WANT?
YOU GUYS CAUGHT THIS? YOU'RE WORKING THE ASSAULT ON MICHAEL BEAUMONT, ON MERCURY?
WE MIGHT, RABBIT. WE MIGHT.
YOU GUYS WORKED THE CRIME SCENE, THE GARAGE OFF SALMON?
YOU GET ANYTHING?
THAT RAPPORT THING, YOU'RE NOT DOING IT VERY WELL.
YOU'VE GOT TO LEAVE THIS ALONE, DEX.
YOU'VE GOT TO LET US DO OUR JOBS AND NOT MUDDY THINGS UP.
GODDAMMIT, HE'S IN A FUCKING COMA, TRACY!
MY FRIEND IS IN A COMA WITH TUBES DRAINING FLUID FROM HIS SKULL, YOU HAVEN'T MADE A FUCKING ARREST!
IF YOU DID YOUR JOB I WOULDN'T BE HERE!

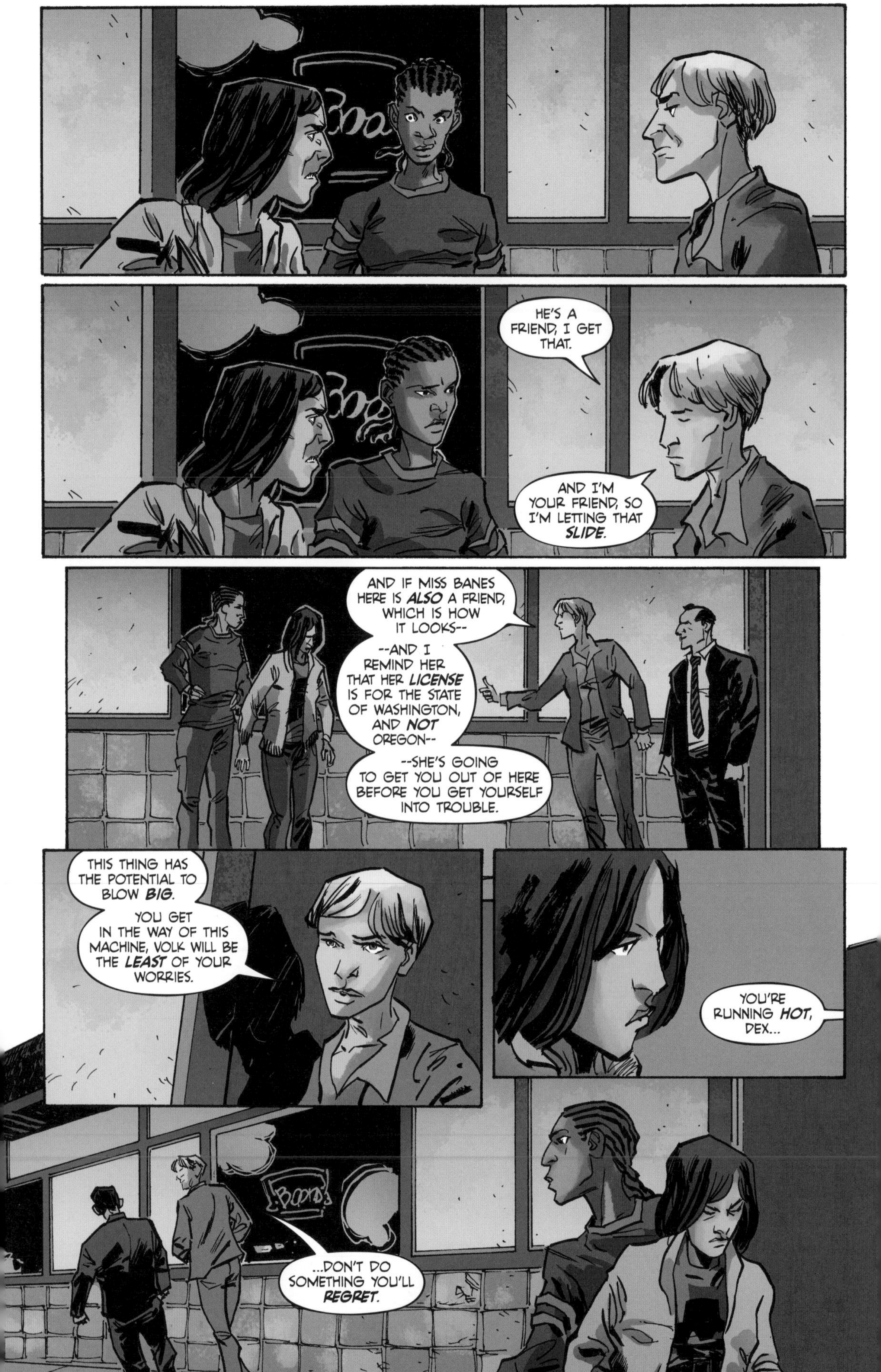
HE'S A FRIEND, I GET THAT.
AND I'M YOUR FRIEND, SO I'M LETTING THAT SLIDE.
AND IF MISS BANES HERE IS ALSO A FRIEND, WHICH IS HOW IT LOOKS--
--AND I REMIND HER THAT HER LICENSE IS FOR THE STATE OF WASHINGTON, AND NOT OREGON--
--SHE'S GOING TO GET YOU OUT OF HERE BEFORE YOU GET YOURSELF INTO TROUBLE.
THIS THING HAS THE POTENTIAL TO BLOW BIG.
YOU GET IN THE WAY OF THIS MACHINE, VOLK WILL BE THE LEAST OF YOUR WORRIES.
YOU'RE RUNNING HOT, DEX...
...DON'T DO SOMETHING YOU'LL REGRET.

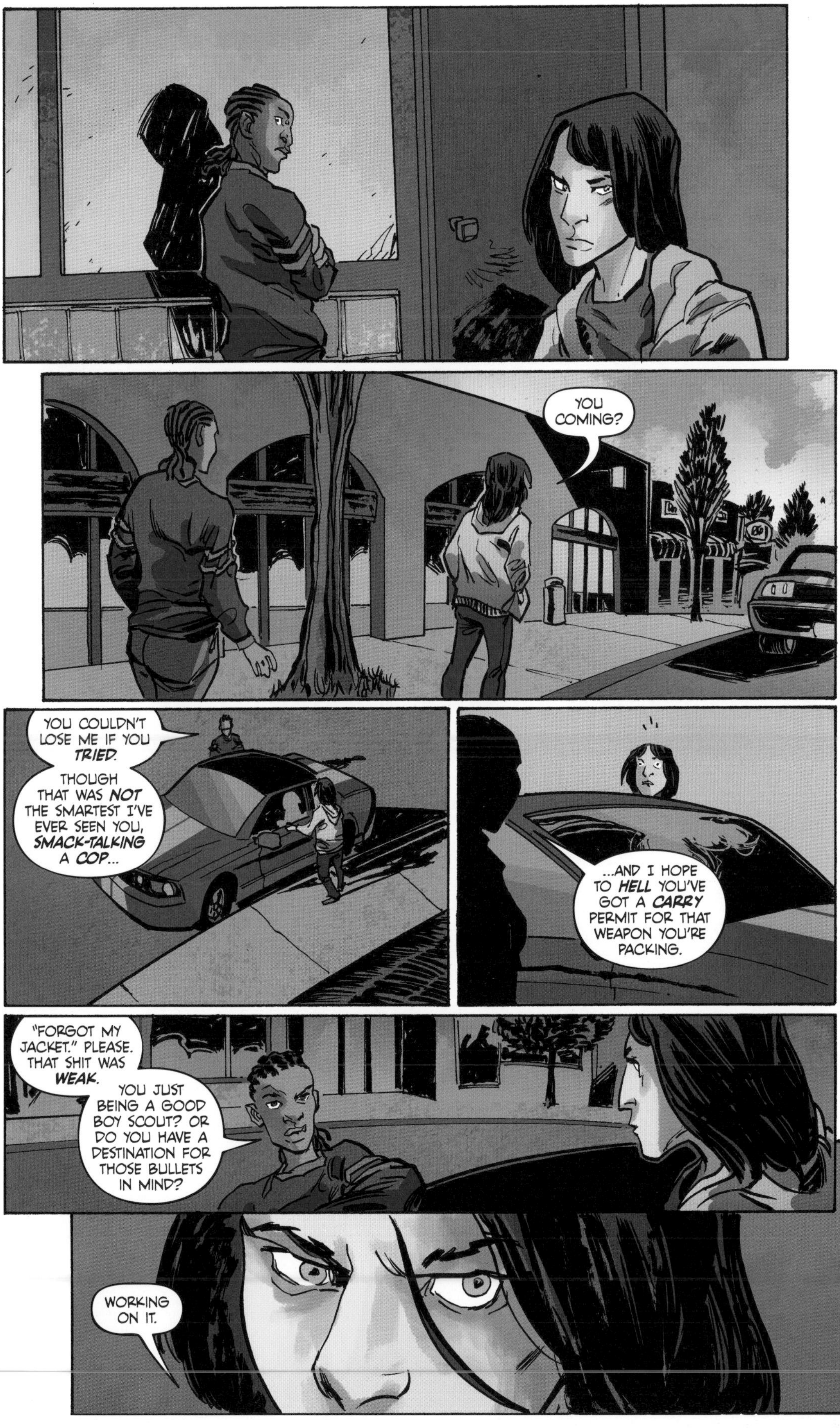
YOU COMING?
YOU COULDN'T LOSE ME IF YOU TRIED.
THOUGH THAT WAS NOT THE SMARTEST I'VE EVER SEEN YOU, SMACK-TALKING A COP...
...AND I HOPE TO HELL YOU'VE GOT A CARRY PERMIT FOR THAT WEAPON YOU'RE PACKING.
"FORGOT MY JACKET." PLEASE. THAT SHIT WAS WEAK.
YOU JUST BEING A GOOD BOY SCOUT? OR DO YOU HAVE A DESTINATION FOR THOSE BULLETS IN MIND?
WORKING ON IT.

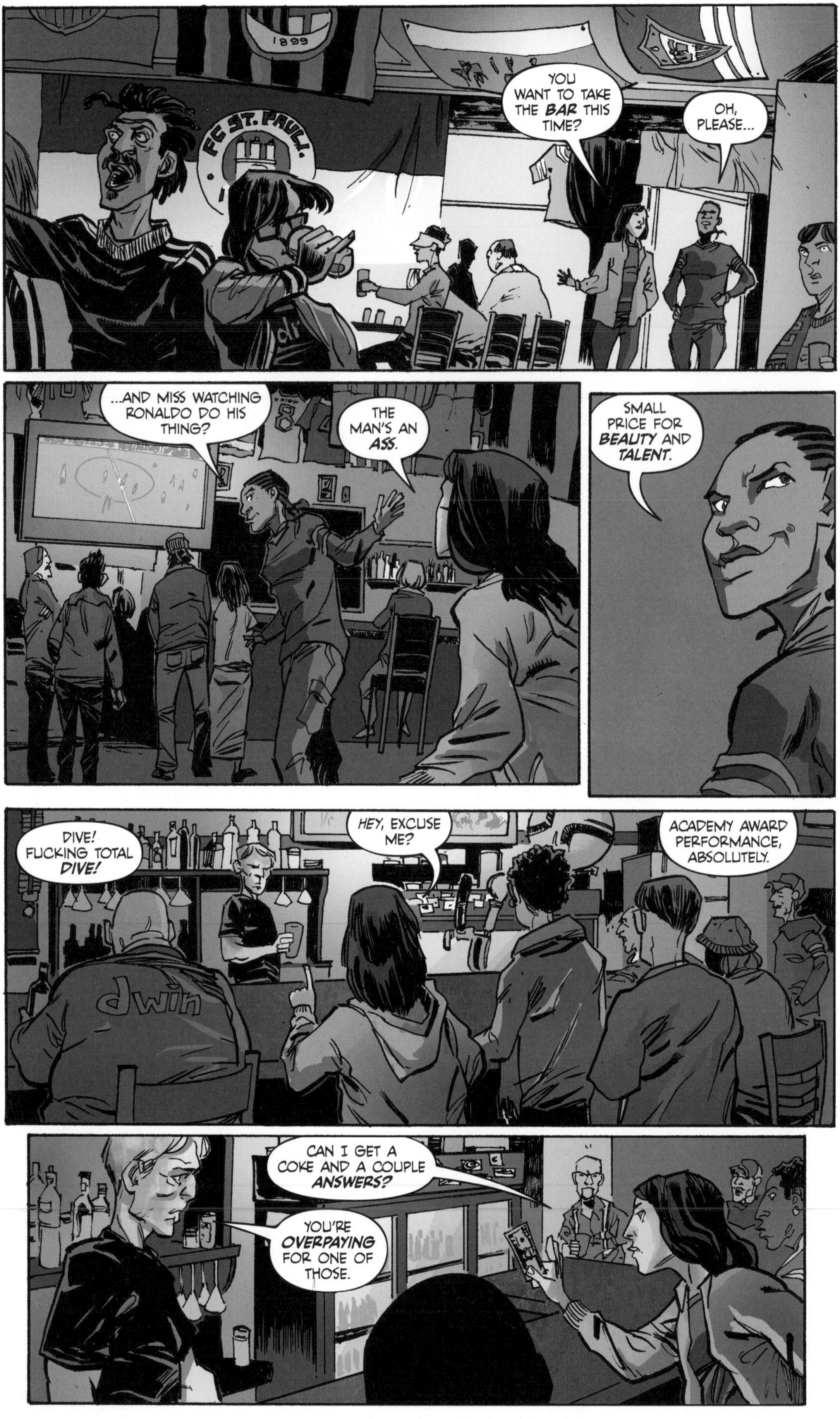
1899
FC ST. PAULI
YOU WANT TO TAKE THE **BAR** THIS TIME?
OH, PLEASE...
...AND MISS WATCHING RONALDO DO HIS THING?
THE MAN'S AN **ASS**.
SMALL PRICE FOR **BEAUTY** AND **TALENT**.
DIVE! FUCKING TOTAL **DIVE!**
HEY, EXCUSE ME?
ACADEMY AWARD PERFORMANCE, ABSOLUTELY.
CAN I GET A COKE AND A COUPLE **ANSWERS?**
YOU'RE **OVERPAYING** FOR ONE OF THOSE.

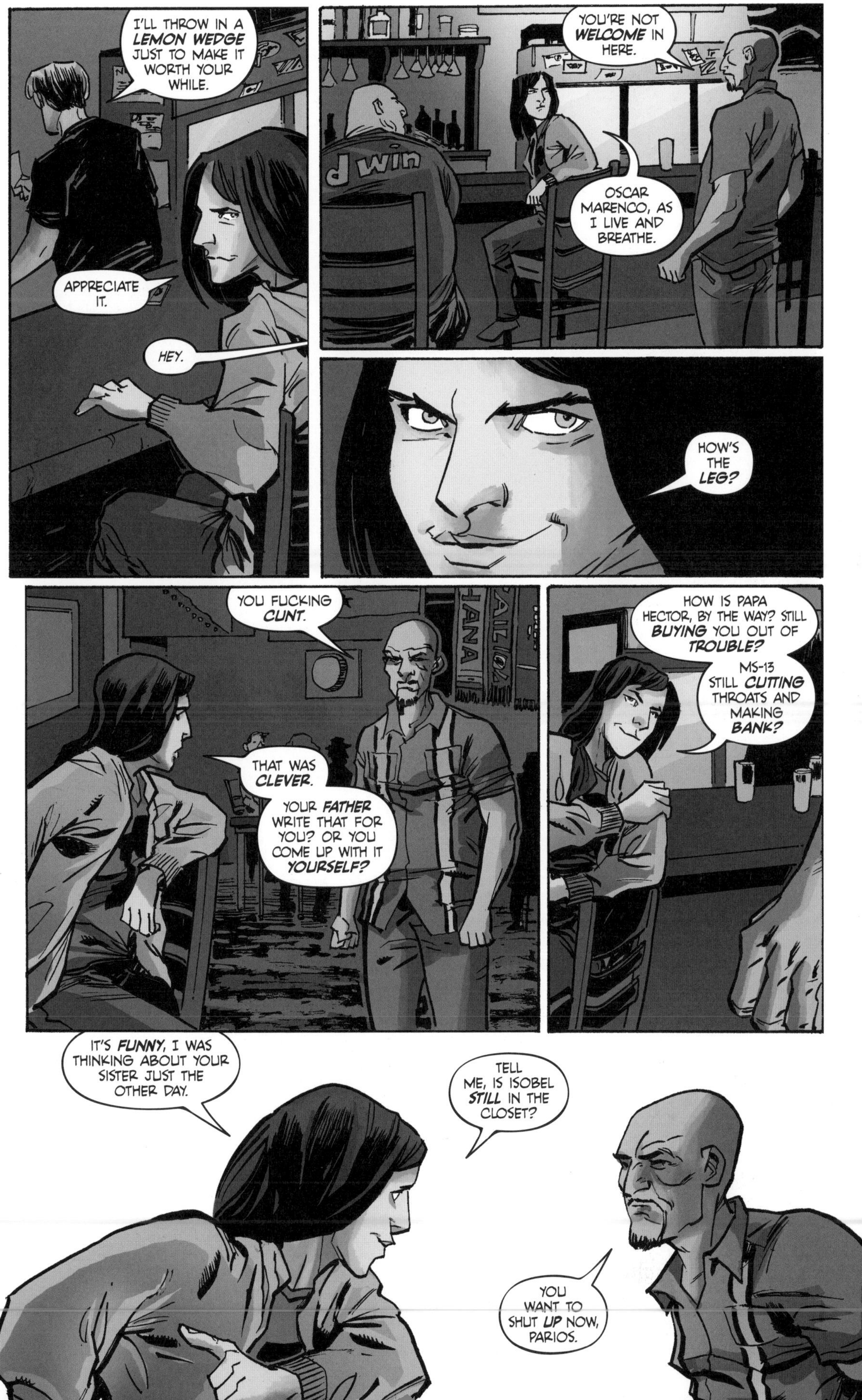
I'LL THROW IN A LEMON WEDGE JUST TO MAKE IT WORTH YOUR WHILE.
APPRECIATE IT.
HEY.
YOU'RE NOT WELCOME IN HERE.
OSCAR MARENCO, AS I LIVE AND BREATHE.
HOW'S THE LEG?
YOU FUCKING CUNT.
THAT WAS CLEVER.
YOUR FATHER WRITE THAT FOR YOU? OR YOU COME UP WITH IT YOURSELF?
HOW IS PAPA HECTOR, BY THE WAY? STILL BUYING YOU OUT OF TROUBLE?
MS-13 STILL CUTTING THROATS AND MAKING BANK?
IT'S FUNNY, I WAS THINKING ABOUT YOUR SISTER JUST THE OTHER DAY.
TELL ME, IS ISOBEL STILL IN THE CLOSET?
YOU WANT TO SHUT UP NOW, PARIOS.

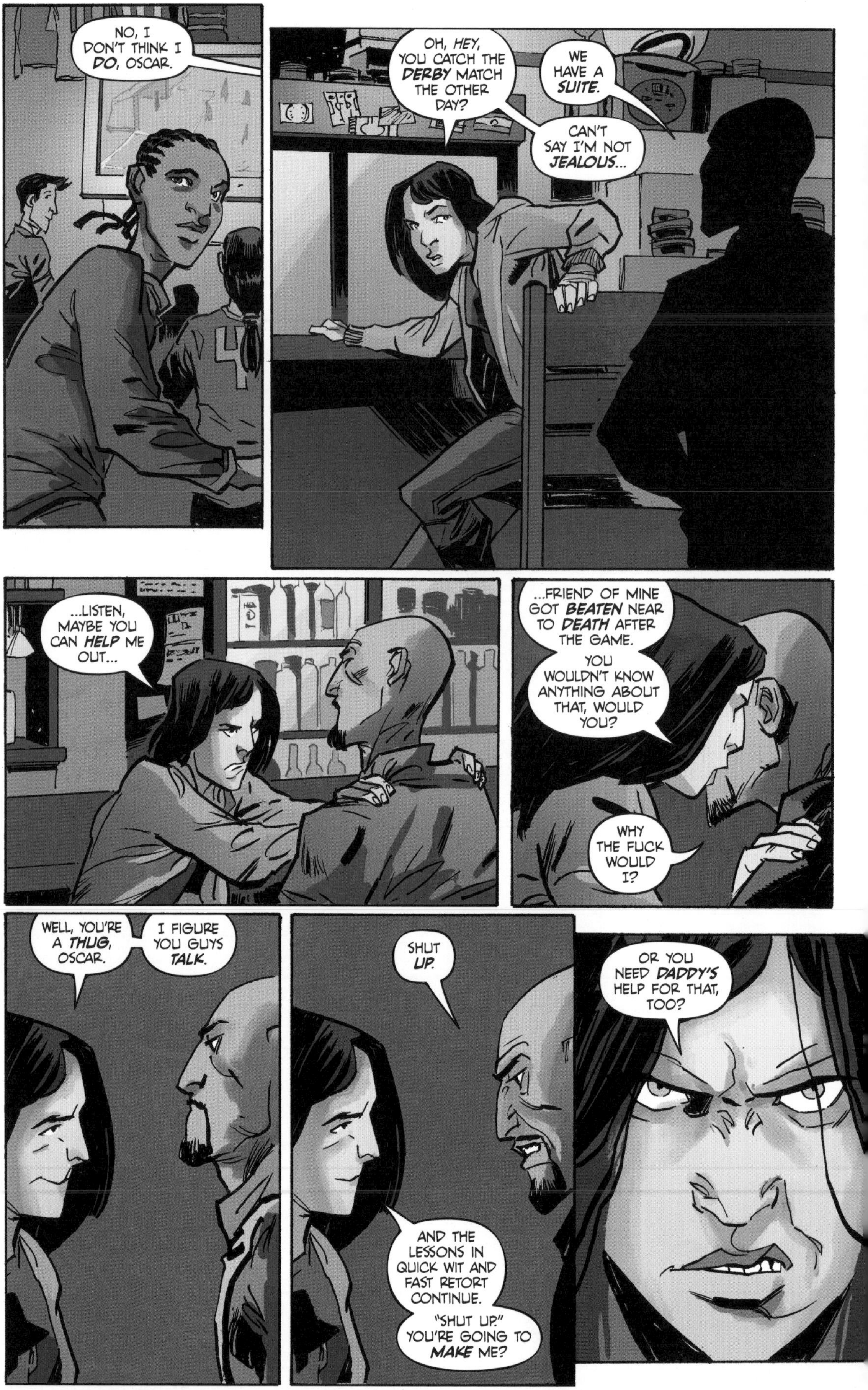

NO, I DON'T THINK I DO, OSCAR.
OH, HEY, YOU CATCH THE DERBY MATCH THE OTHER DAY?
WE HAVE A SUITE.
CAN'T SAY I'M NOT JEALOUS...
...LISTEN, MAYBE YOU CAN HELP ME OUT...
...FRIEND OF MINE GOT BEATEN NEAR TO DEATH AFTER THE GAME.
YOU WOULDN'T KNOW ANYTHING ABOUT THAT, WOULD YOU?
WHY THE FUCK WOULD I?
WELL, YOU'RE A THUG, OSCAR.
I FIGURE YOU GUYS TALK.
SHUT UP.
AND THE LESSONS IN QUICK WIT AND FAST RETORT CONTINUE.
"SHUT UP." YOU'RE GOING TO MAKE ME?
OR YOU NEED DADDY'S HELP FOR THAT, TOO?

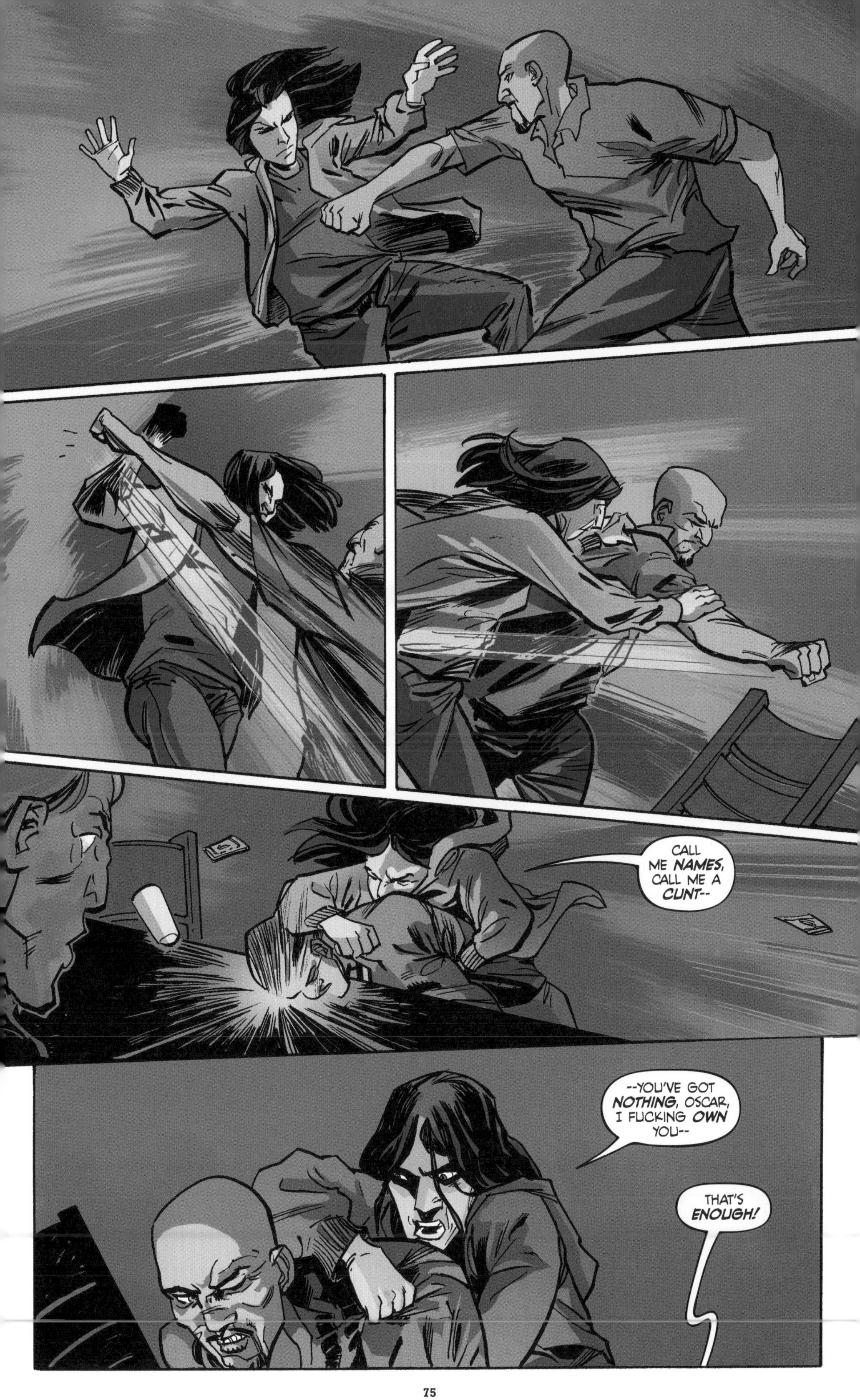
CALL ME *NAMES*, CALL ME A *CUNT*--
--YOU'VE GOT *NOTHING*, OSCAR, I FUCKING *OWN* YOU--
THAT'S *ENOUGH!*

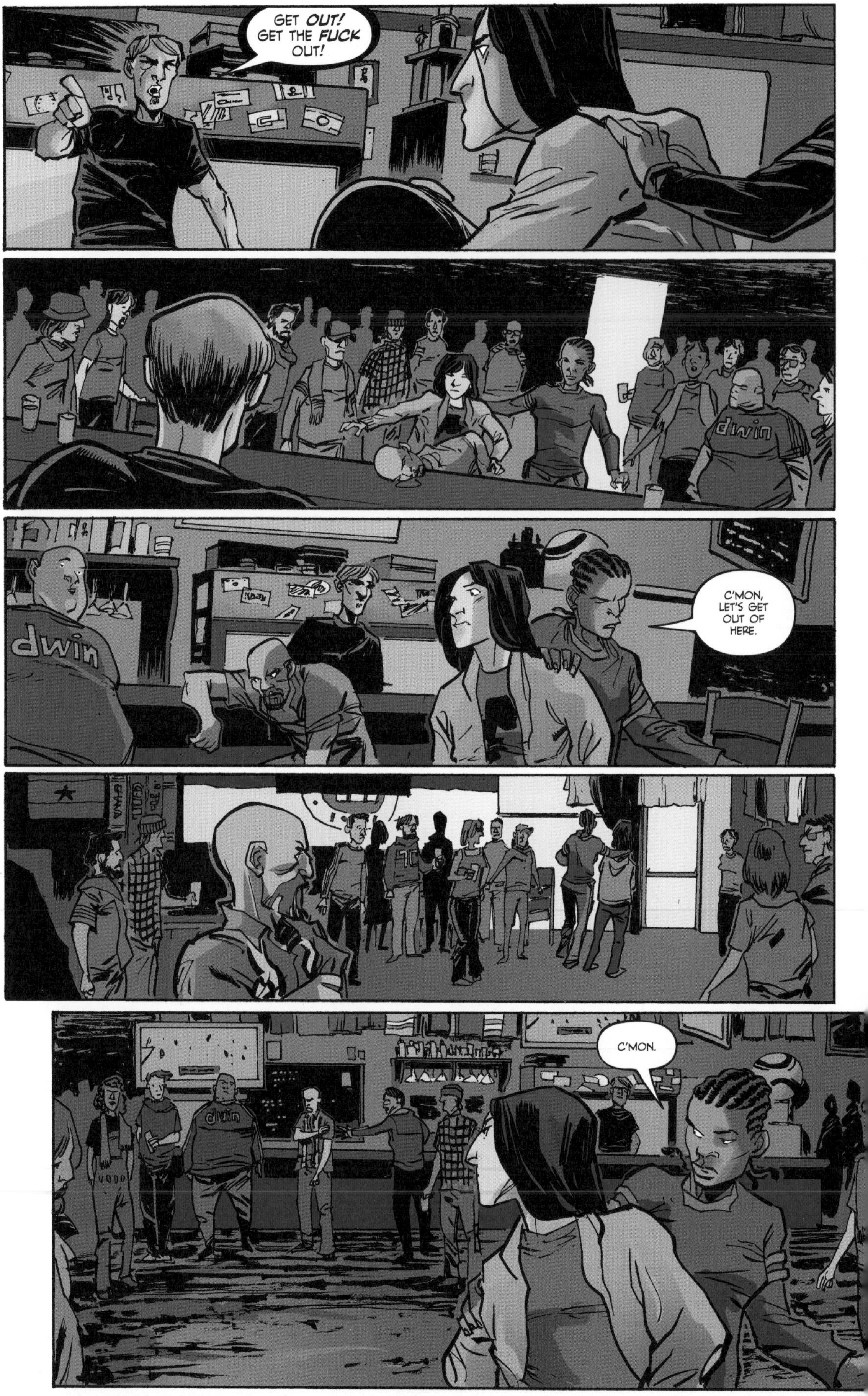
GET OUT! GET THE FUCK OUT!
C'MON, LET'S GET OUT OF HERE.
C'MON.

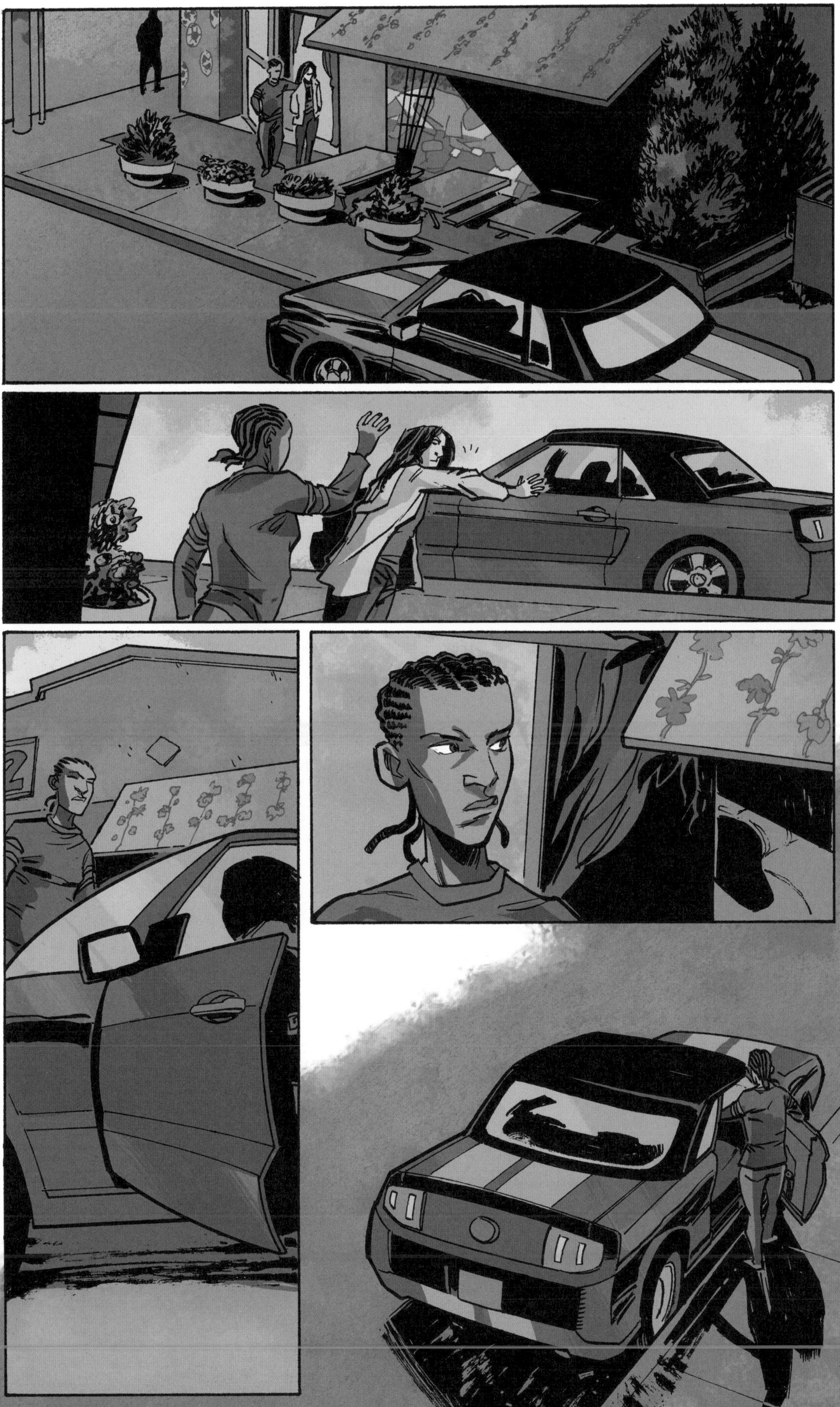

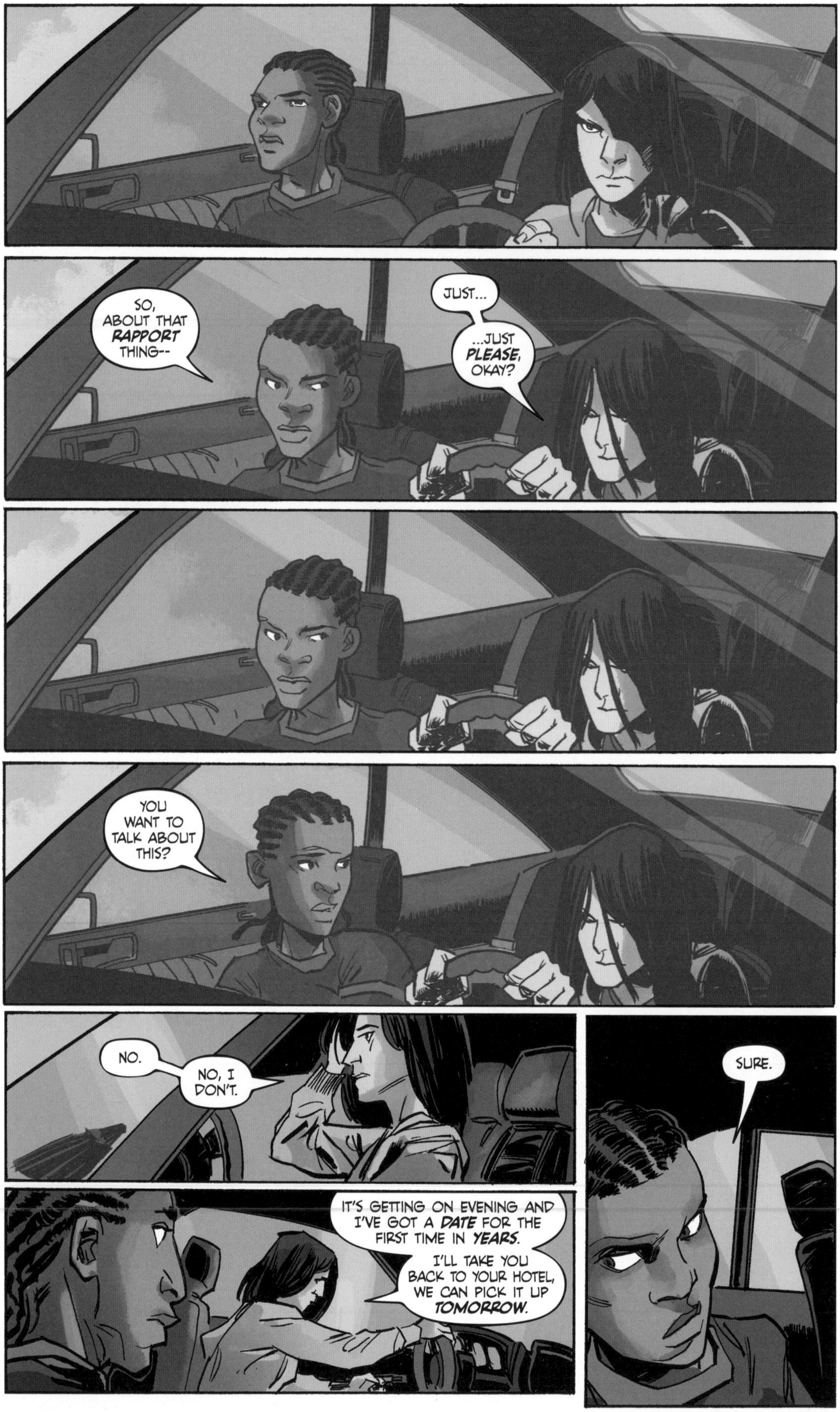
SO, ABOUT THAT RAPPORT THING--
JUST...
...JUST PLEASE, OKAY?
YOU WANT TO TALK ABOUT THIS?
NO.
NO, I DON'T.
SURE.
IT'S GETTING ON EVENING AND I'VE GOT A DATE FOR THE FIRST TIME IN YEARS.
I'LL TAKE YOU BACK TO YOUR HOTEL, WE CAN PICK IT UP TOMORROW.

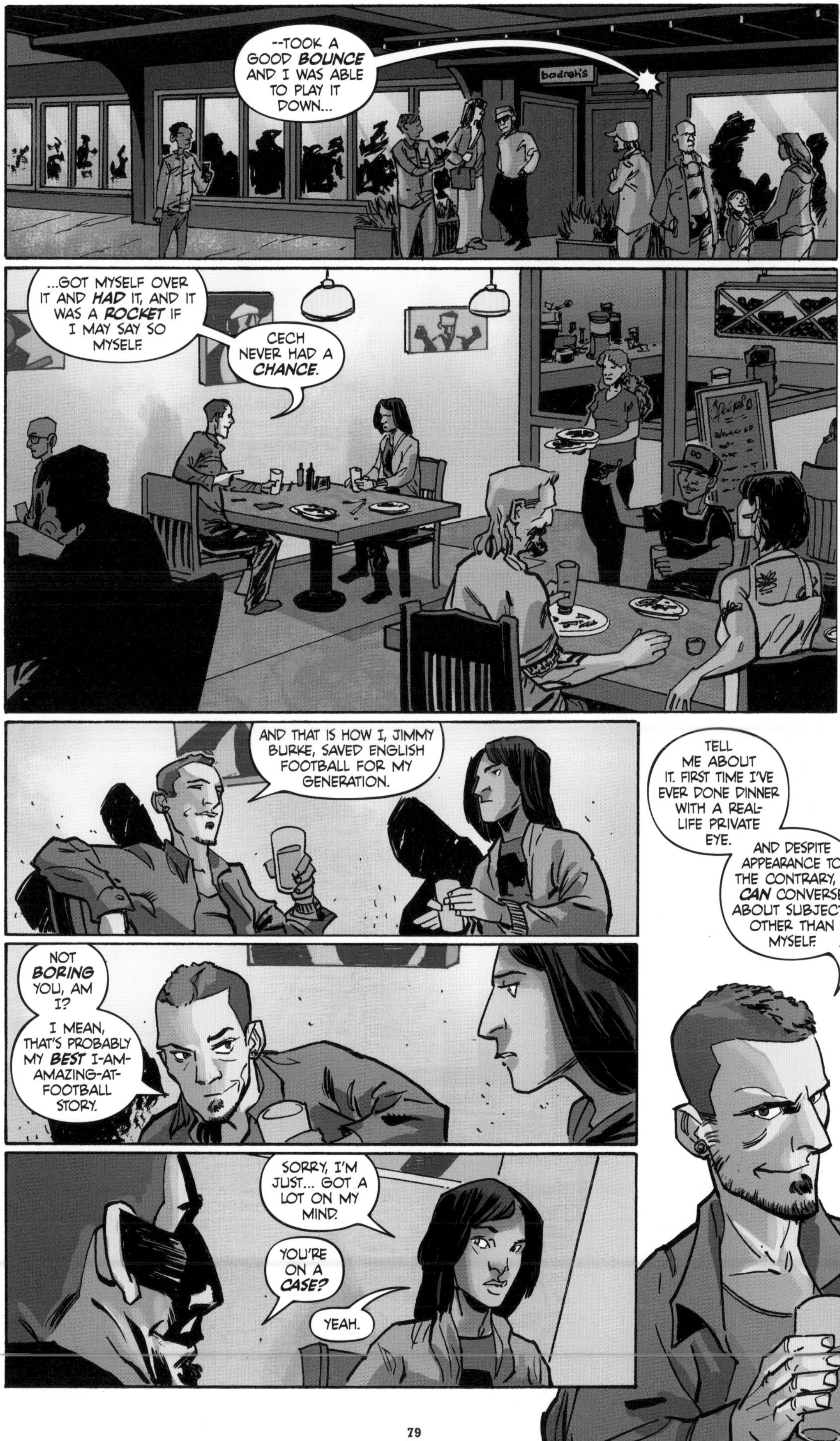
--TOOK A GOOD BOUNCE AND I WAS ABLE TO PLAY IT DOWN...
bodrah's
...GOT MYSELF OVER IT AND HAD IT, AND IT WAS A ROCKET IF I MAY SAY SO MYSELF.
CECH NEVER HAD A CHANCE.
AND THAT IS HOW I, JIMMY BURKE, SAVED ENGLISH FOOTBALL FOR MY GENERATION.
TELL ME ABOUT IT. FIRST TIME I'VE EVER DONE DINNER WITH A REAL-LIFE PRIVATE EYE.
AND DESPITE APPEARANCE TO THE CONTRARY, I CAN CONVERSE ABOUT SUBJECTS OTHER THAN MYSELF.
NOT BORING YOU, AM I?
I MEAN, THAT'S PROBABLY MY BEST I-AM-AMAZING-AT-FOOTBALL STORY.
SORRY, I'M JUST... GOT A LOT ON MY MIND.
YOU'RE ON A CASE?
YEAH.

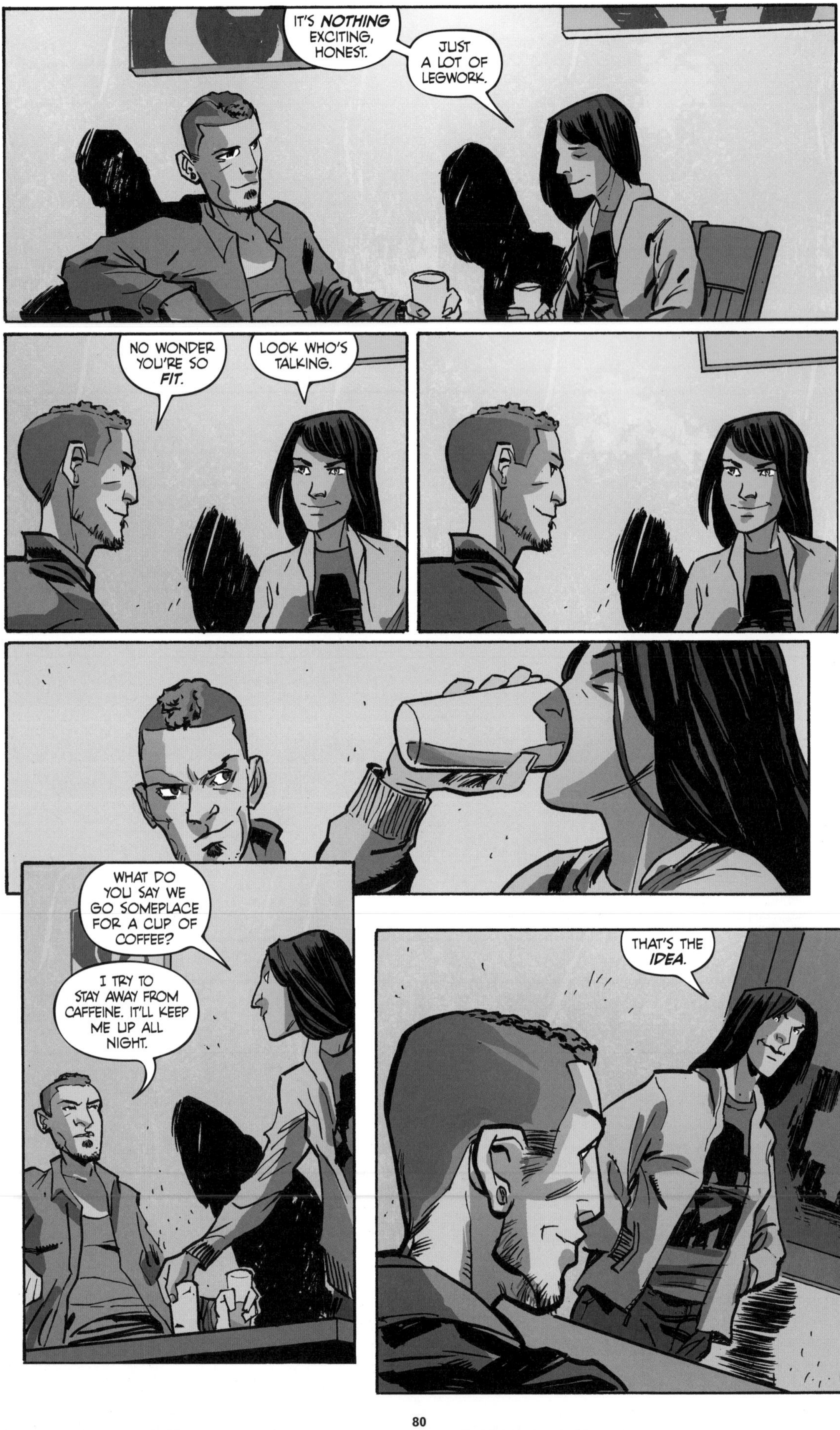
IT'S NOTHING EXCITING, HONEST.
JUST A LOT OF LEGWORK.
NO WONDER YOU'RE SO FIT.
LOOK WHO'S TALKING.
WHAT DO YOU SAY WE GO SOMEPLACE FOR A CUP OF COFFEE?
I TRY TO STAY AWAY FROM CAFFEINE. IT'LL KEEP ME UP ALL NIGHT.
THAT'S THE IDEA.

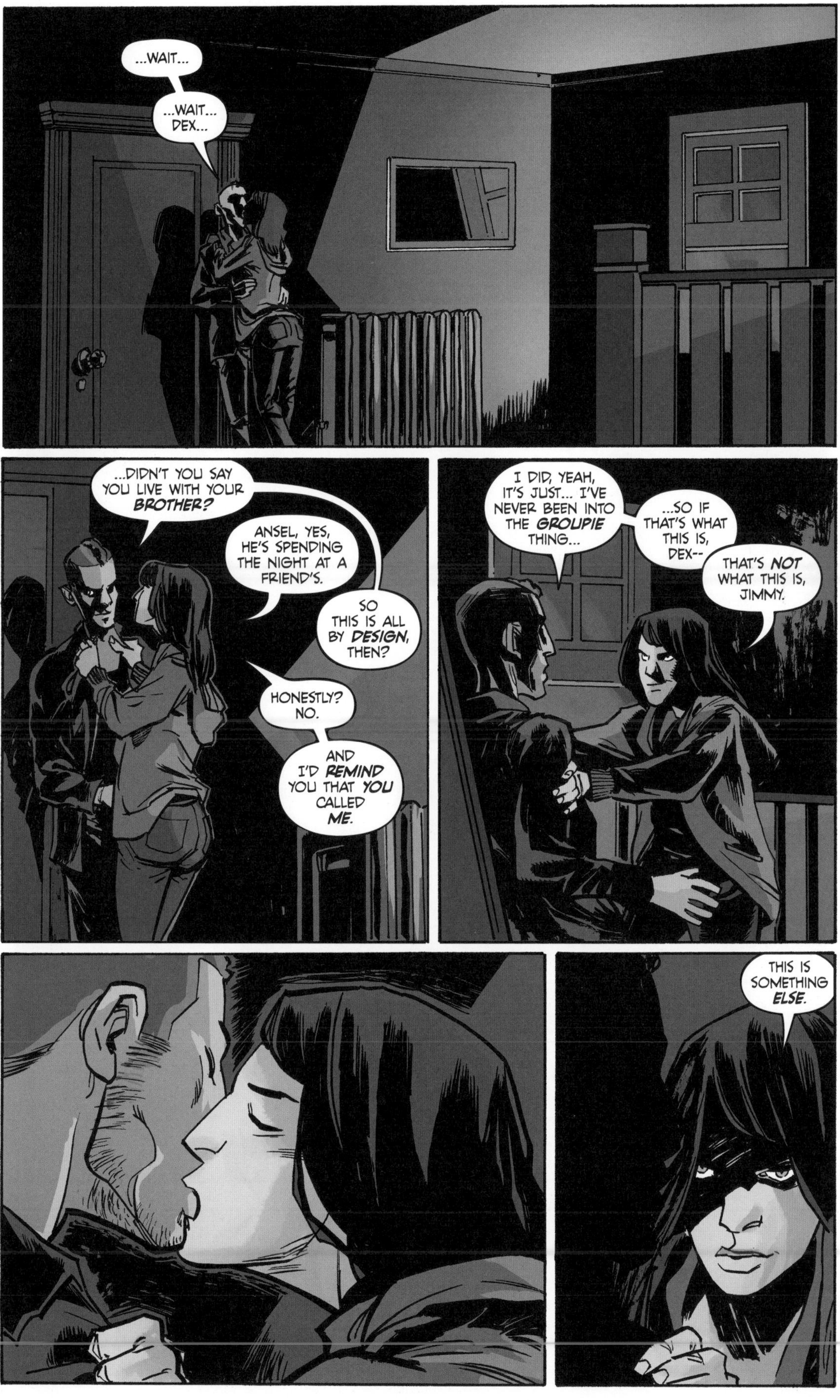
...WAIT...
...WAIT... DEX...
...DIDN'T YOU SAY YOU LIVE WITH YOUR BROTHER?
ANSEL, YES, HE'S SPENDING THE NIGHT AT A FRIEND'S.
SO THIS IS ALL BY DESIGN, THEN?
HONESTLY? NO.
AND I'D REMIND YOU THAT YOU CALLED ME.
I DID, YEAH, IT'S JUST... I'VE NEVER BEEN INTO THE GROUPIE THING...
...SO IF THAT'S WHAT THIS IS, DEX--
THAT'S NOT WHAT THIS IS, JIMMY.
THIS IS SOMETHING ELSE.

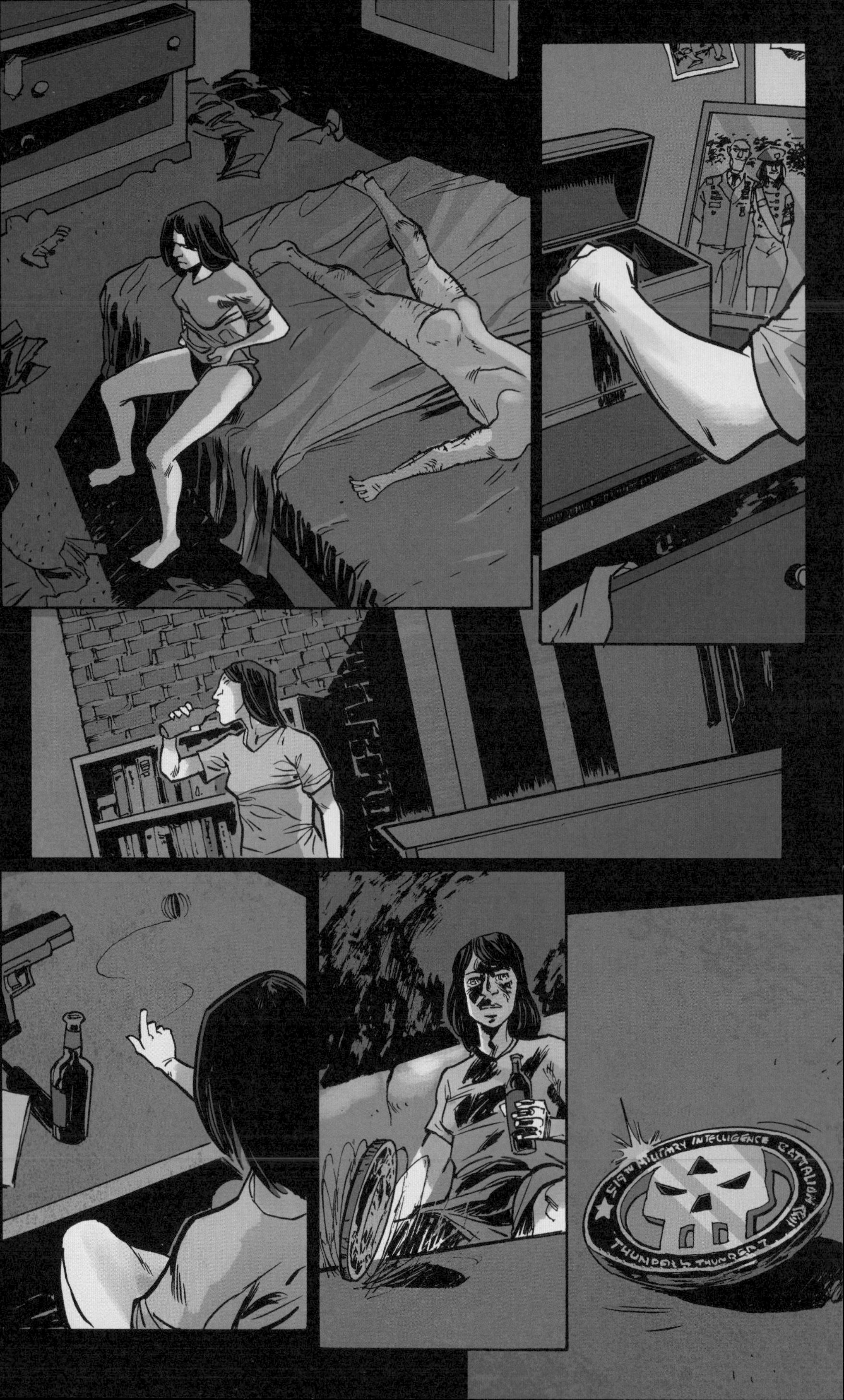
519th MILITARY INTELLIGENCE BATTALION

Chapter Four

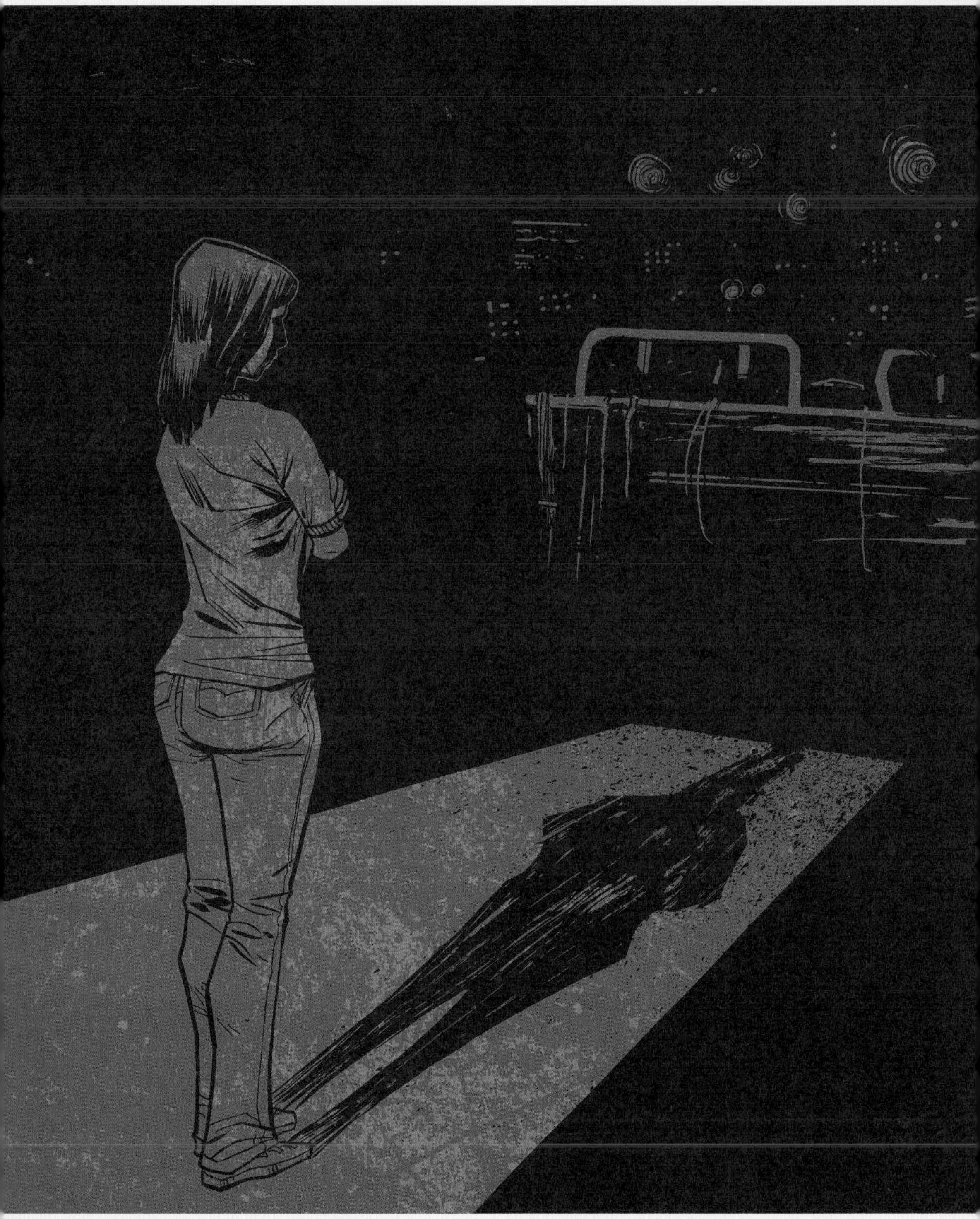

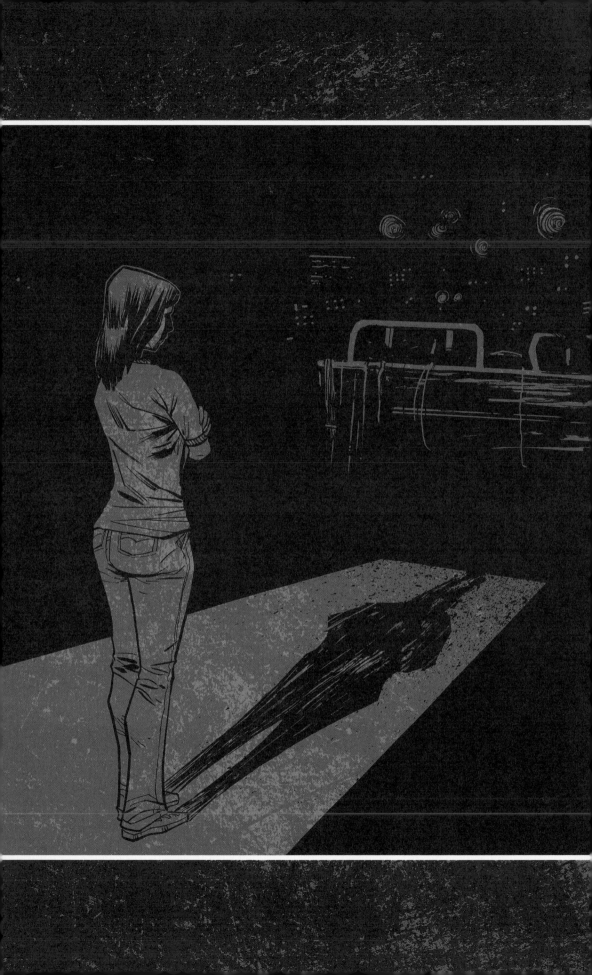

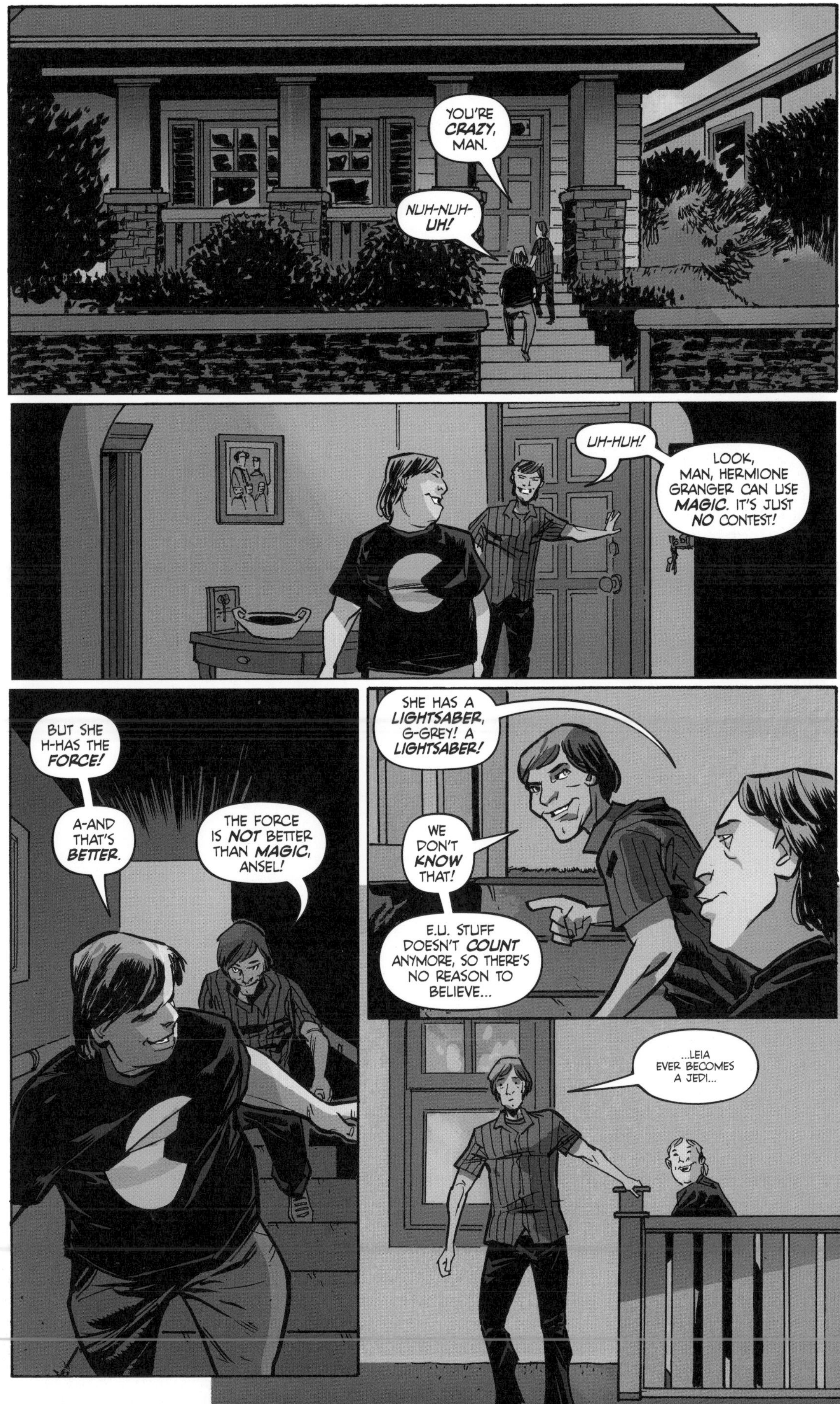
YOU'RE CRAZY, MAN.
NUH-NUH-UH!
UH-HUH!
LOOK, MAN, HERMIONE GRANGER CAN USE MAGIC. IT'S JUST NO CONTEST!
BUT SHE H-HAS THE FORCE!
A-AND THAT'S BETTER.
THE FORCE IS NOT BETTER THAN MAGIC, ANSEL!
SHE HAS A LIGHTSABER, G-GREY! A LIGHTSABER!
WE DON'T KNOW THAT!
E.U. STUFF DOESN'T COUNT ANYMORE, SO THERE'S NO REASON TO BELIEVE...
...LEIA EVER BECOMES A JEDI...

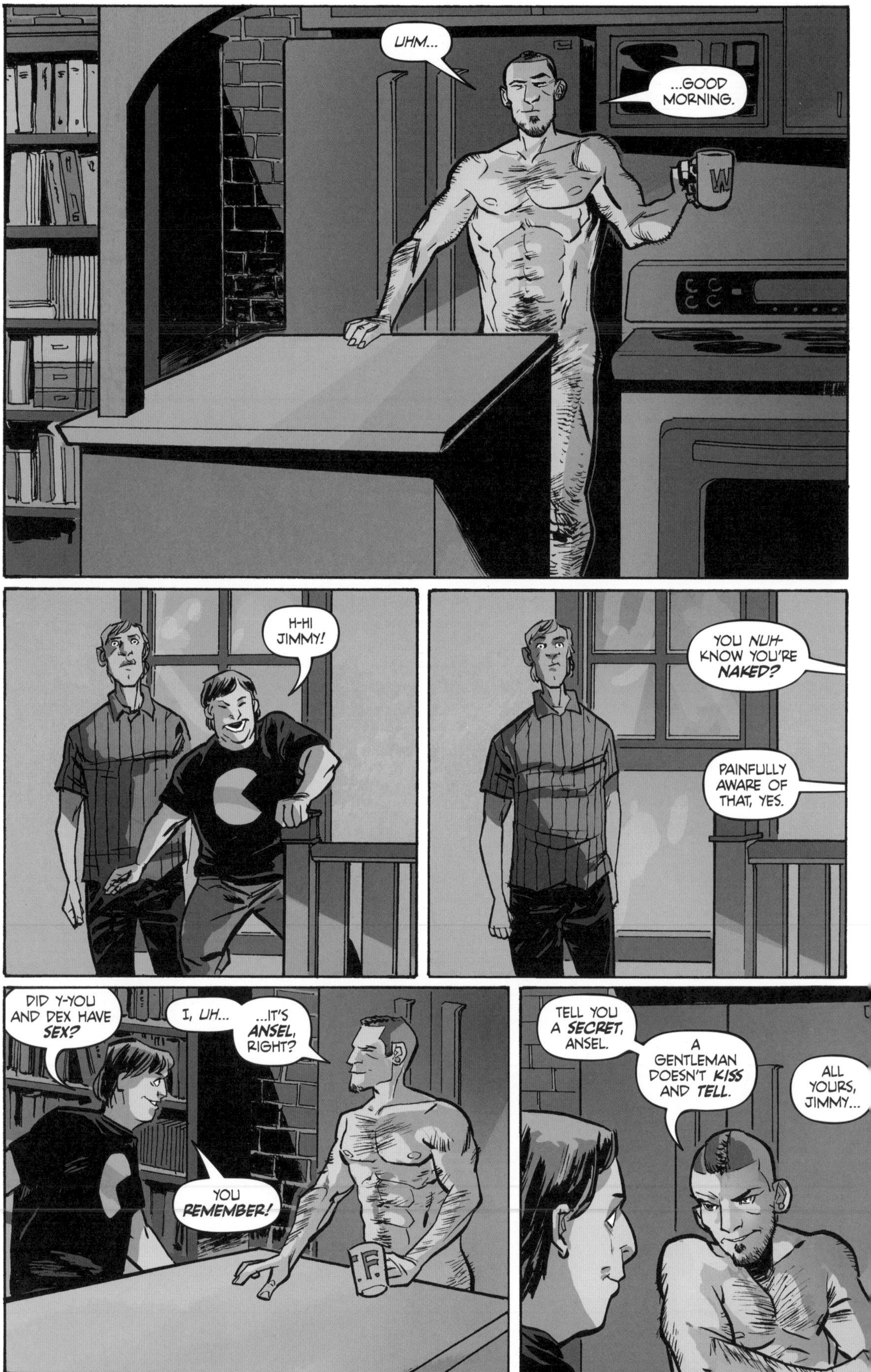
UHM...
...GOOD MORNING.
H-HI JIMMY!
YOU NUH-KNOW YOU'RE NAKED?
PAINFULLY AWARE OF THAT, YES.
DID Y-YOU AND DEX HAVE SEX?
I, UH...
...IT'S ANSEL, RIGHT?
YOU REMEMBER!
TELL YOU A SECRET, ANSEL.
A GENTLEMAN DOESN'T KISS AND TELL.
ALL YOURS, JIMMY...

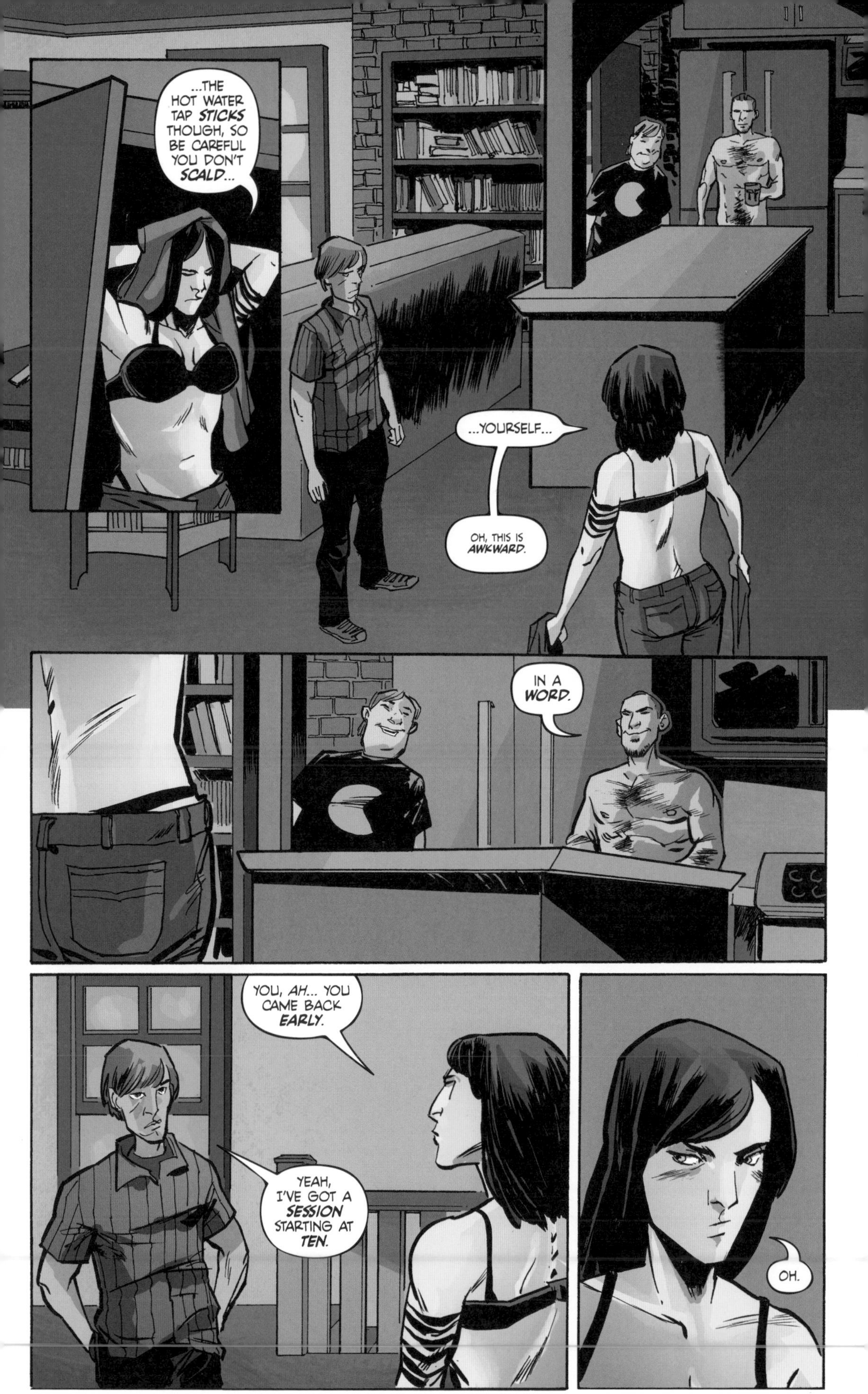
...THE HOT WATER TAP STICKS THOUGH, SO BE CAREFUL YOU DON'T SCALD...
...YOURSELF...
OH, THIS IS AWKWARD.
IN A WORD.
YOU, AH... YOU CAME BACK EARLY.
YEAH, I'VE GOT A SESSION STARTING AT TEN.
OH.

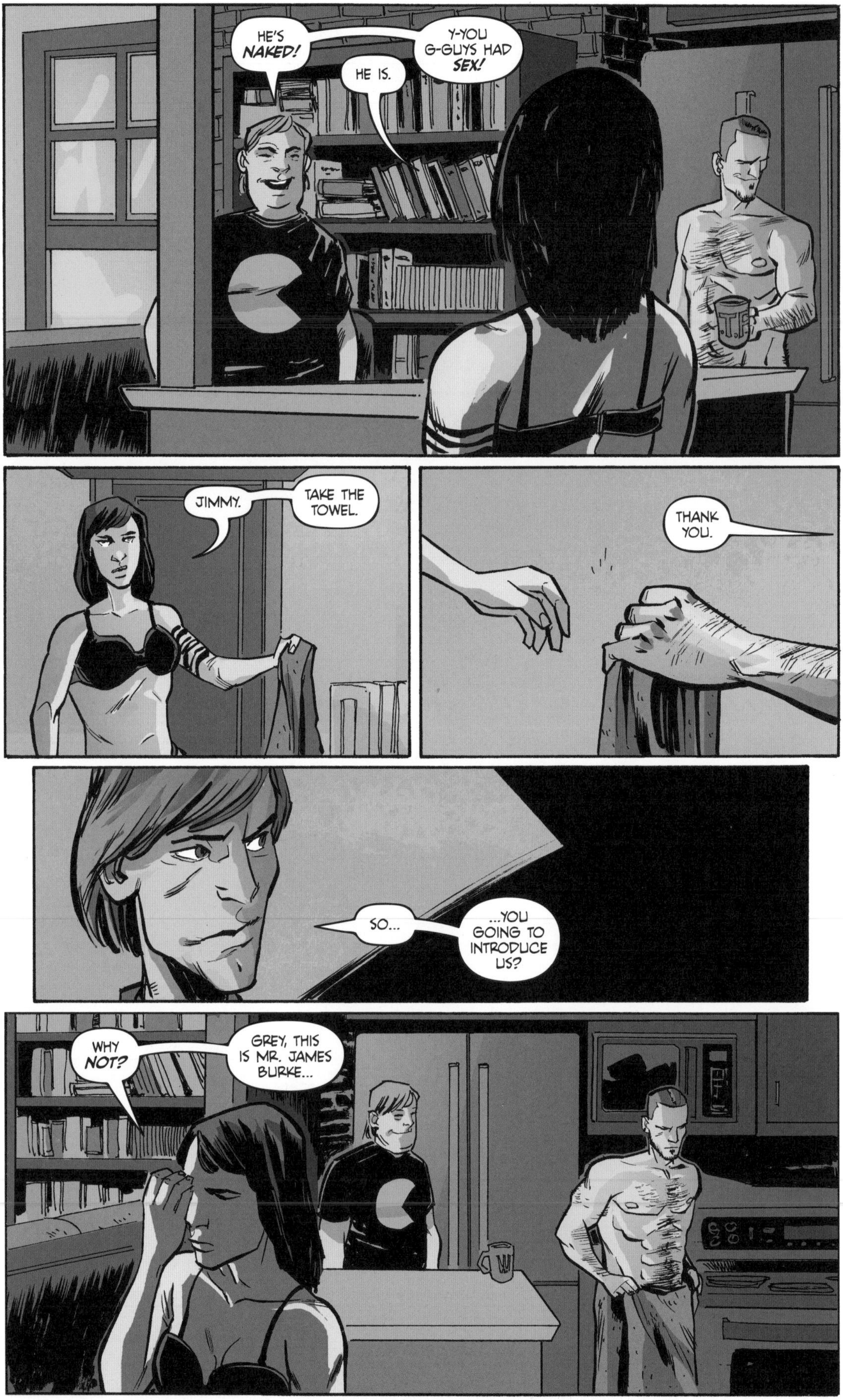
HE'S NAKED!
Y-YOU G-GUYS HAD SEX!
HE IS.
JIMMY.
TAKE THE TOWEL.
THANK YOU.
SO...
...YOU GOING TO INTRODUCE US?
WHY NOT?
GREY, THIS IS MR. JAMES BURKE...

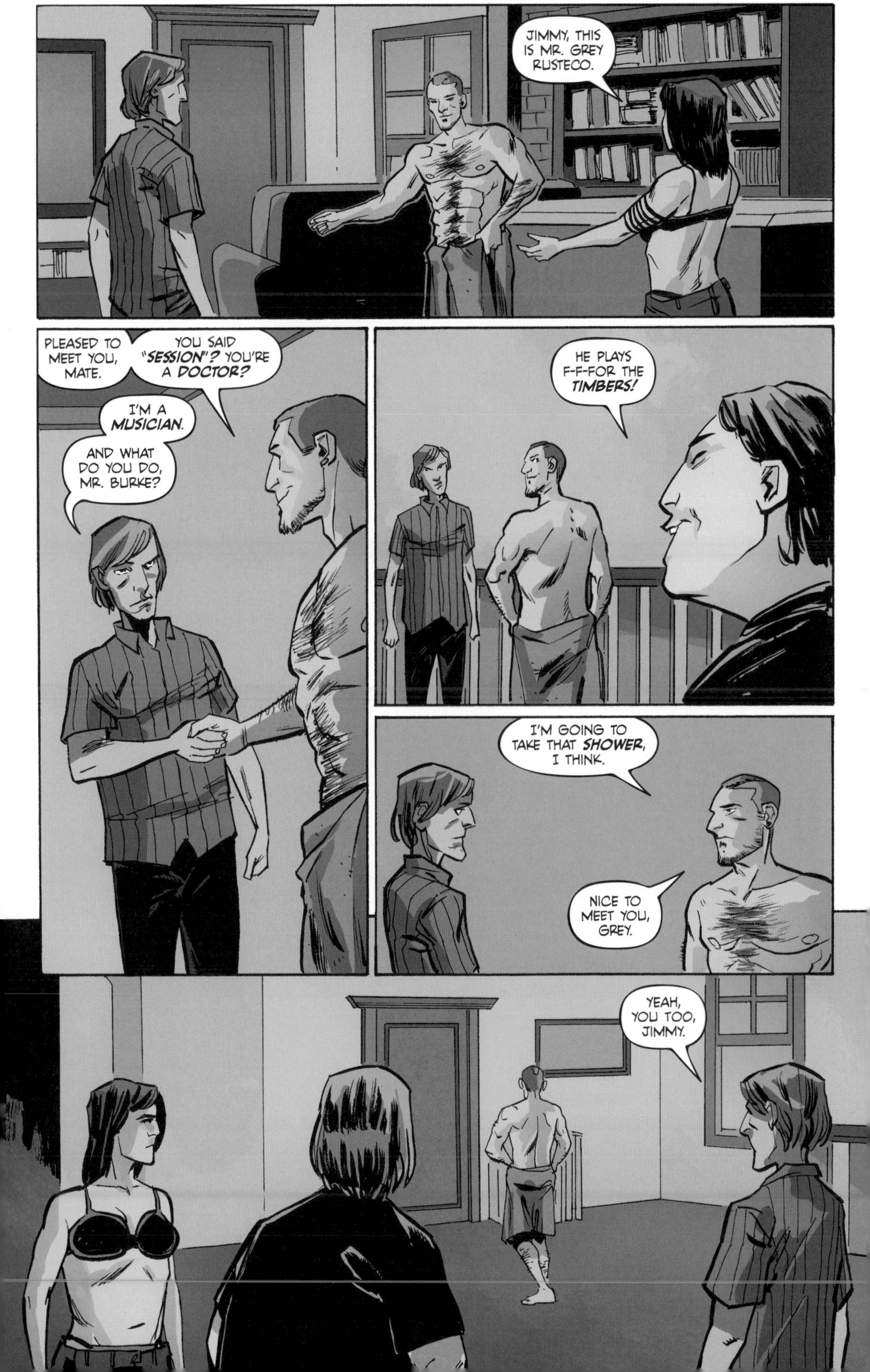
JIMMY, THIS IS MR. GREY RUSTECO.
PLEASED TO MEET YOU, MATE.
YOU SAID "SESSION"? YOU'RE A DOCTOR?
I'M A MUSICIAN.
AND WHAT DO YOU DO, MR. BURKE?
HE PLAYS F-F-FOR THE TIMBERS!
I'M GOING TO TAKE THAT SHOWER, I THINK.
NICE TO MEET YOU, GREY.
YEAH, YOU TOO, JIMMY.

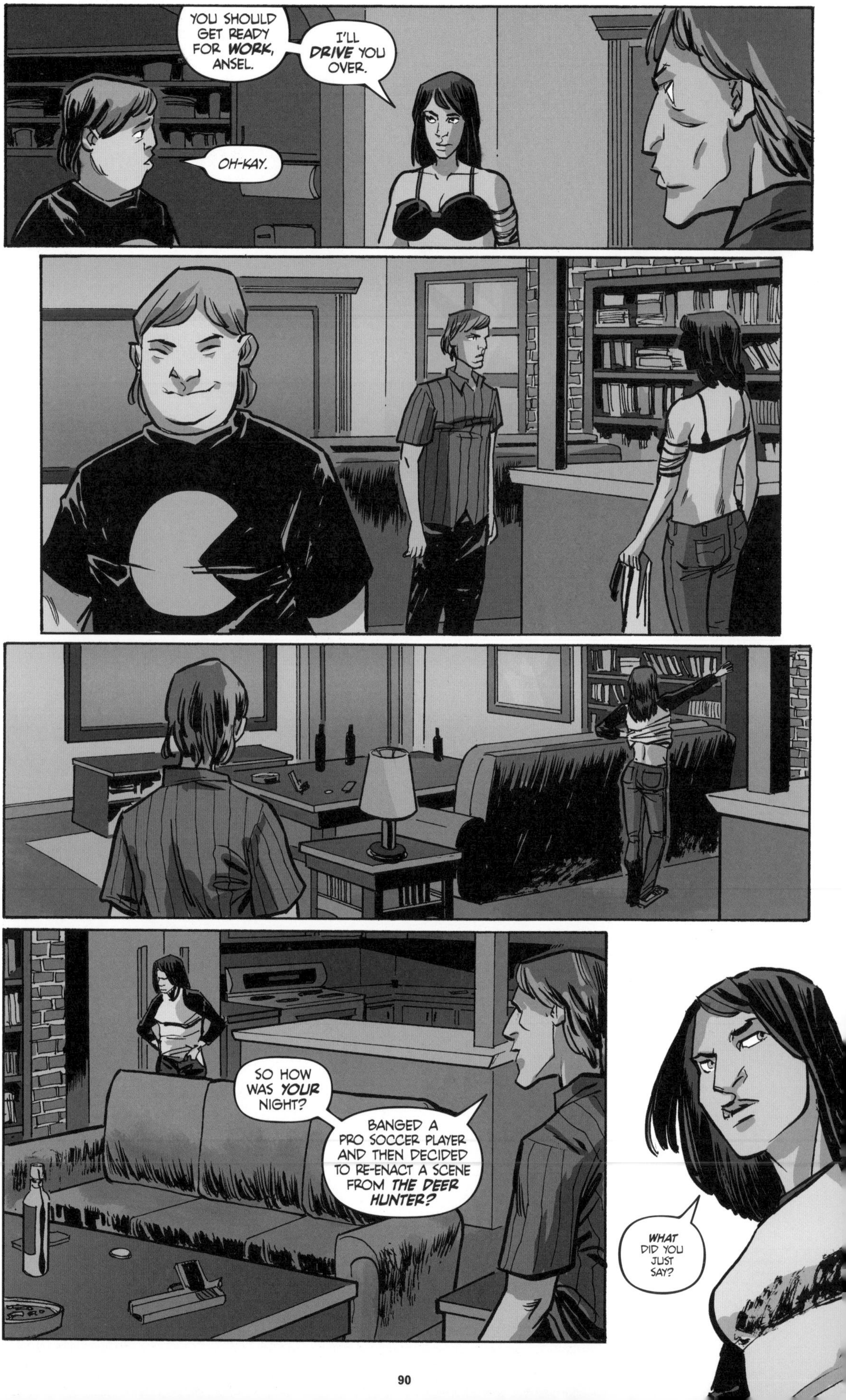
YOU SHOULD GET READY FOR WORK, ANSEL.
I'LL DRIVE YOU OVER.
OH-KAY.
SO HOW WAS YOUR NIGHT?
BANGED A PRO SOCCER PLAYER AND THEN DECIDED TO RE-ENACT A SCENE FROM THE DEER HUNTER?
WHAT DID YOU JUST SAY?

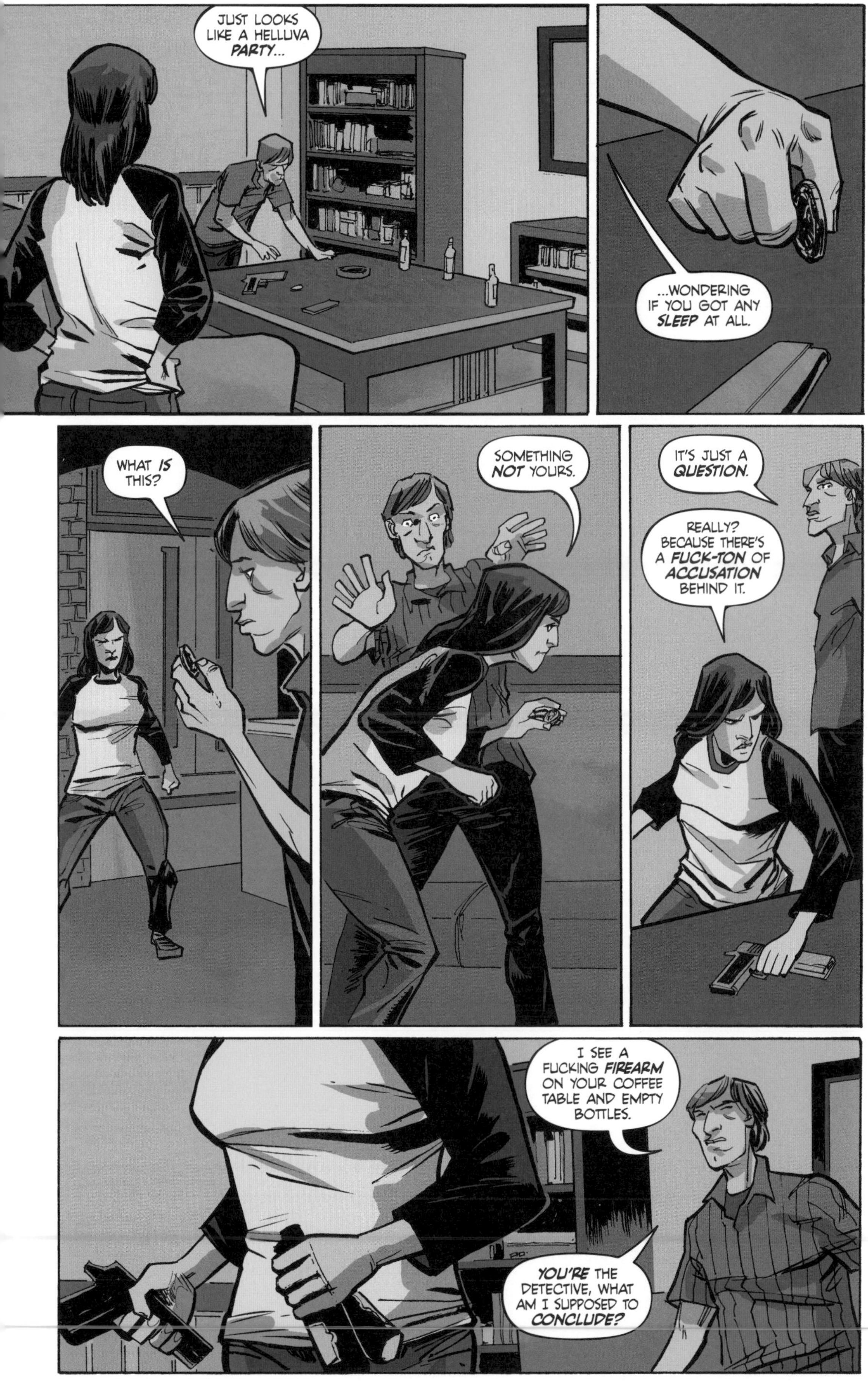
JUST LOOKS LIKE A HELLUVA PARTY...
...WONDERING IF YOU GOT ANY SLEEP AT ALL.
WHAT IS THIS?
SOMETHING NOT YOURS.
IT'S JUST A QUESTION.
REALLY? BECAUSE THERE'S A FUCK-TON OF ACCUSATION BEHIND IT.
I SEE A FUCKING FIREARM ON YOUR COFFEE TABLE AND EMPTY BOTTLES.
YOU'RE THE DETECTIVE, WHAT AM I SUPPOSED TO CONCLUDE?

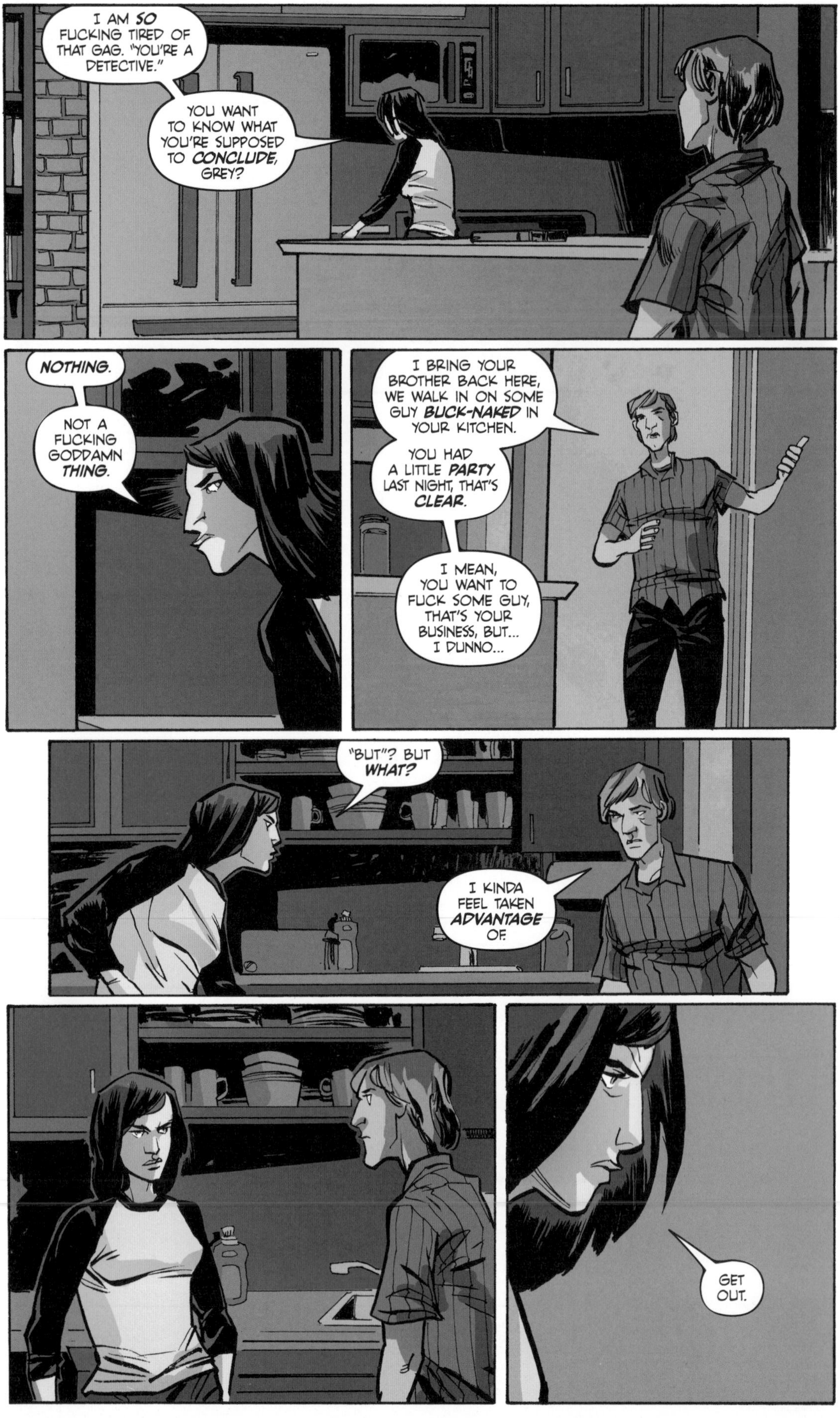

I AM SO FUCKING TIRED OF THAT GAG. "YOU'RE A DETECTIVE."
YOU WANT TO KNOW WHAT YOU'RE SUPPOSED TO CONCLUDE, GREY?
NOTHING.
NOT A FUCKING GODDAMN THING.
I BRING YOUR BROTHER BACK HERE, WE WALK IN ON SOME GUY BUCK-NAKED IN YOUR KITCHEN.
YOU HAD A LITTLE PARTY LAST NIGHT, THAT'S CLEAR.
I MEAN, YOU WANT TO FUCK SOME GUY, THAT'S YOUR BUSINESS, BUT... I DUNNO...
"BUT"? BUT WHAT?
I KINDA FEEL TAKEN ADVANTAGE OF.
GET OUT.

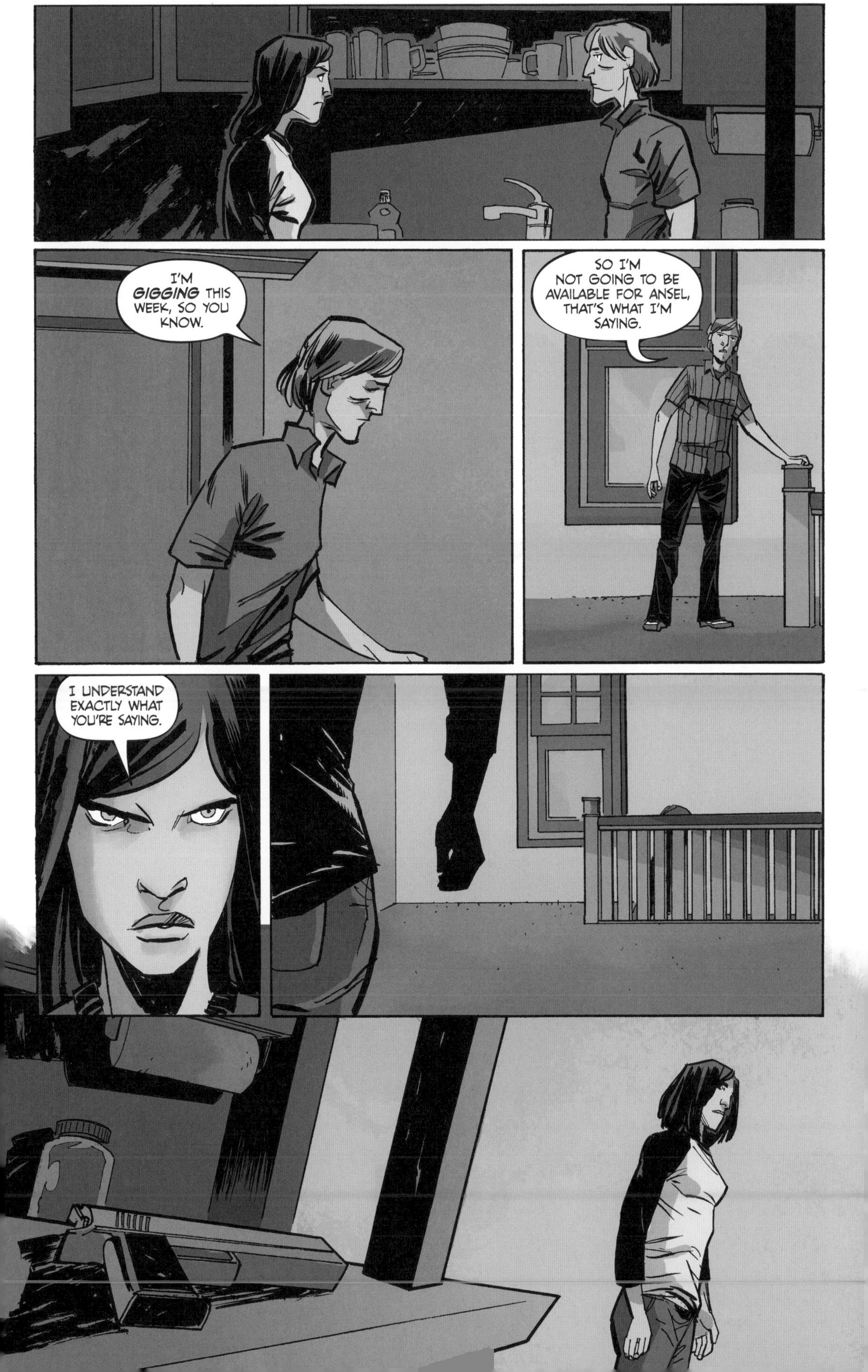
I'M GIGGING THIS WEEK, SO YOU KNOW.
SO I'M NOT GOING TO BE AVAILABLE FOR ANSEL, THAT'S WHAT I'M SAYING.
I UNDERSTAND EXACTLY WHAT YOU'RE SAYING.

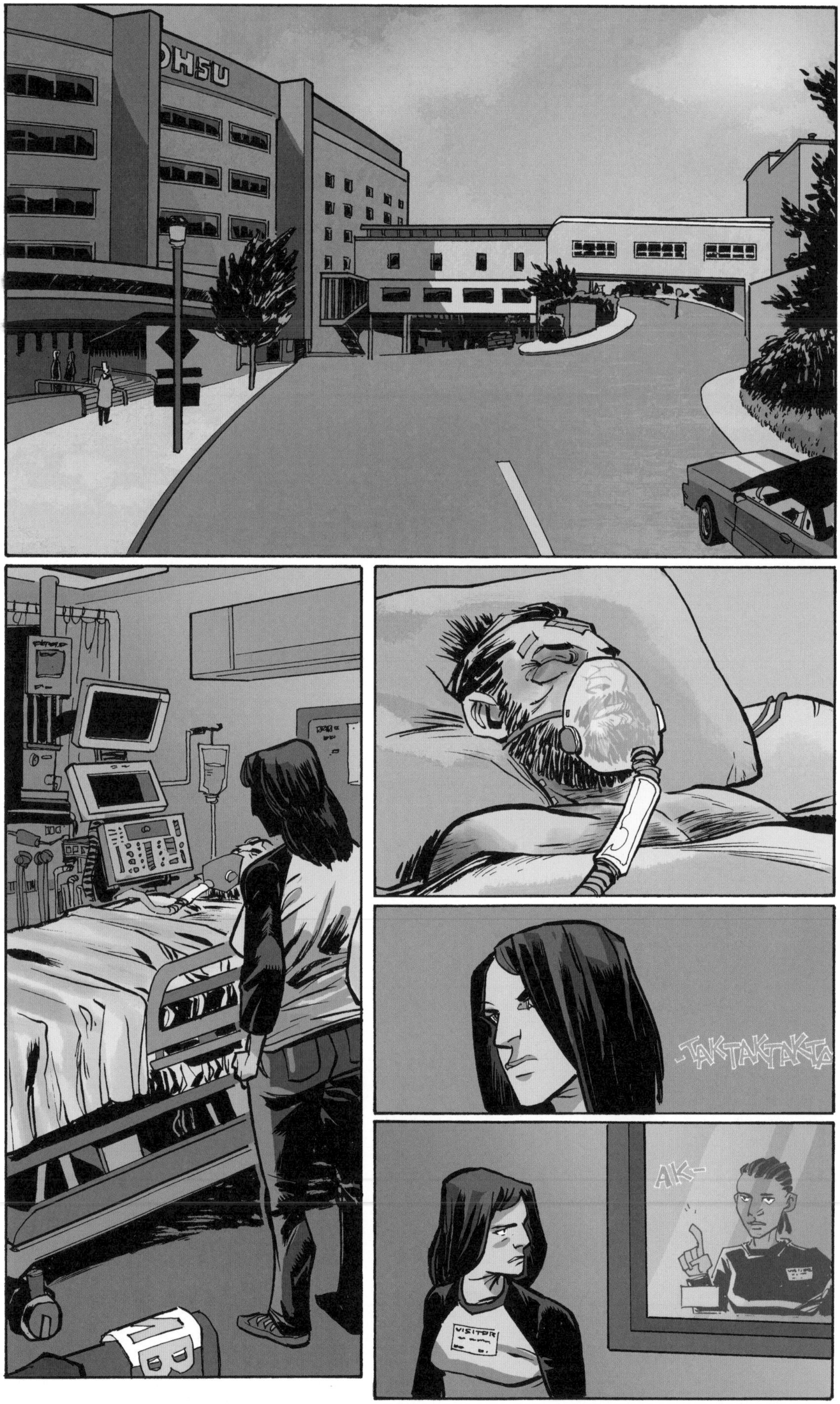
OHSU
-TAKTAKTAKTA
AK-
VISITOR

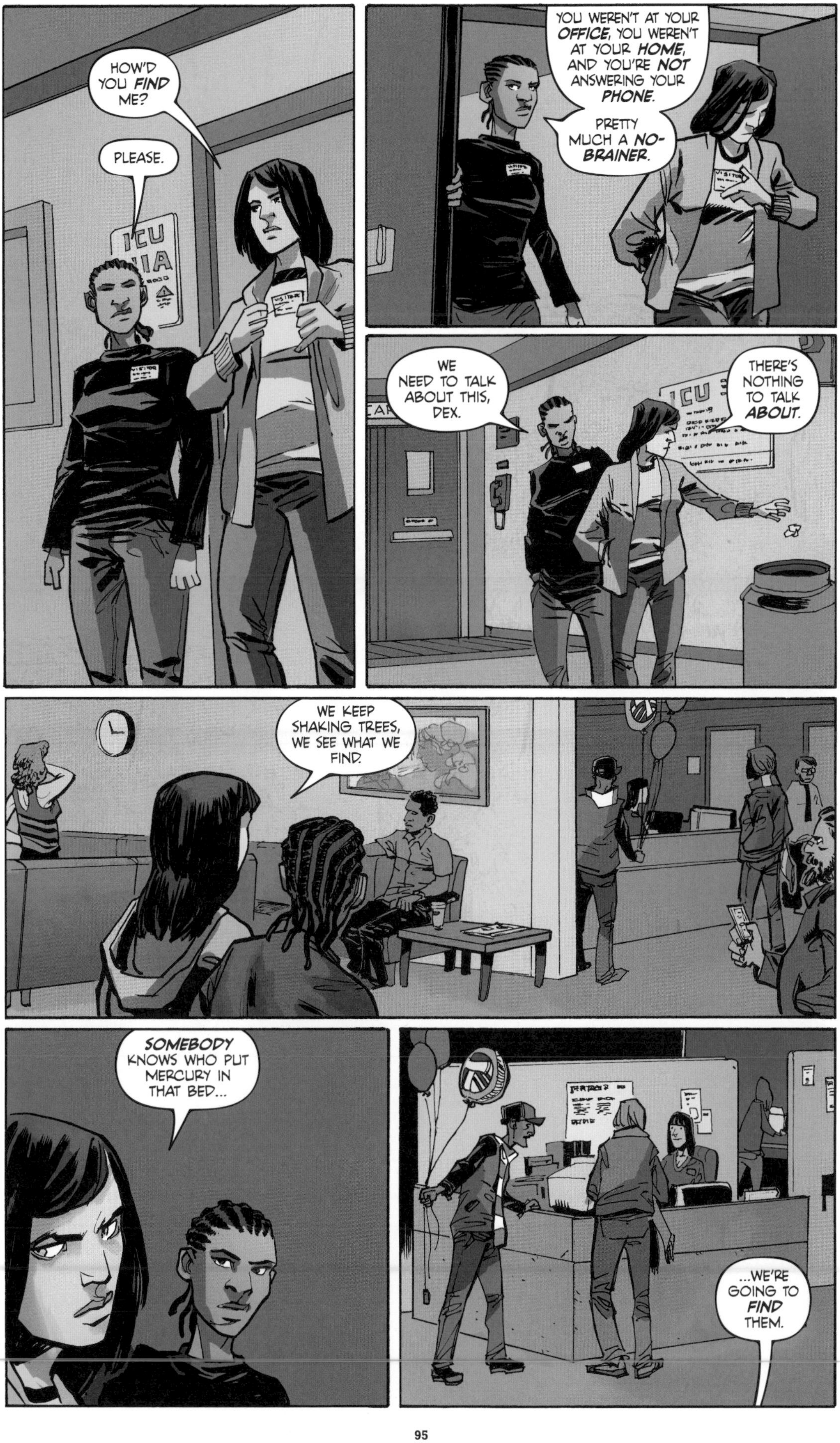
HOW'D YOU *FIND* ME?
PLEASE.
YOU WEREN'T AT YOUR *OFFICE*, YOU WEREN'T AT YOUR *HOME*, AND YOU'RE *NOT* ANSWERING YOUR *PHONE*.
PRETTY MUCH A *NO-BRAINER*.
WE NEED TO TALK ABOUT THIS, DEX.
THERE'S NOTHING TO TALK *ABOUT*.
ICU
WE KEEP SHAKING TREES, WE SEE WHAT WE FIND.
SOMEBODY KNOWS WHO PUT MERCURY IN THAT BED...
...WE'RE GOING TO *FIND* THEM.

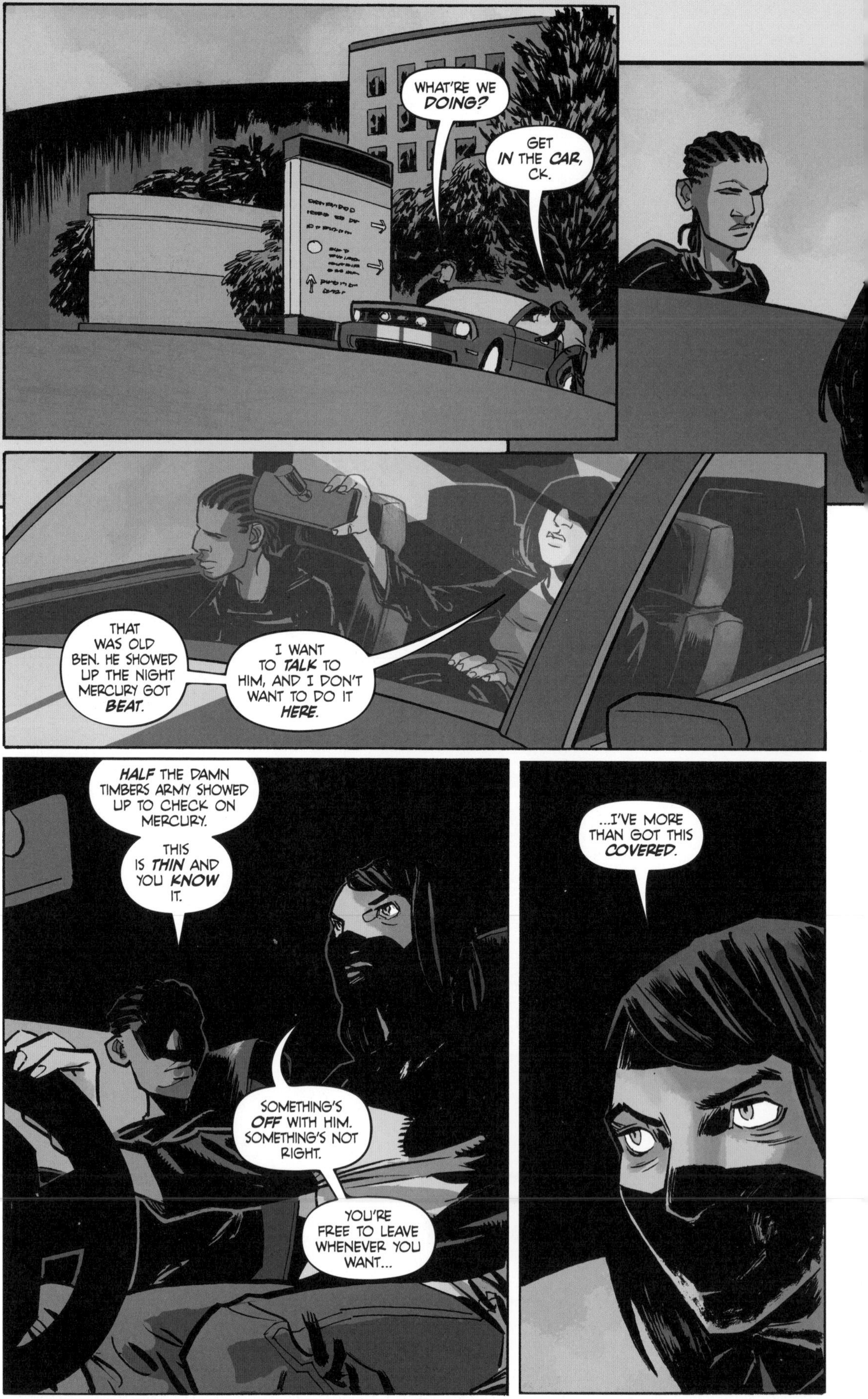
WHAT'RE WE DOING?
GET IN THE CAR, CK.
THAT WAS OLD BEN. HE SHOWED UP THE NIGHT MERCURY GOT BEAT.
I WANT TO TALK TO HIM, AND I DON'T WANT TO DO IT HERE.
HALF THE DAMN TIMBERS ARMY SHOWED UP TO CHECK ON MERCURY.
THIS IS THIN AND YOU KNOW IT.
SOMETHING'S OFF WITH HIM. SOMETHING'S NOT RIGHT.
YOU'RE FREE TO LEAVE WHENEVER YOU WANT...
...I'VE MORE THAN GOT THIS COVERED.

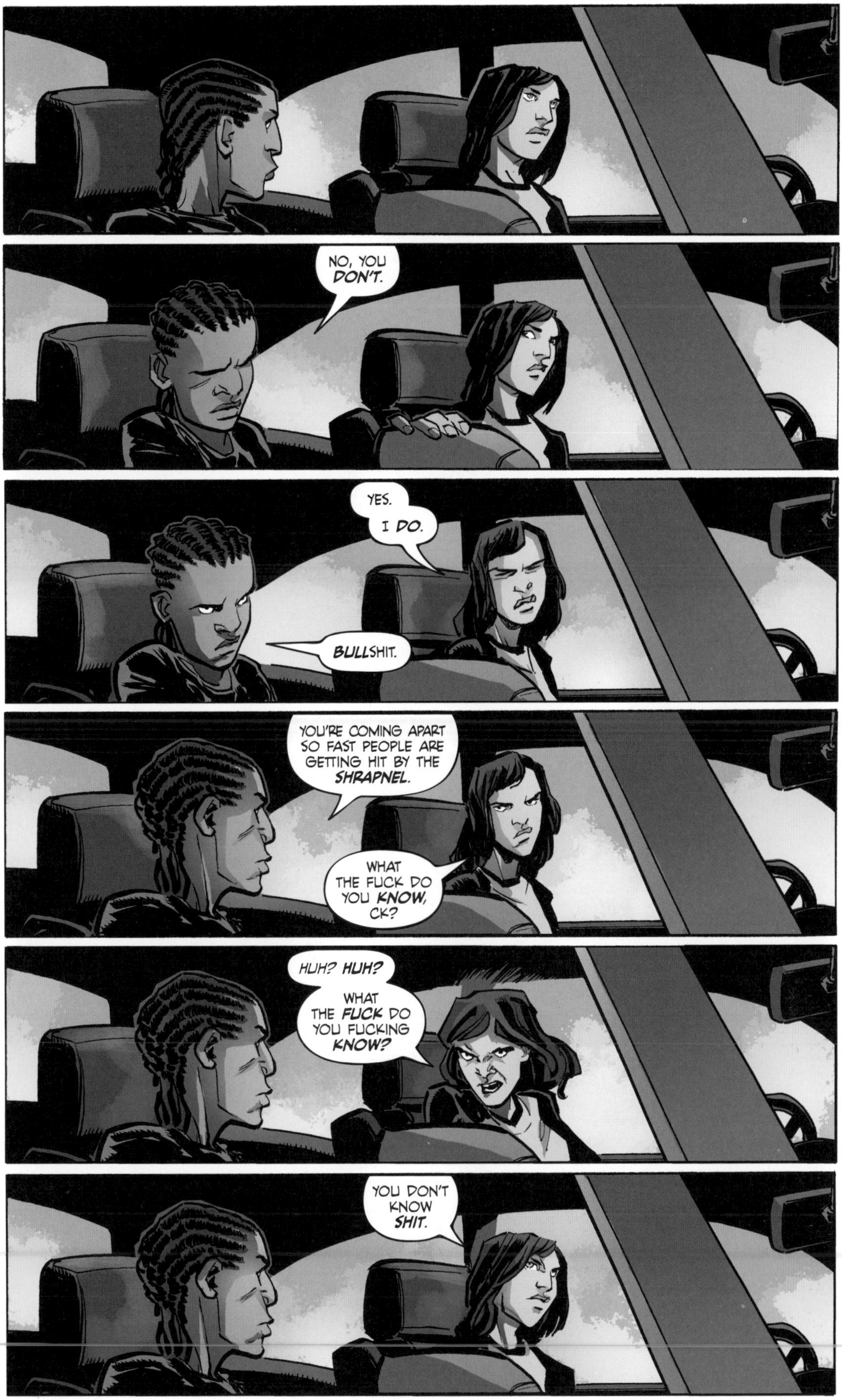
NO, YOU *DON'T*.
YES.
I *DO*.
*BULL*SHIT.
YOU'RE COMING APART SO FAST PEOPLE ARE GETTING HIT BY THE *SHRAPNEL*.
WHAT THE FUCK DO YOU *KNOW*, CK?
HUH? HUH?
WHAT THE *FUCK* DO YOU FUCKING *KNOW?*
YOU DON'T KNOW *SHIT*.

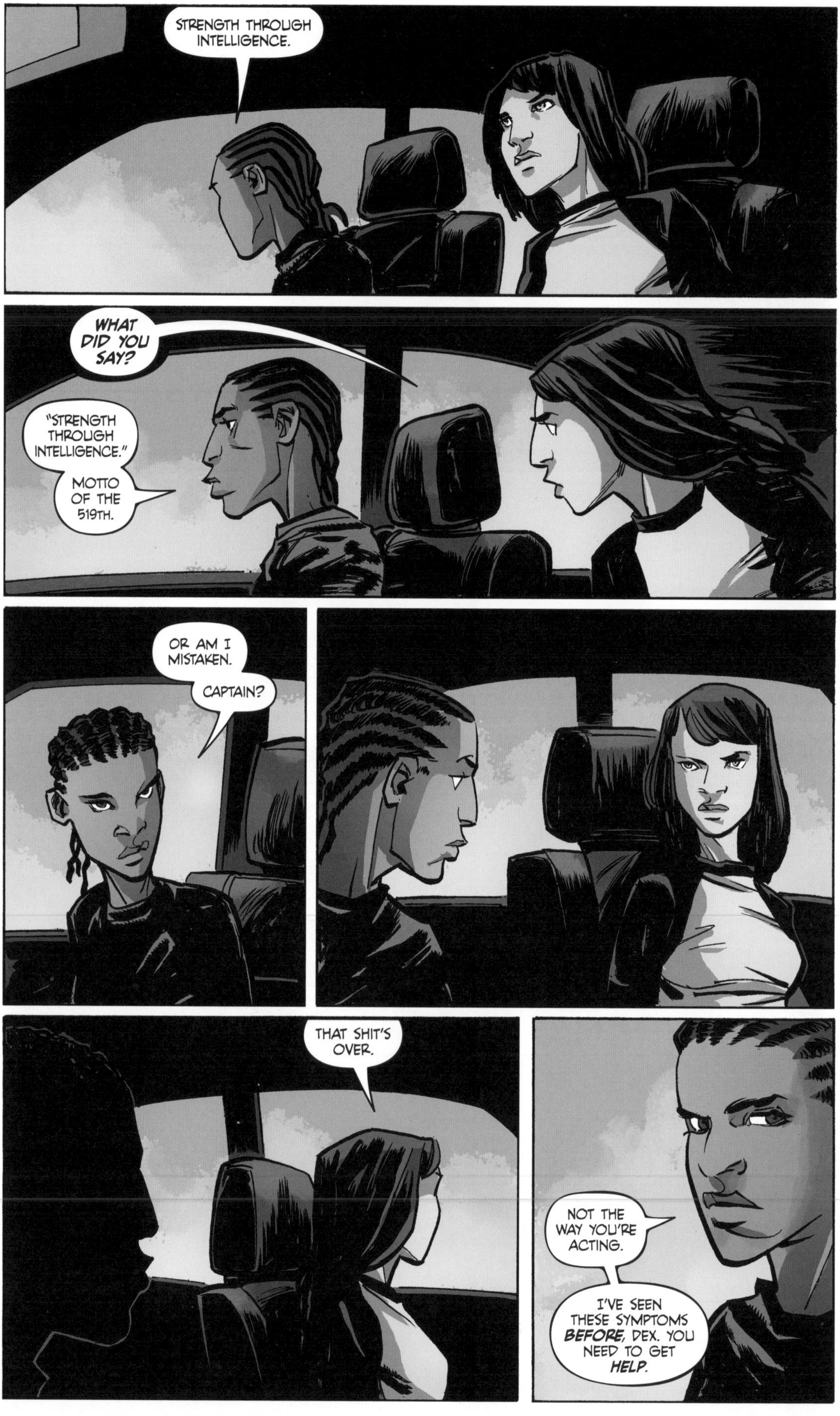
STRENGTH THROUGH INTELLIGENCE.
WHAT DID YOU SAY?
"STRENGTH THROUGH INTELLIGENCE."
MOTTO OF THE 519TH.
OR AM I MISTAKEN.
CAPTAIN?
THAT SHIT'S OVER.
NOT THE WAY YOU'RE ACTING.
I'VE SEEN THESE SYMPTOMS BEFORE, DEX. YOU NEED TO GET HELP.

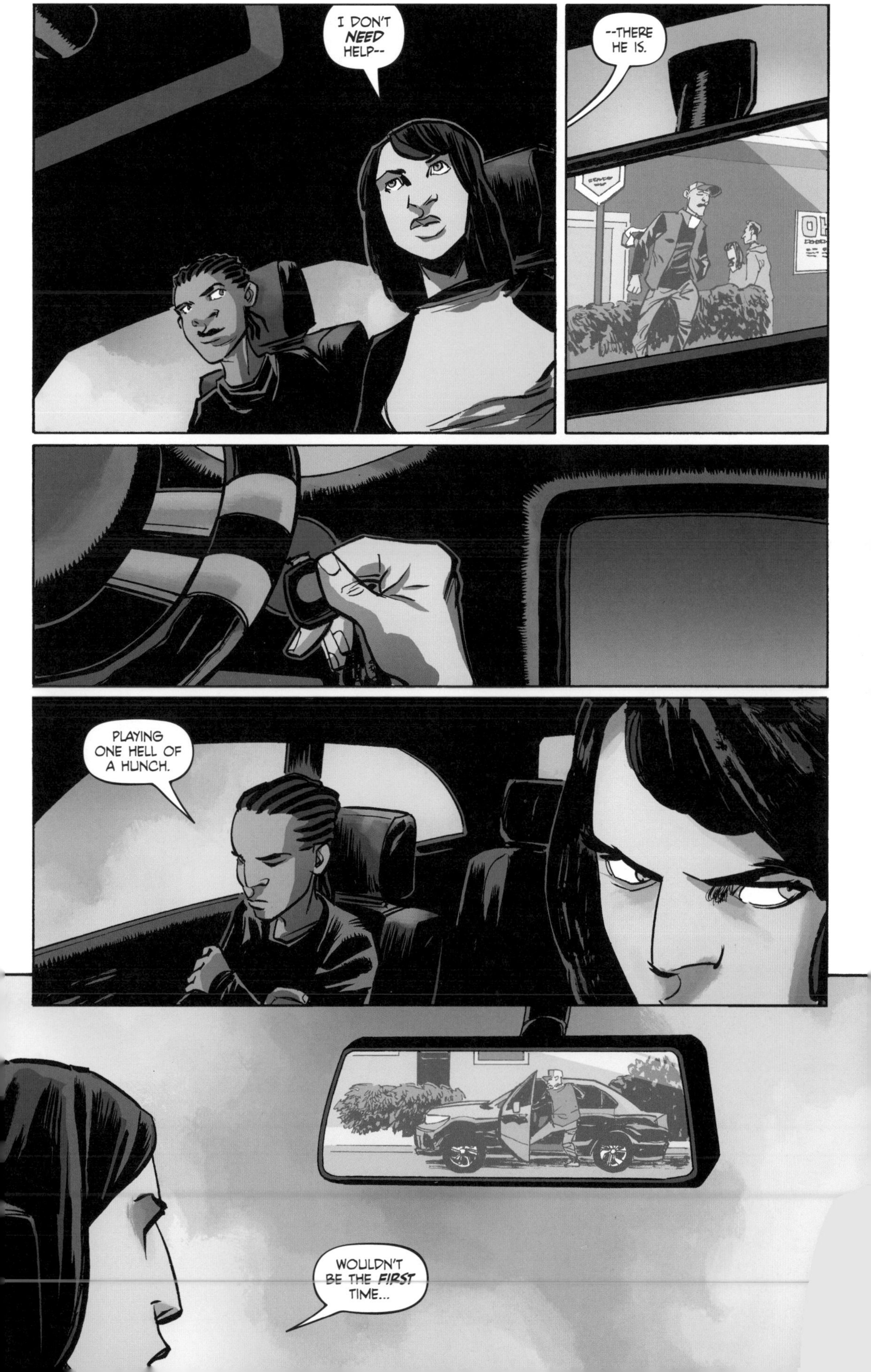
I DON'T NEED HELP--
--THERE HE IS.
PLAYING ONE HELL OF A HUNCH.
WOULDN'T BE THE FIRST TIME...

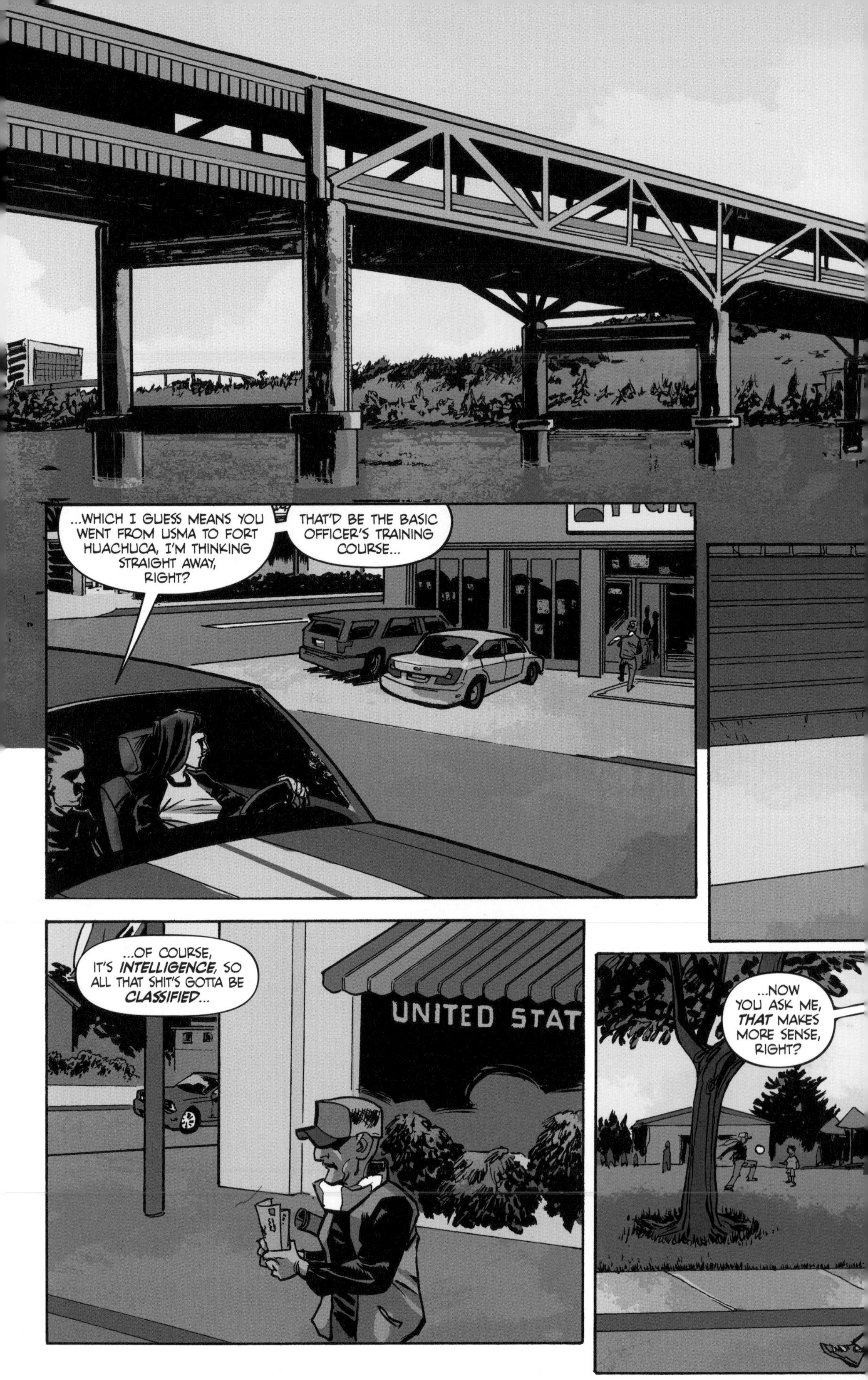
...WHICH I GUESS MEANS YOU WENT FROM USMA TO FORT HUACHUCA, I'M THINKING STRAIGHT AWAY, RIGHT?
THAT'D BE THE BASIC OFFICER'S TRAINING COURSE...
...OF COURSE, IT'S INTELLIGENCE, SO ALL THAT SHIT'S GOTTA BE CLASSIFIED...
UNITED STAT
...NOW YOU ASK ME, THAT MAKES MORE SENSE, RIGHT?

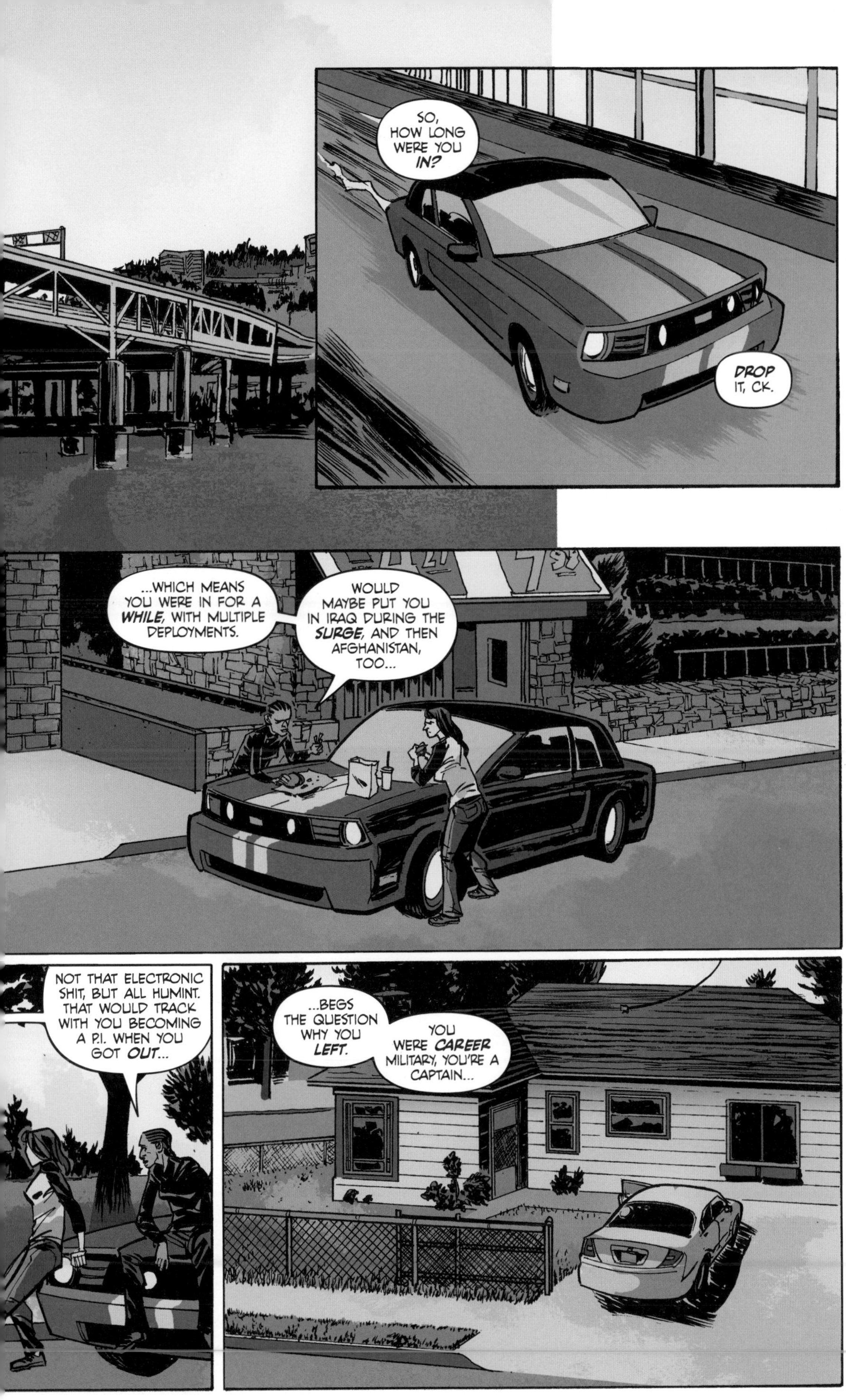
SO, HOW LONG WERE YOU *IN?*
DROP IT, CK.
...WHICH MEANS YOU WERE IN FOR A *WHILE,* WITH MULTIPLE DEPLOYMENTS.
WOULD MAYBE PUT YOU IN IRAQ DURING THE *SURGE,* AND THEN AFGHANISTAN, TOO...
NOT THAT ELECTRONIC SHIT, BUT ALL HUMINT. THAT WOULD TRACK WITH YOU BECOMING A P.I. WHEN YOU GOT *OUT*...
...BEGS THE QUESTION WHY YOU *LEFT.*
YOU WERE *CAREER* MILITARY, YOU'RE A CAPTAIN...

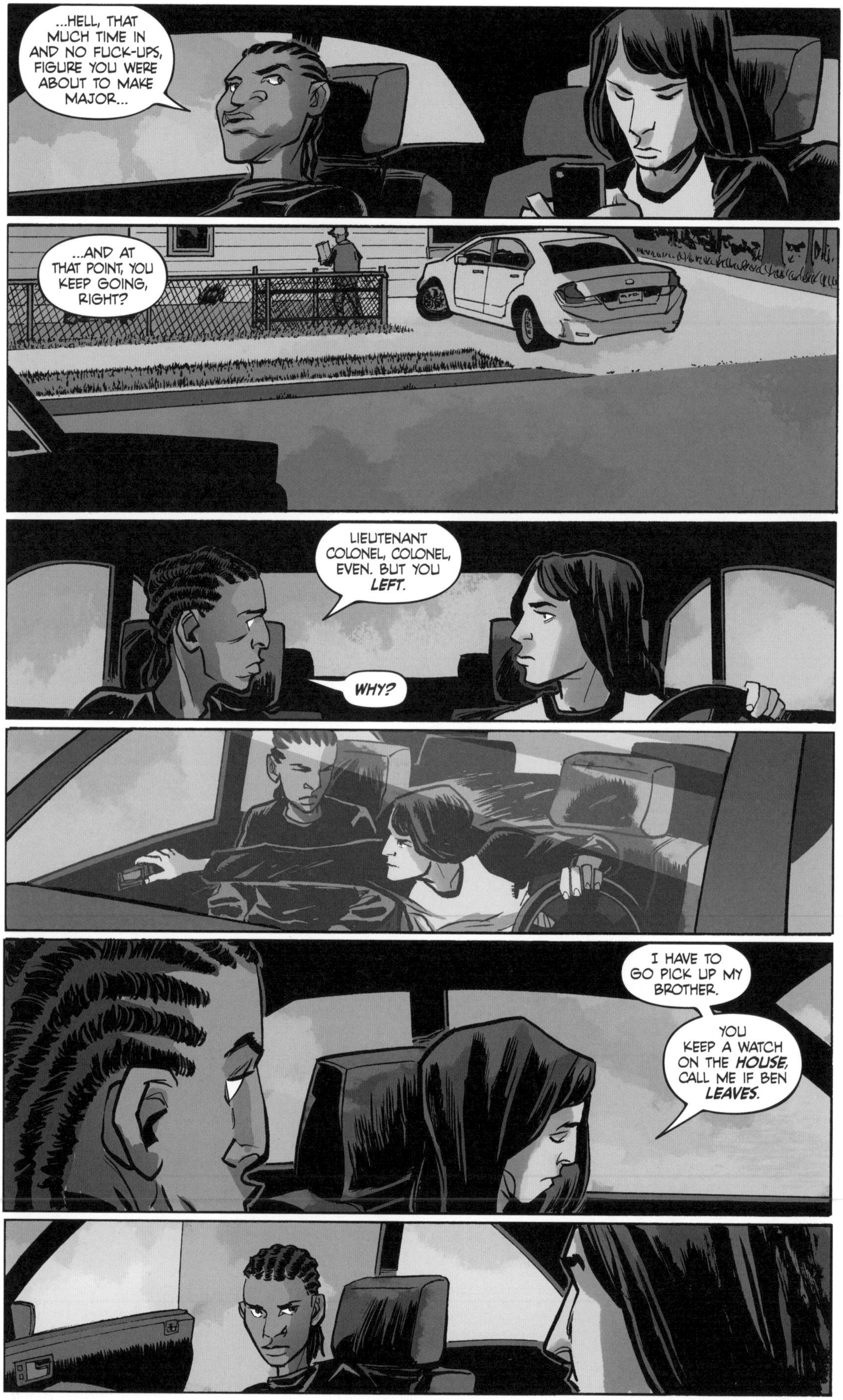
...HELL, THAT MUCH TIME IN AND NO FUCK-UPS, FIGURE YOU WERE ABOUT TO MAKE MAJOR...
...AND AT THAT POINT, YOU KEEP GOING, RIGHT?
LIEUTENANT COLONEL, COLONEL, EVEN. BUT YOU LEFT.
WHY?
I HAVE TO GO PICK UP MY BROTHER.
YOU KEEP A WATCH ON THE HOUSE, CALL ME IF BEN LEAVES.

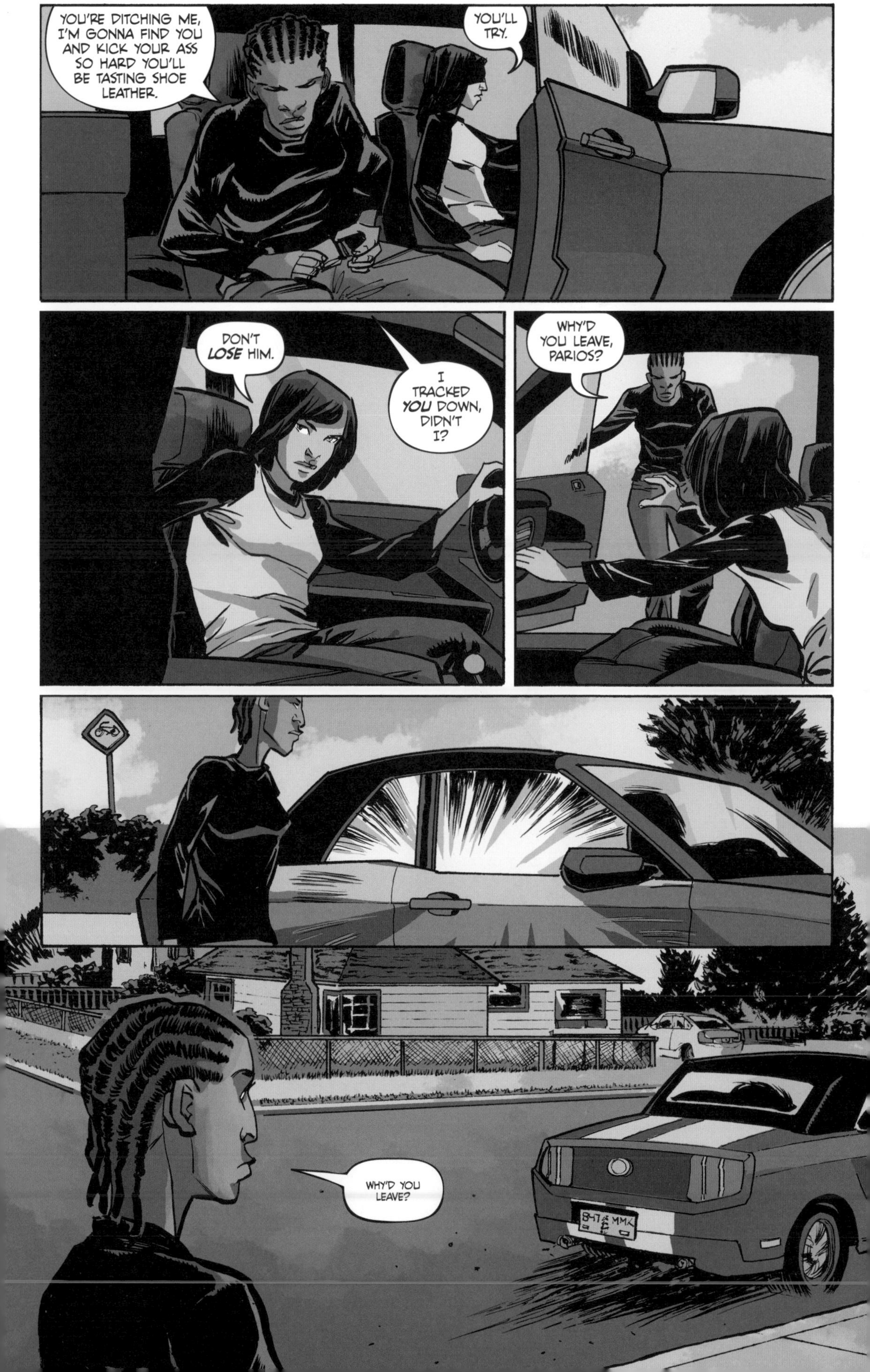
YOU'RE DITCHING ME, I'M GONNA FIND YOU AND KICK YOUR ASS SO HARD YOU'LL BE TASTING SHOE LEATHER.
YOU'LL TRY.
DON'T *LOSE* HIM.
I TRACKED *YOU* DOWN, DIDN'T I?
WHY'D YOU LEAVE, PARIOS?
WHY'D YOU LEAVE?

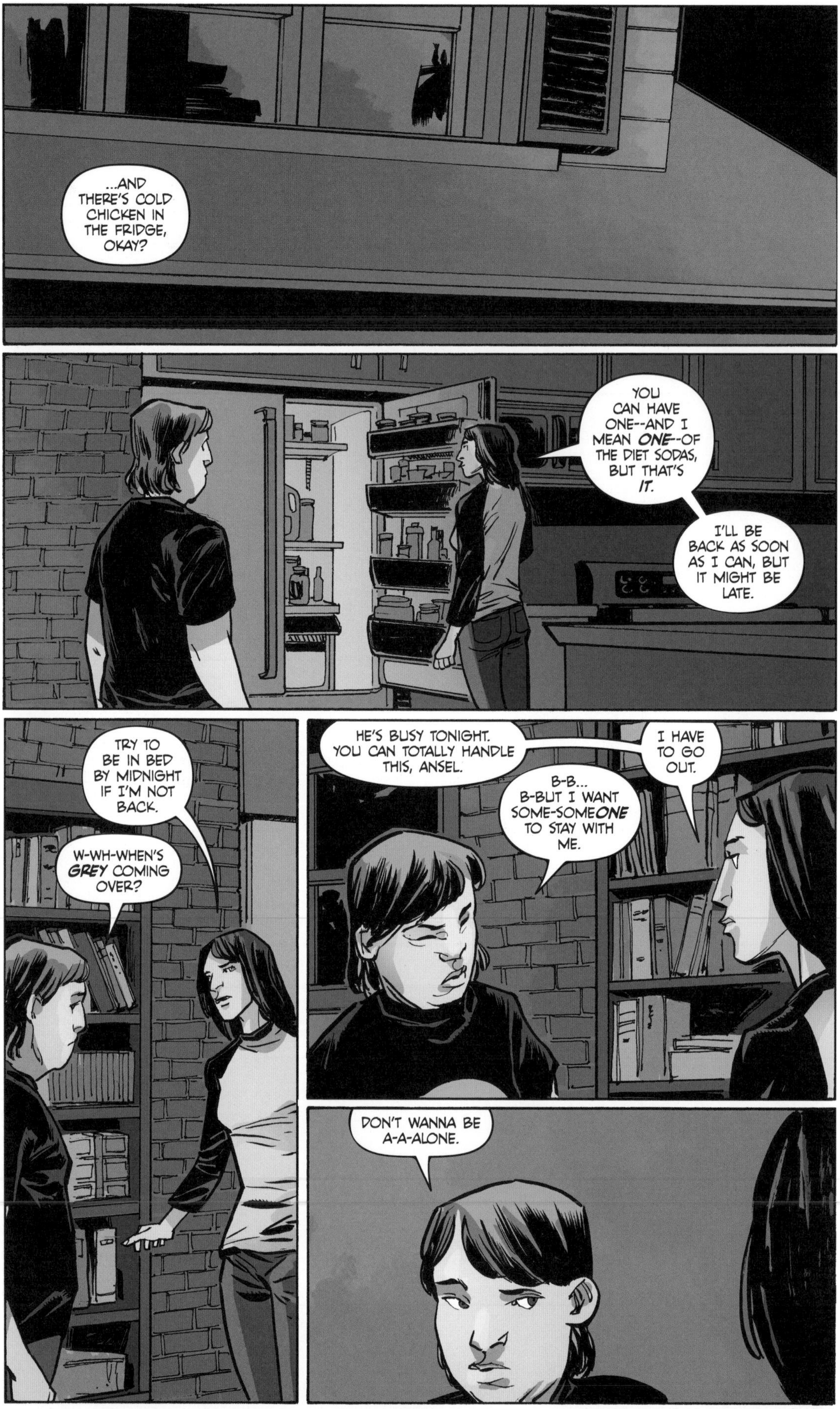
...AND THERE'S COLD CHICKEN IN THE FRIDGE, OKAY?
YOU CAN HAVE ONE--AND I MEAN *ONE*--OF THE DIET SODAS, BUT THAT'S *IT*.
I'LL BE BACK AS SOON AS I CAN, BUT IT MIGHT BE LATE.
TRY TO BE IN BED BY MIDNIGHT IF I'M NOT BACK.
W-WH-WHEN'S *GREY* COMING OVER?
HE'S BUSY TONIGHT. YOU CAN TOTALLY HANDLE THIS, ANSEL.
I HAVE TO GO OUT.
B-B... B-BUT I WANT SOME-SOME*ONE* TO STAY WITH ME.
DON'T WANNA BE A-A-ALONE.

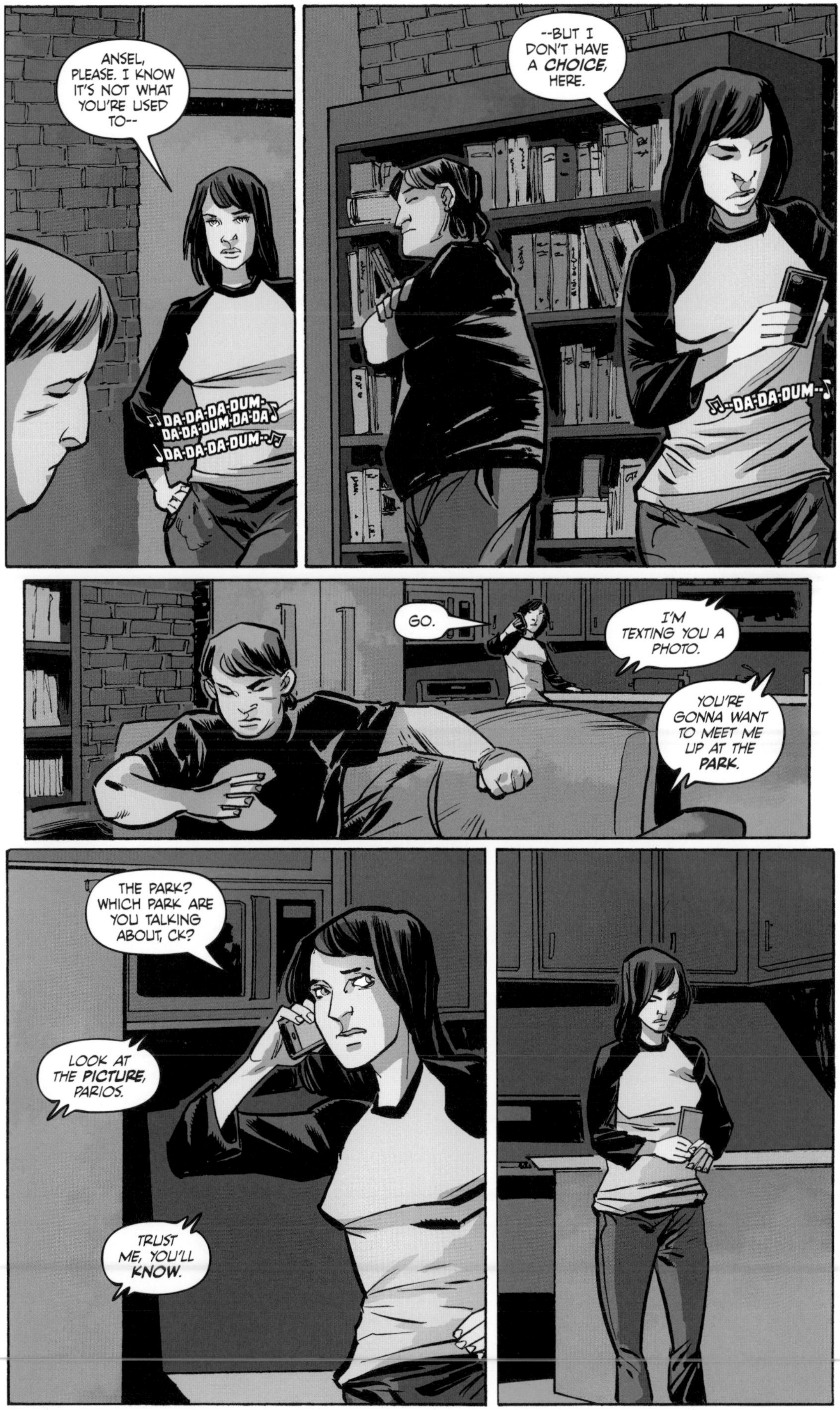
ANSEL, PLEASE. I KNOW IT'S NOT WHAT YOU'RE USED TO--
DA-DA-DA-DUM-DA-DA-DUM-DA-DA
DA-DA-DA-DUM--
--BUT I DON'T HAVE A CHOICE, HERE.
--DA-DA-DUM--
GO.
I'M TEXTING YOU A PHOTO.
YOU'RE GONNA WANT TO MEET ME UP AT THE PARK.
THE PARK? WHICH PARK ARE YOU TALKING ABOUT, CK?
LOOK AT THE PICTURE, PARIOS.
TRUST ME, YOU'LL KNOW.

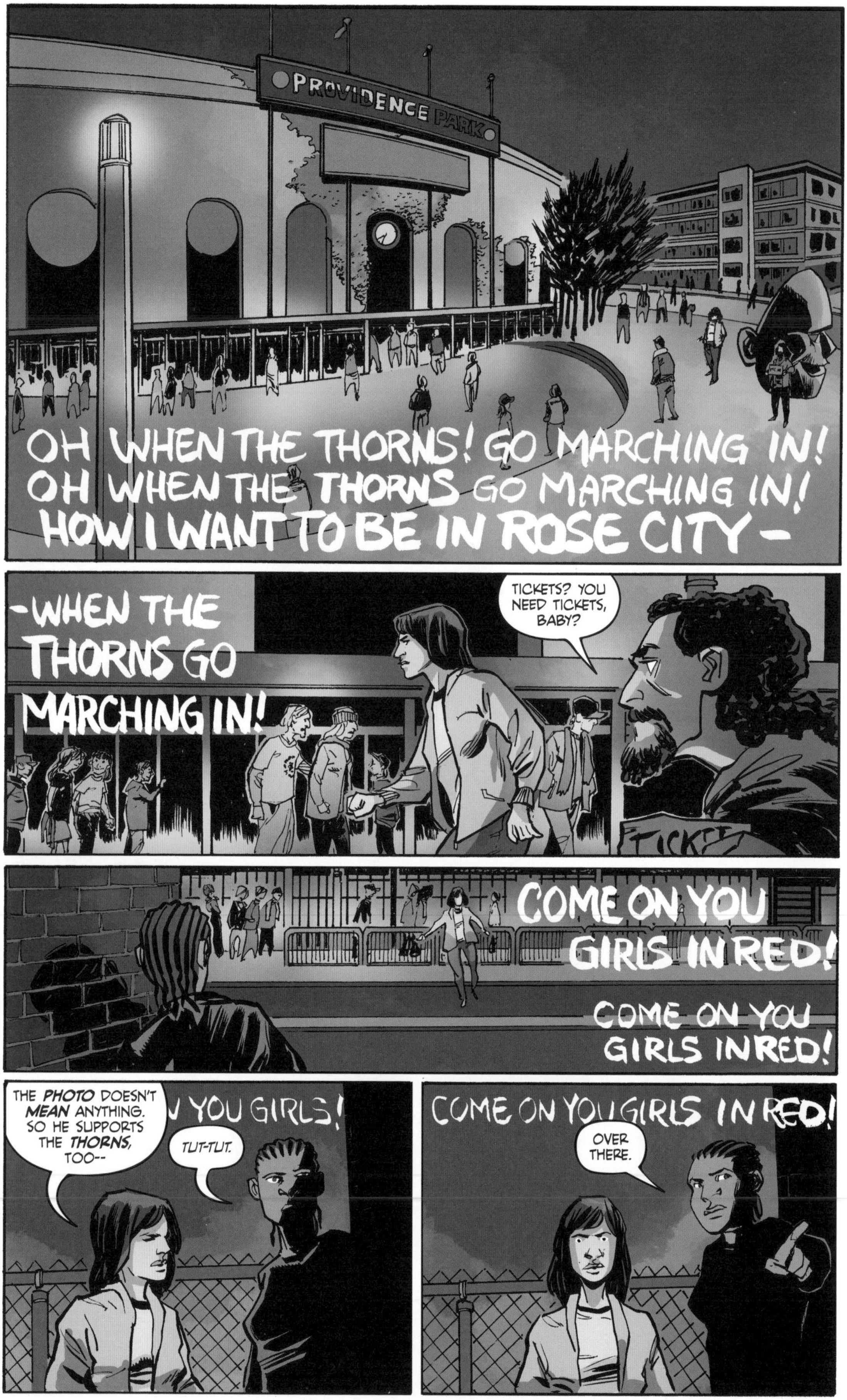
PROVIDENCE PARK
OH WHEN THE THORNS! GO MARCHING IN!
OH WHEN THE THORNS GO MARCHING IN!
HOW I WANT TO BE IN ROSE CITY -
-WHEN THE THORNS GO MARCHING IN!
TICKETS? YOU NEED TICKETS, BABY?
COME ON YOU GIRLS IN RED!
COME ON YOU GIRLS IN RED!
THE PHOTO DOESN'T MEAN ANYTHING. SO HE SUPPORTS THE THORNS, TOO--
TUT-TUT.
COME ON YOU GIRLS IN RED!
OVER THERE.

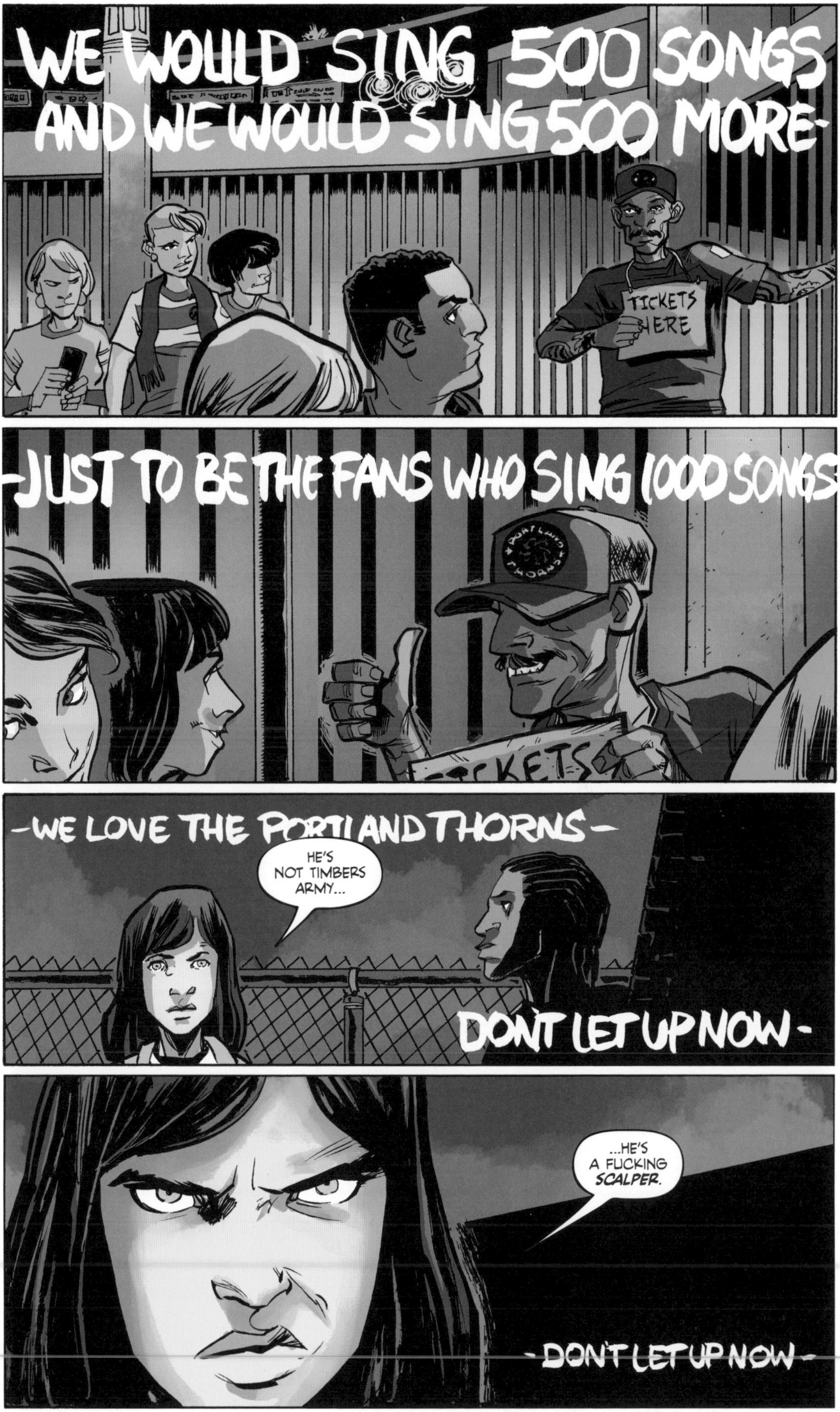
WE WOULD SING 500 SONGS
AND WE WOULD SING 500 MORE-
TICKETS HERE
-JUST TO BE THE FANS WHO SING 1000 SONGS
TICKETS
-WE LOVE THE PORTLAND THORNS-
HE'S NOT TIMBERS ARMY...
DON'T LET UP NOW-
...HE'S A FUCKING SCALPER.
-DON'T LET UP NOW-

Chapter Five

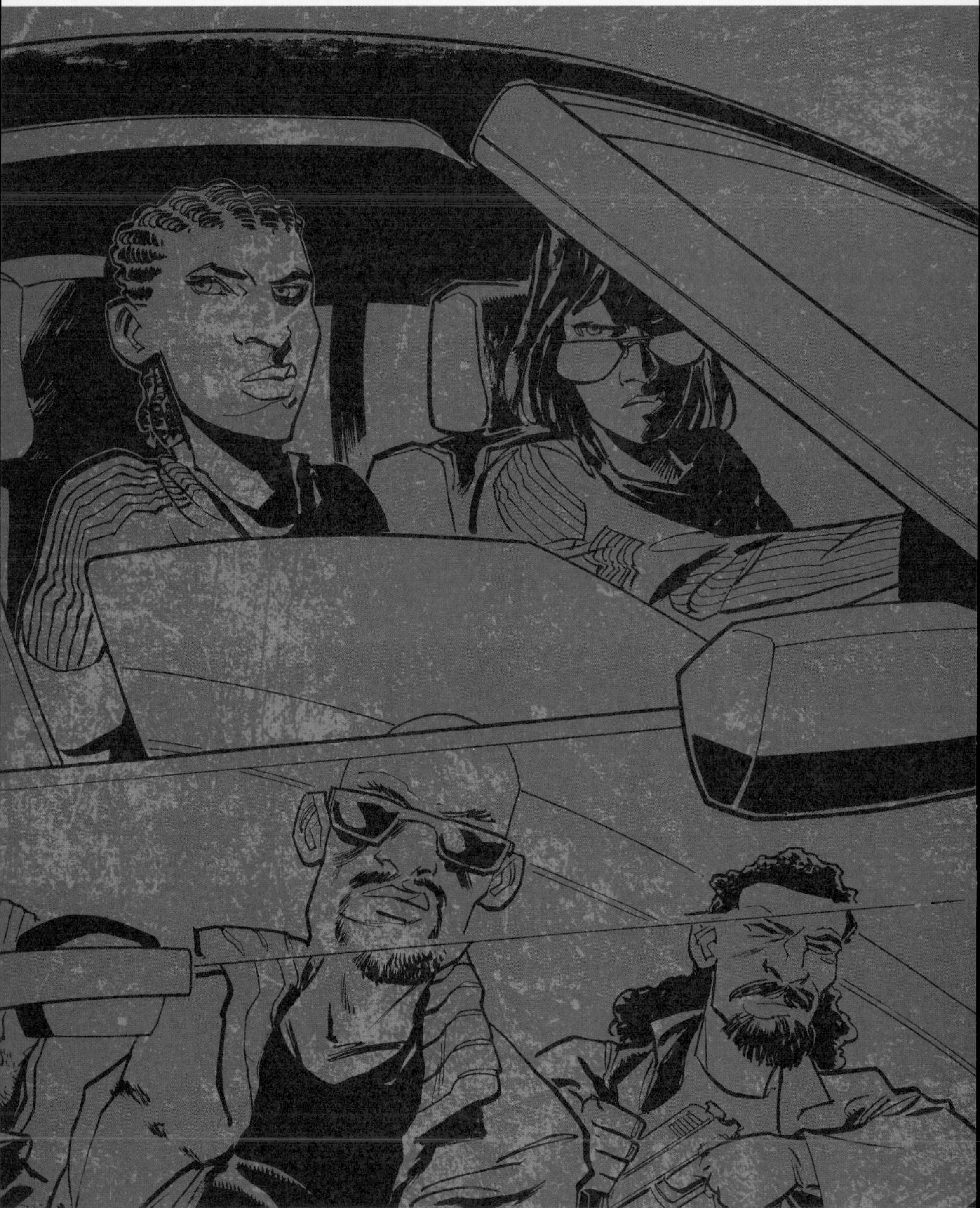

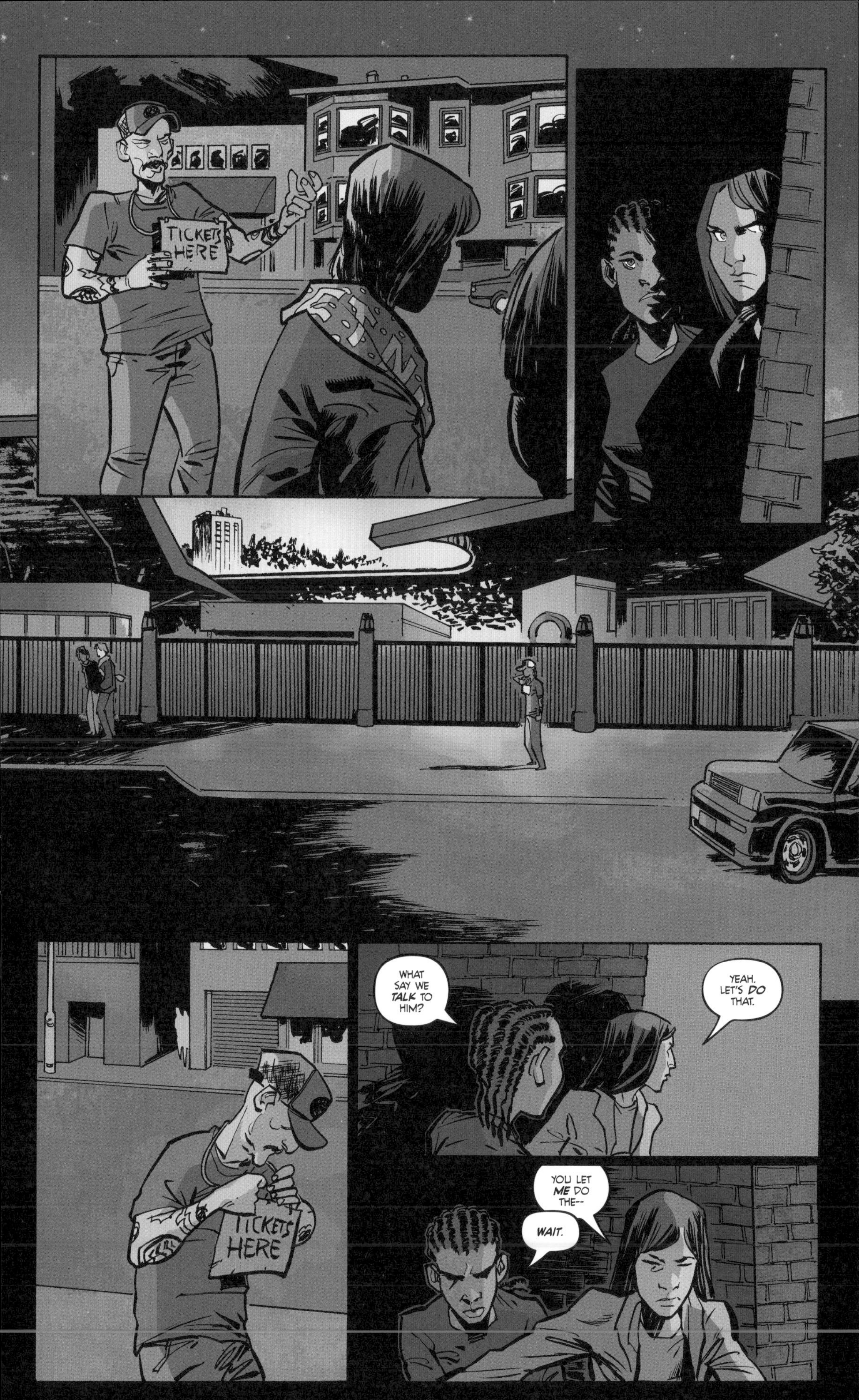

TICKETS HERE
TICKETS HERE
WHAT SAY WE TALK TO HIM?
YEAH. LET'S DO THAT.
YOU LET ME DO THE--
WAIT.

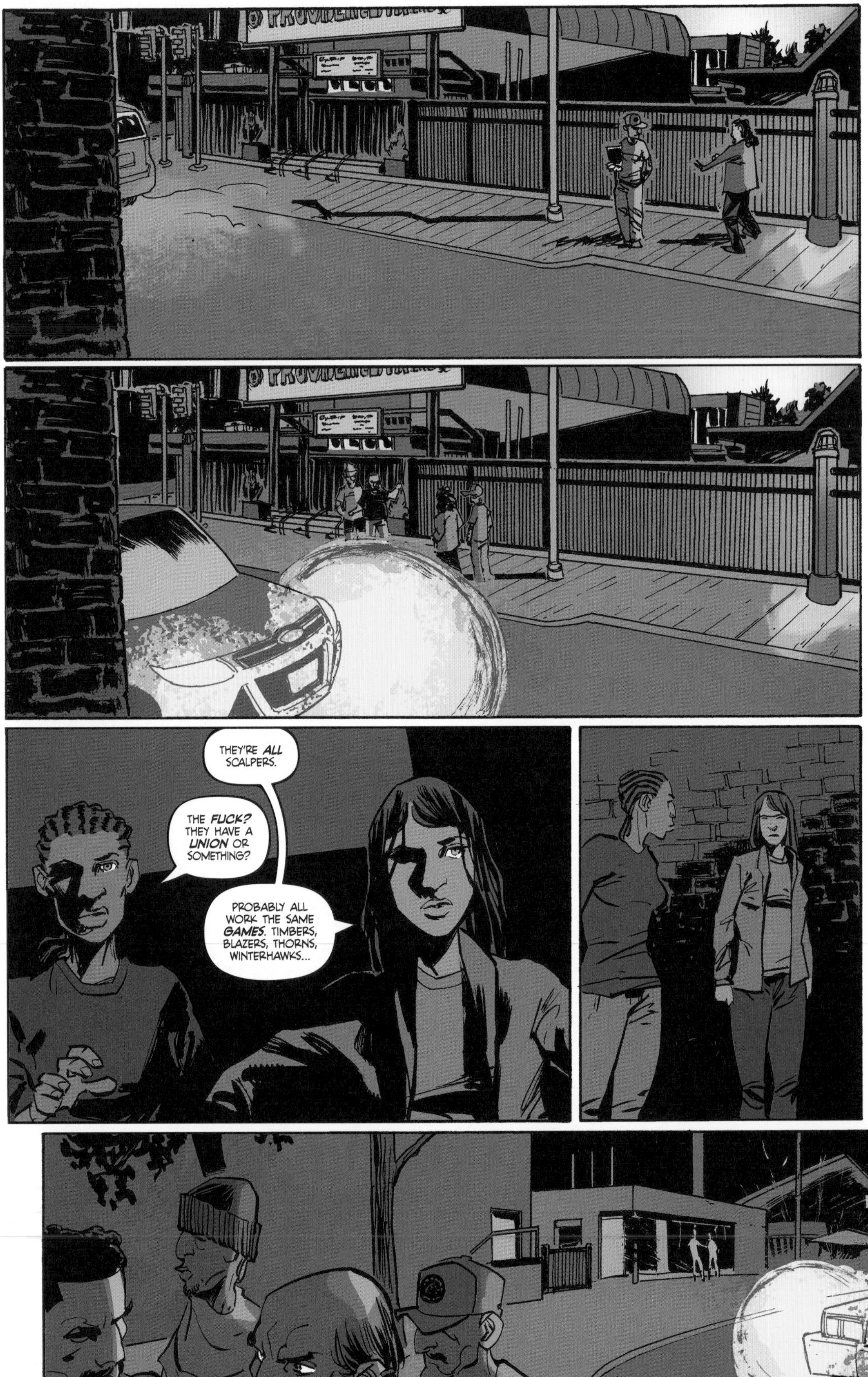
THEY'RE ALL SCALPERS.
THE FUCK? THEY HAVE A UNION OR SOMETHING?
PROBABLY ALL WORK THE SAME GAMES. TIMBERS, BLAZERS, THORNS, WINTERHAWKS...

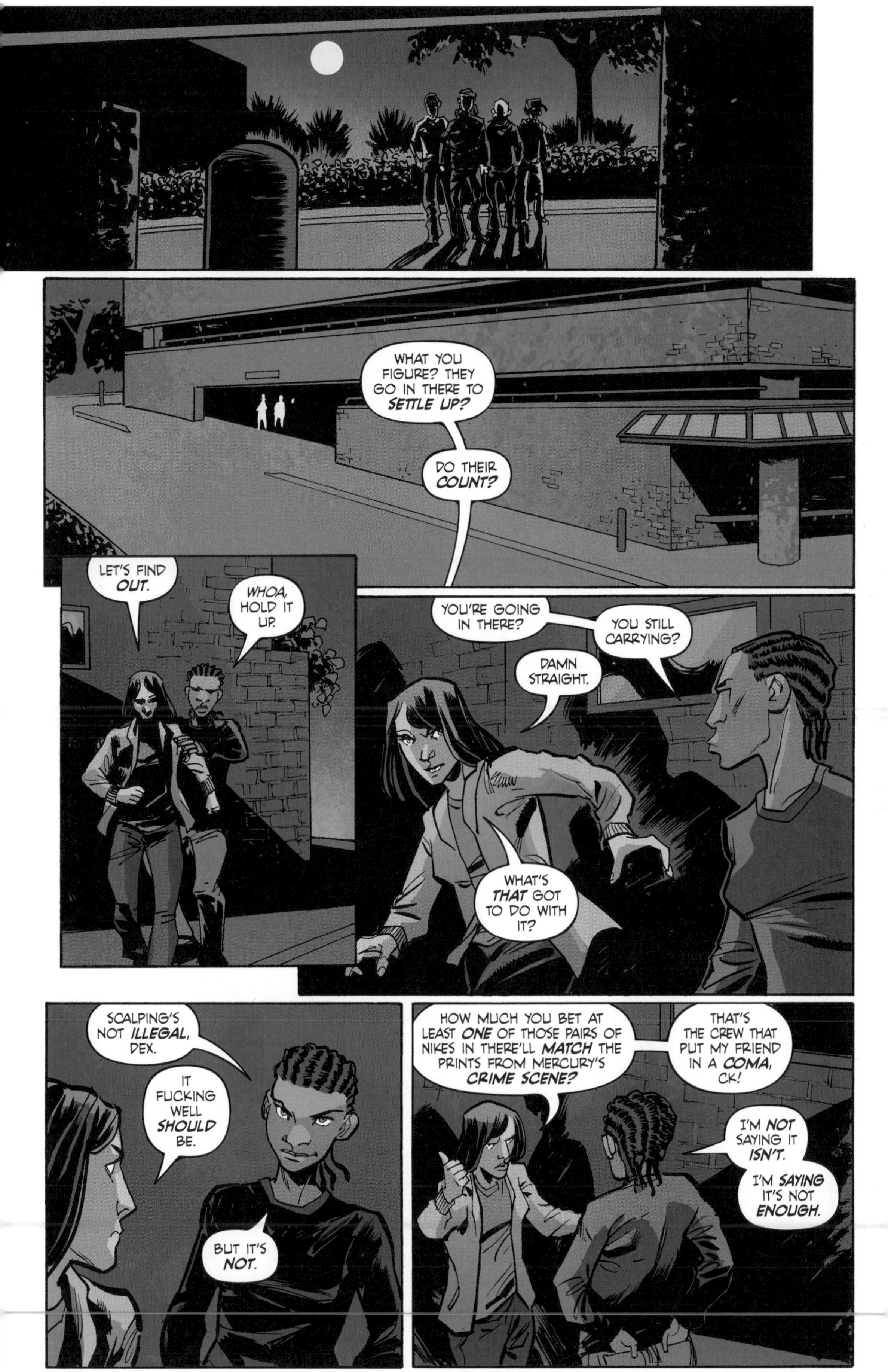
WHAT YOU FIGURE? THEY GO IN THERE TO SETTLE UP?
DO THEIR COUNT?
LET'S FIND OUT.
WHOA, HOLD IT UP.
YOU'RE GOING IN THERE?
YOU STILL CARRYING?
DAMN STRAIGHT.
WHAT'S THAT GOT TO DO WITH IT?
SCALPING'S NOT ILLEGAL, DEX.
IT FUCKING WELL SHOULD BE.
BUT IT'S NOT.
HOW MUCH YOU BET AT LEAST ONE OF THOSE PAIRS OF NIKES IN THERE'LL MATCH THE PRINTS FROM MERCURY'S CRIME SCENE?
THAT'S THE CREW THAT PUT MY FRIEND IN A COMA, CK!
I'M NOT SAYING IT ISN'T.
I'M SAYING IT'S NOT ENOUGH.

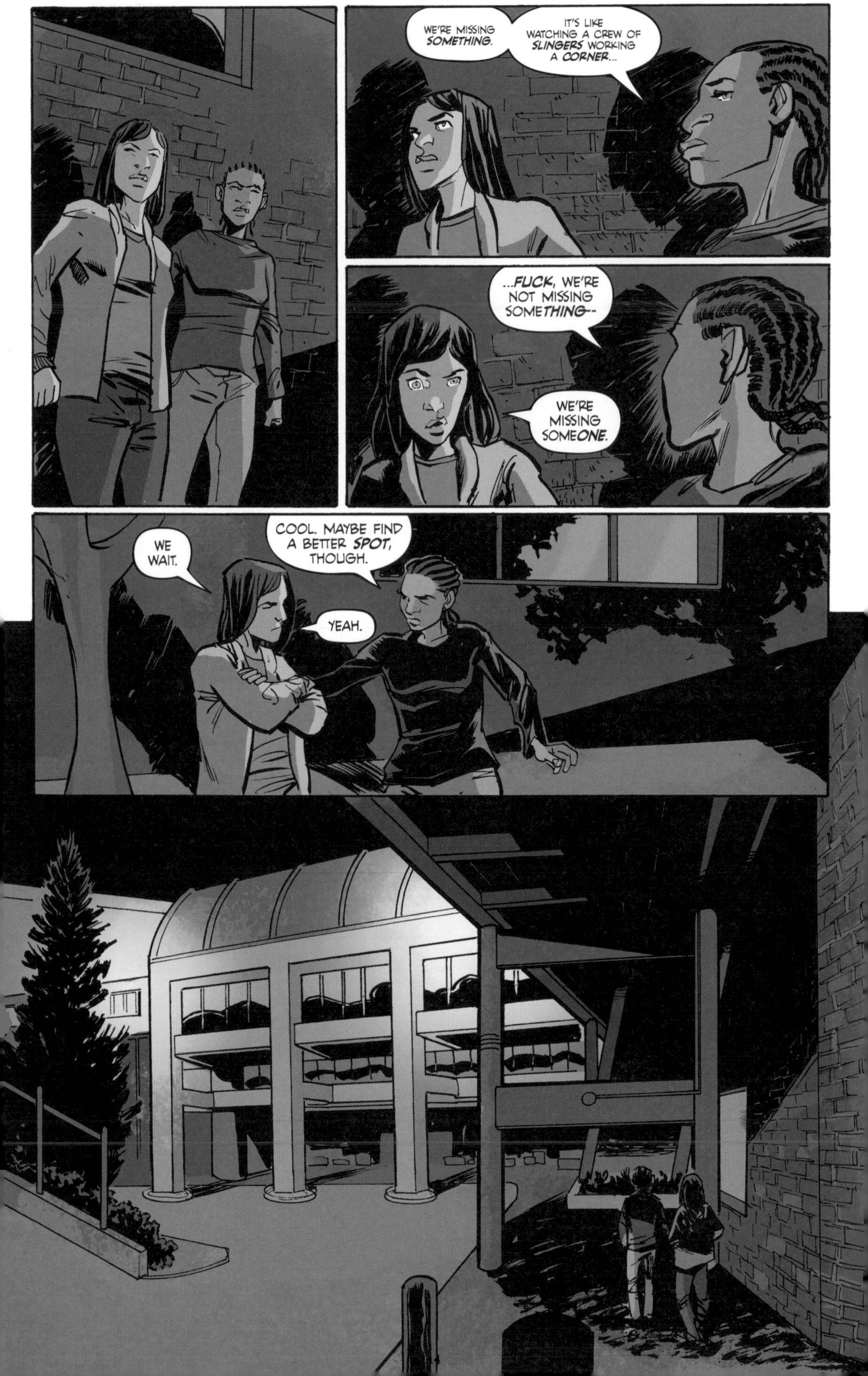
WE'RE MISSING SOMETHING.
IT'S LIKE WATCHING A CREW OF SLINGERS WORKING A CORNER...
...FUCK, WE'RE NOT MISSING SOMETHING--
WE'RE MISSING SOMEONE.
WE WAIT.
COOL. MAYBE FIND A BETTER SPOT, THOUGH.
YEAH.

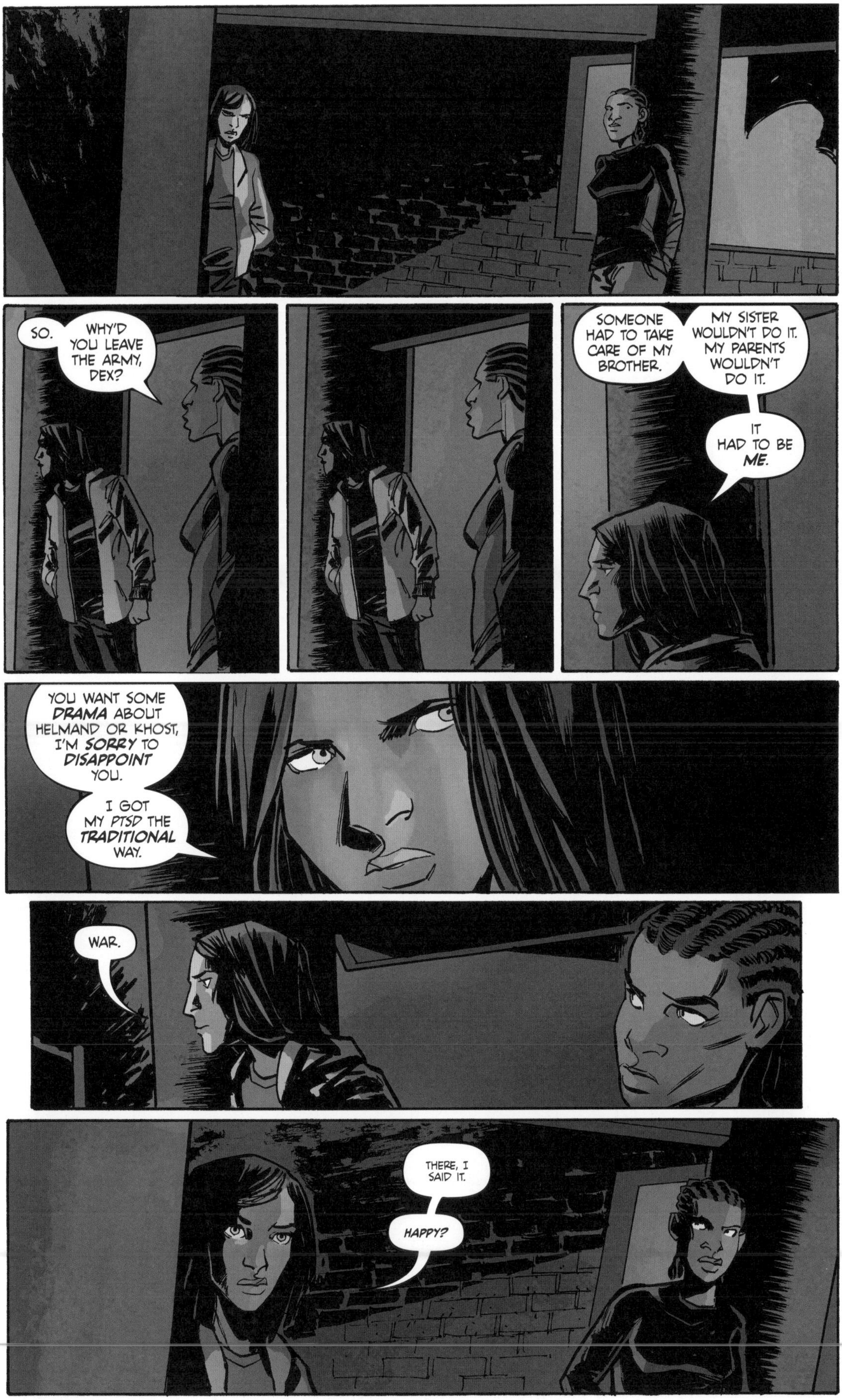
SO.
WHY'D YOU LEAVE THE ARMY, DEX?
SOMEONE HAD TO TAKE CARE OF MY BROTHER.
MY SISTER WOULDN'T DO IT. MY PARENTS WOULDN'T DO IT.
IT HAD TO BE ME.
YOU WANT SOME DRAMA ABOUT HELMAND OR KHOST, I'M SORRY TO DISAPPOINT YOU.
I GOT MY PTSD THE TRADITIONAL WAY.
WAR.
THERE, I SAID IT.
HAPPY?

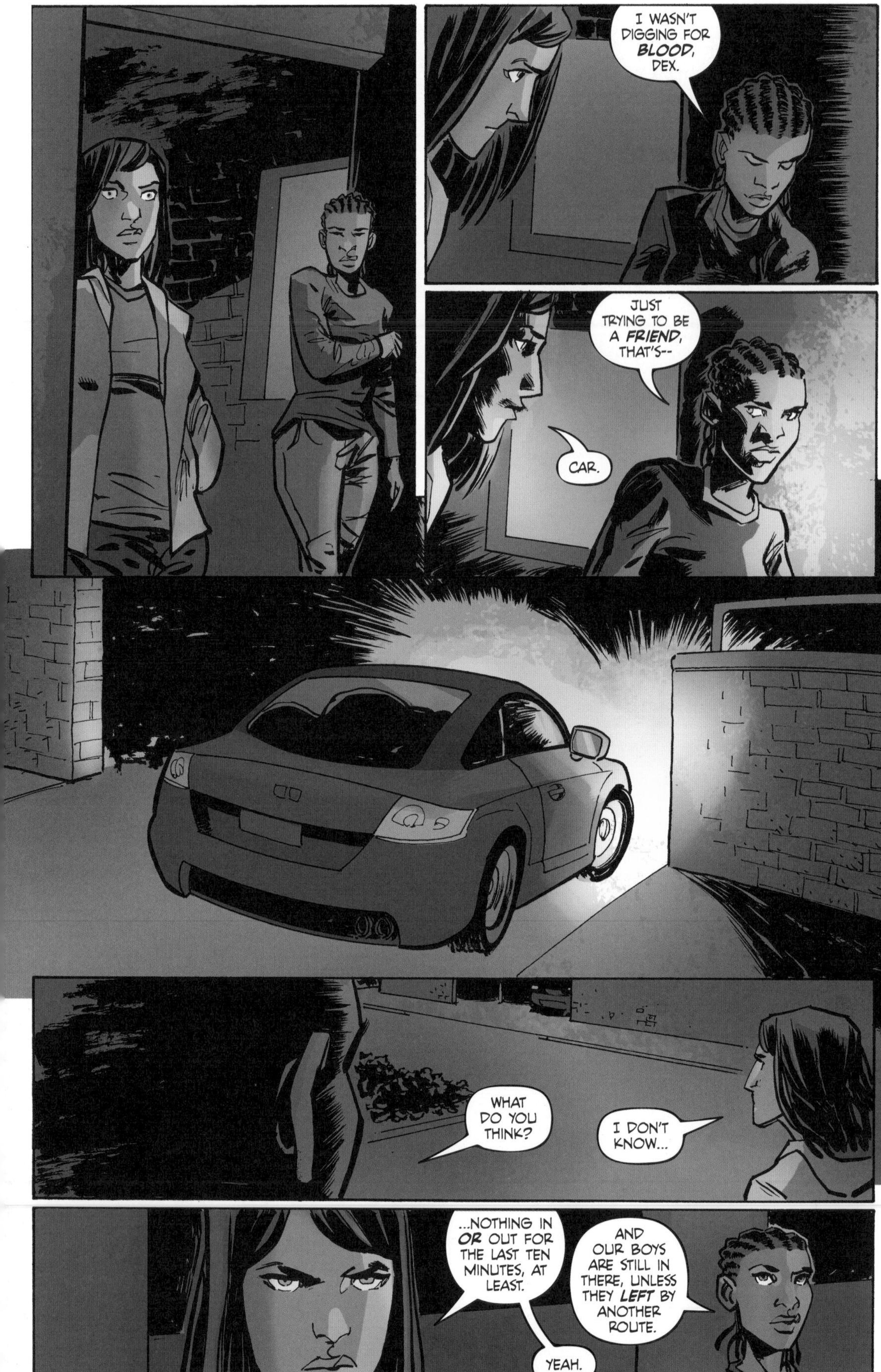
I WASN'T DIGGING FOR BLOOD, DEX.
JUST TRYING TO BE A FRIEND, THAT'S--
CAR.
WHAT DO YOU THINK?
I DON'T KNOW...
...NOTHING IN OR OUT FOR THE LAST TEN MINUTES, AT LEAST.
AND OUR BOYS ARE STILL IN THERE, UNLESS THEY LEFT BY ANOTHER ROUTE.
YEAH.

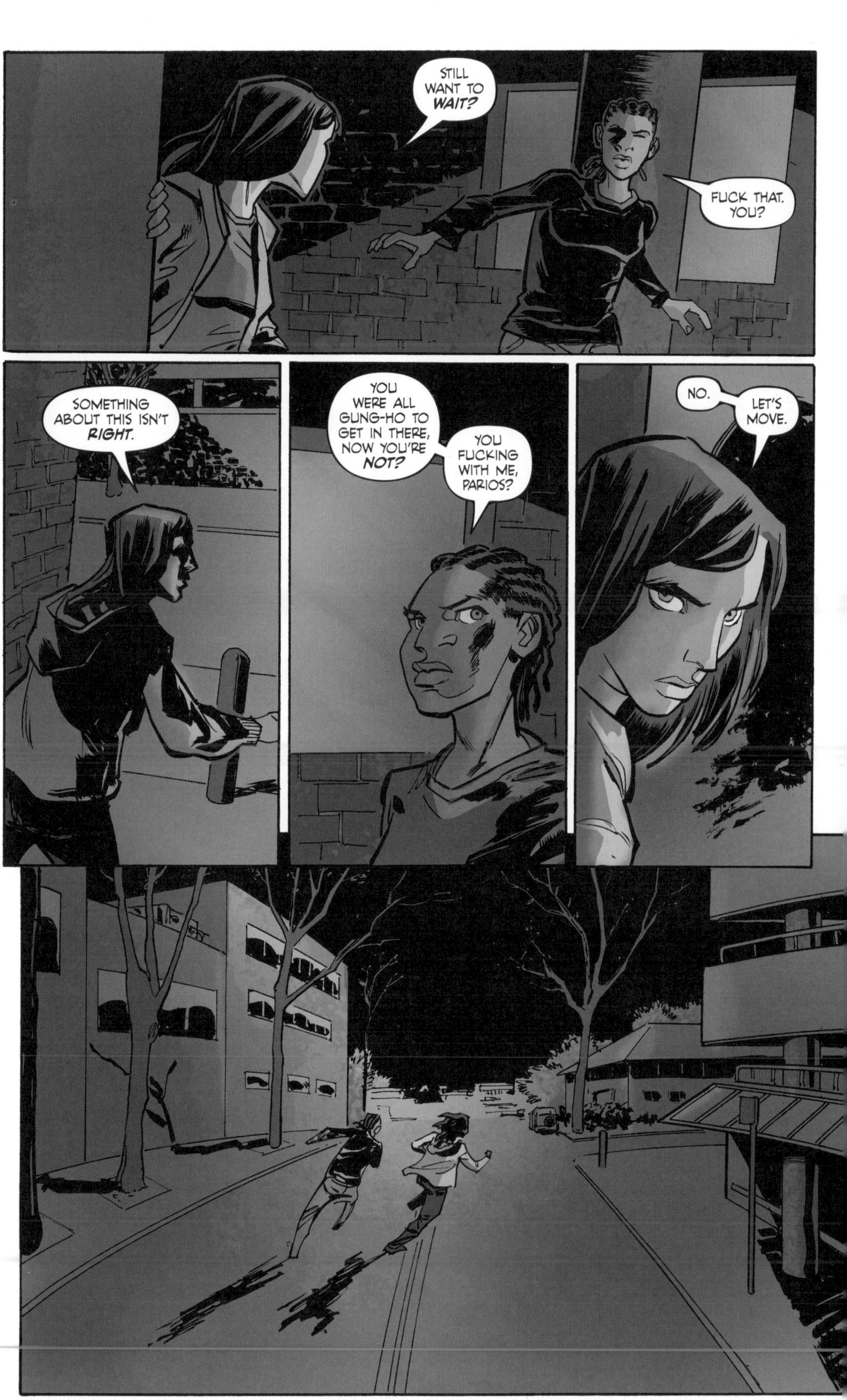
STILL WANT TO WAIT?
FUCK THAT. YOU?
SOMETHING ABOUT THIS ISN'T RIGHT.
YOU WERE ALL GUNG-HO TO GET IN THERE, NOW YOU'RE NOT?
YOU FUCKING WITH ME, PARIOS?
NO.
LET'S MOVE.

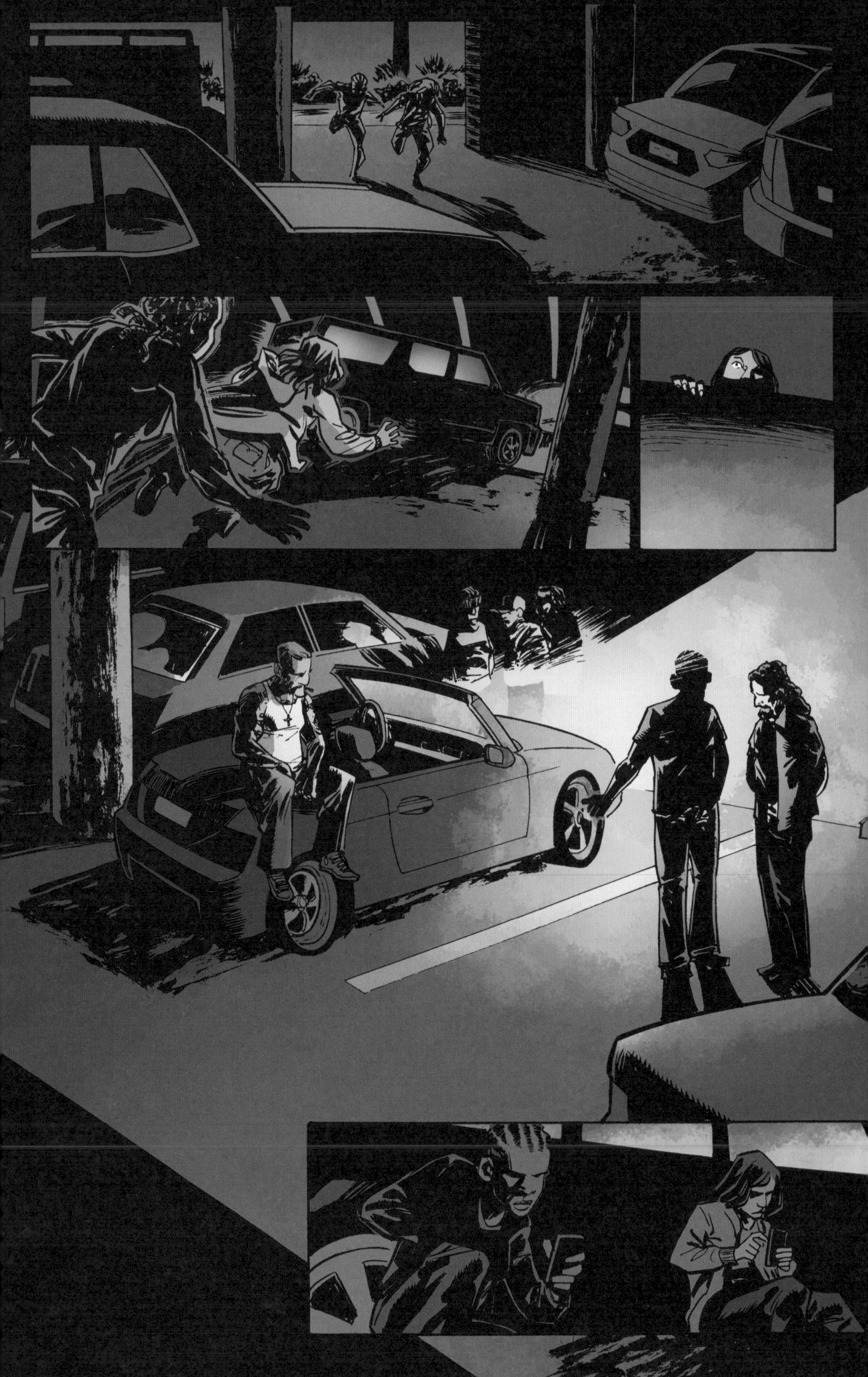

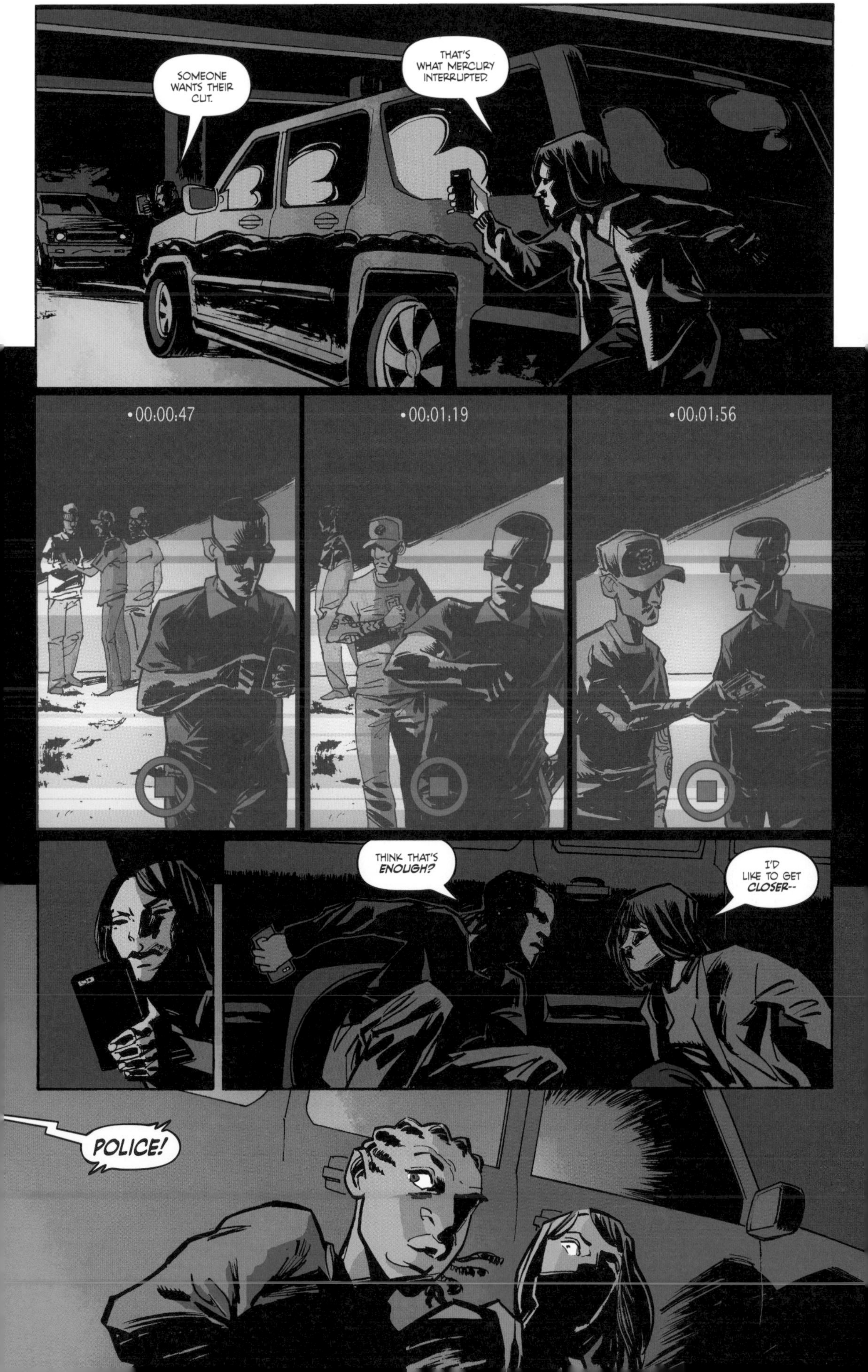
SOMEONE WANTS THEIR CUT.
THAT'S WHAT MERCURY INTERRUPTED.
•00:00:47
•00:01:19
•00:01:56
THINK THAT'S *ENOUGH?*
I'D LIKE TO GET *CLOSER--*
POLICE!

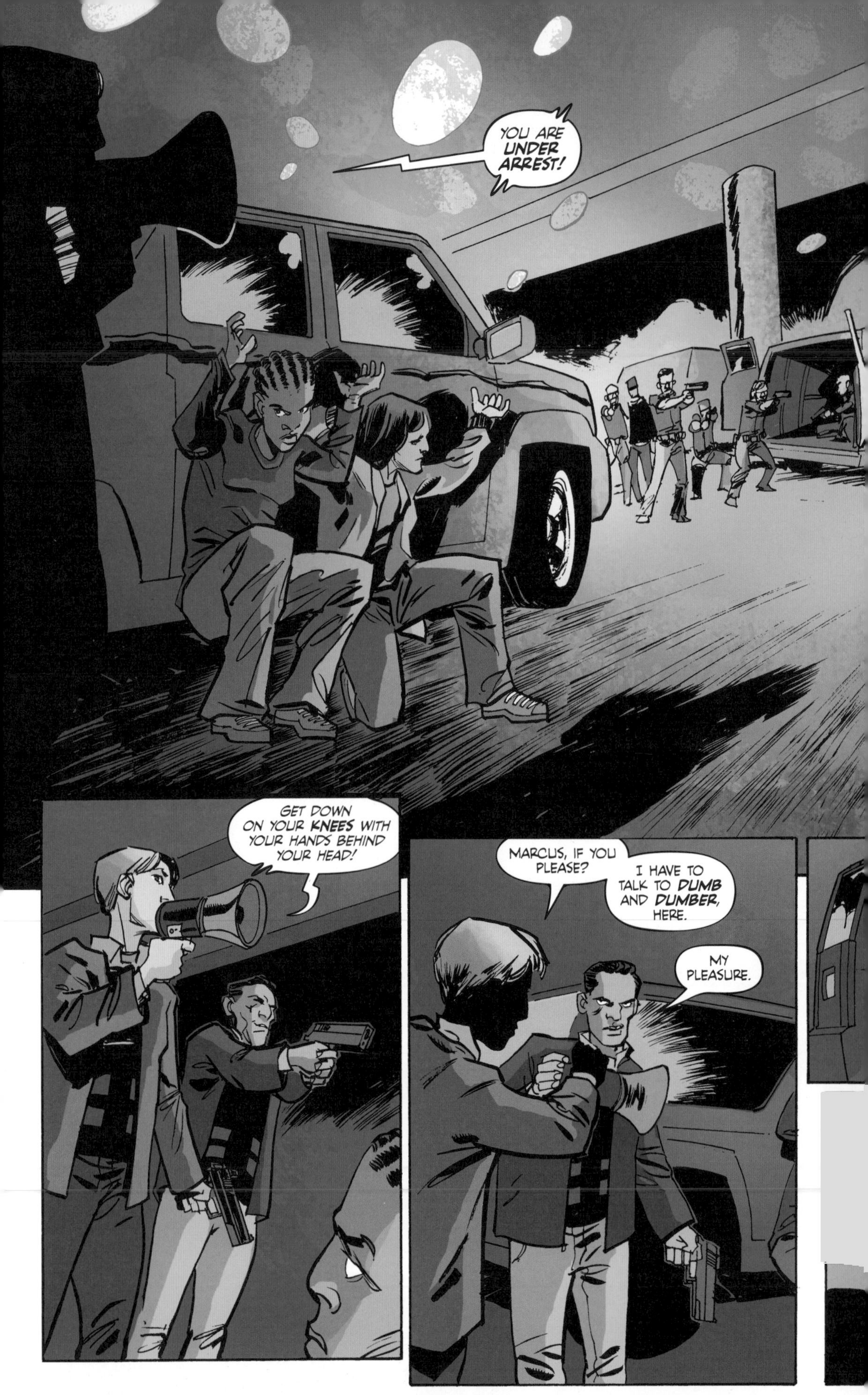
YOU ARE UNDER ARREST!
GET DOWN ON YOUR KNEES WITH YOUR HANDS BEHIND YOUR HEAD!
MARCUS, IF YOU PLEASE?
I HAVE TO TALK TO DUMB AND DUMBER, HERE.
MY PLEASURE.

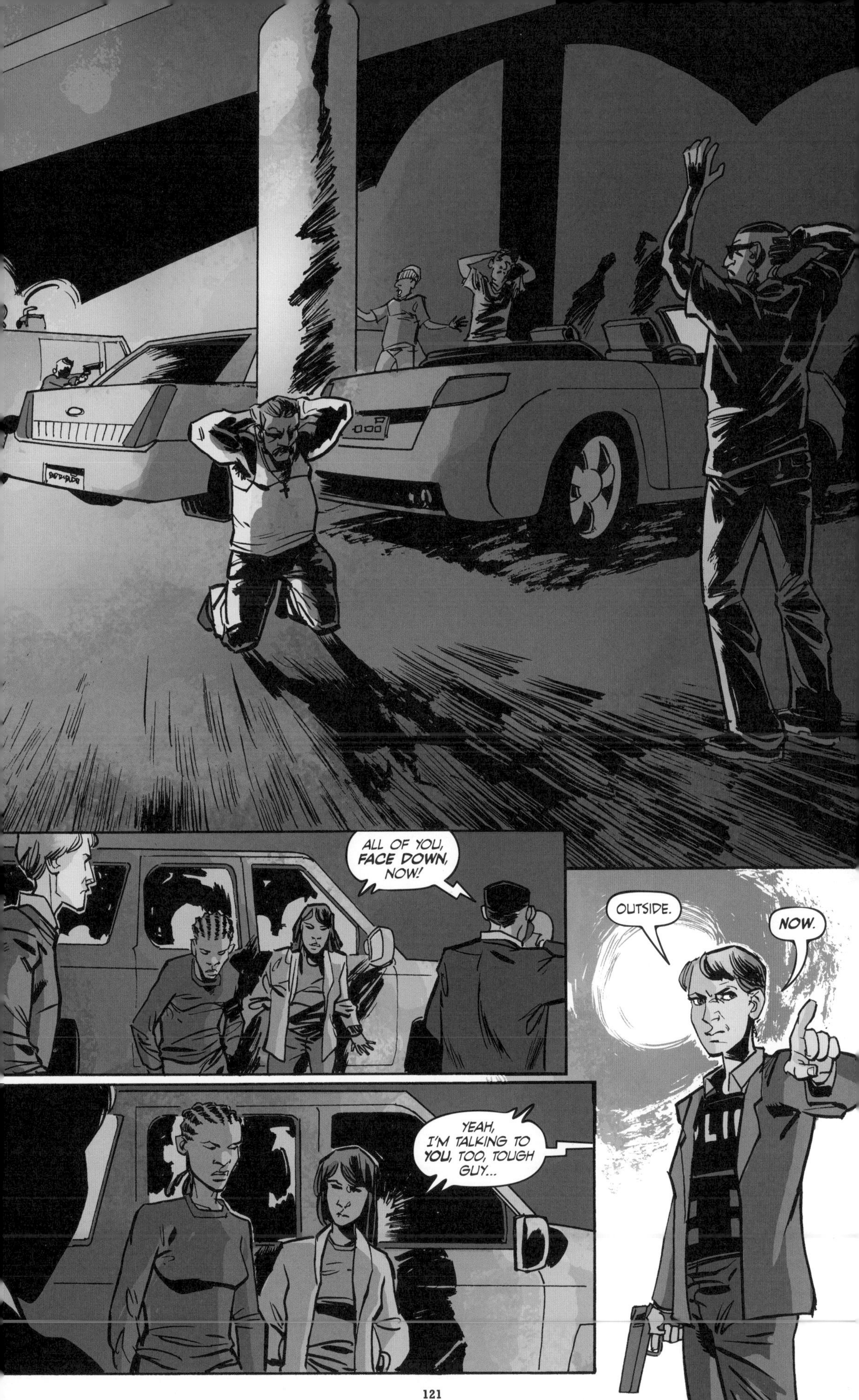
ALL OF YOU, FACE DOWN, NOW!
OUTSIDE.
NOW.
YEAH, I'M TALKING TO YOU, TOO, TOUGH GUY...

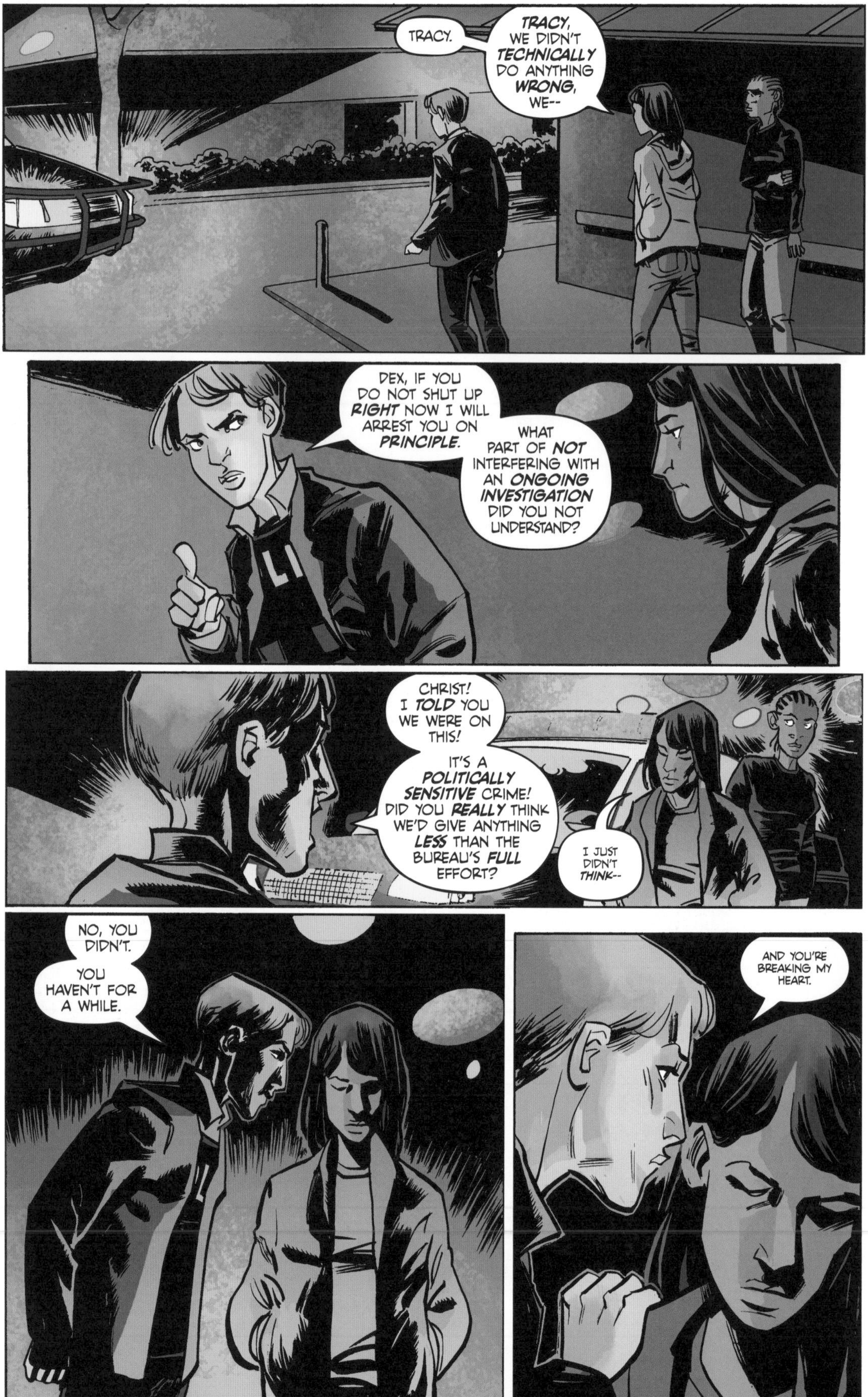

TRACY.
TRACY, WE DIDN'T TECHNICALLY DO ANYTHING WRONG, WE--
DEX, IF YOU DO NOT SHUT UP RIGHT NOW I WILL ARREST YOU ON PRINCIPLE.
WHAT PART OF NOT INTERFERING WITH AN ONGOING INVESTIGATION DID YOU NOT UNDERSTAND?
CHRIST! I TOLD YOU WE WERE ON THIS!
IT'S A POLITICALLY SENSITIVE CRIME! DID YOU REALLY THINK WE'D GIVE ANYTHING LESS THAN THE BUREAU'S FULL EFFORT?
I JUST DIDN'T THINK--
NO, YOU DIDN'T.
YOU HAVEN'T FOR A WHILE.
AND YOU'RE BREAKING MY HEART.

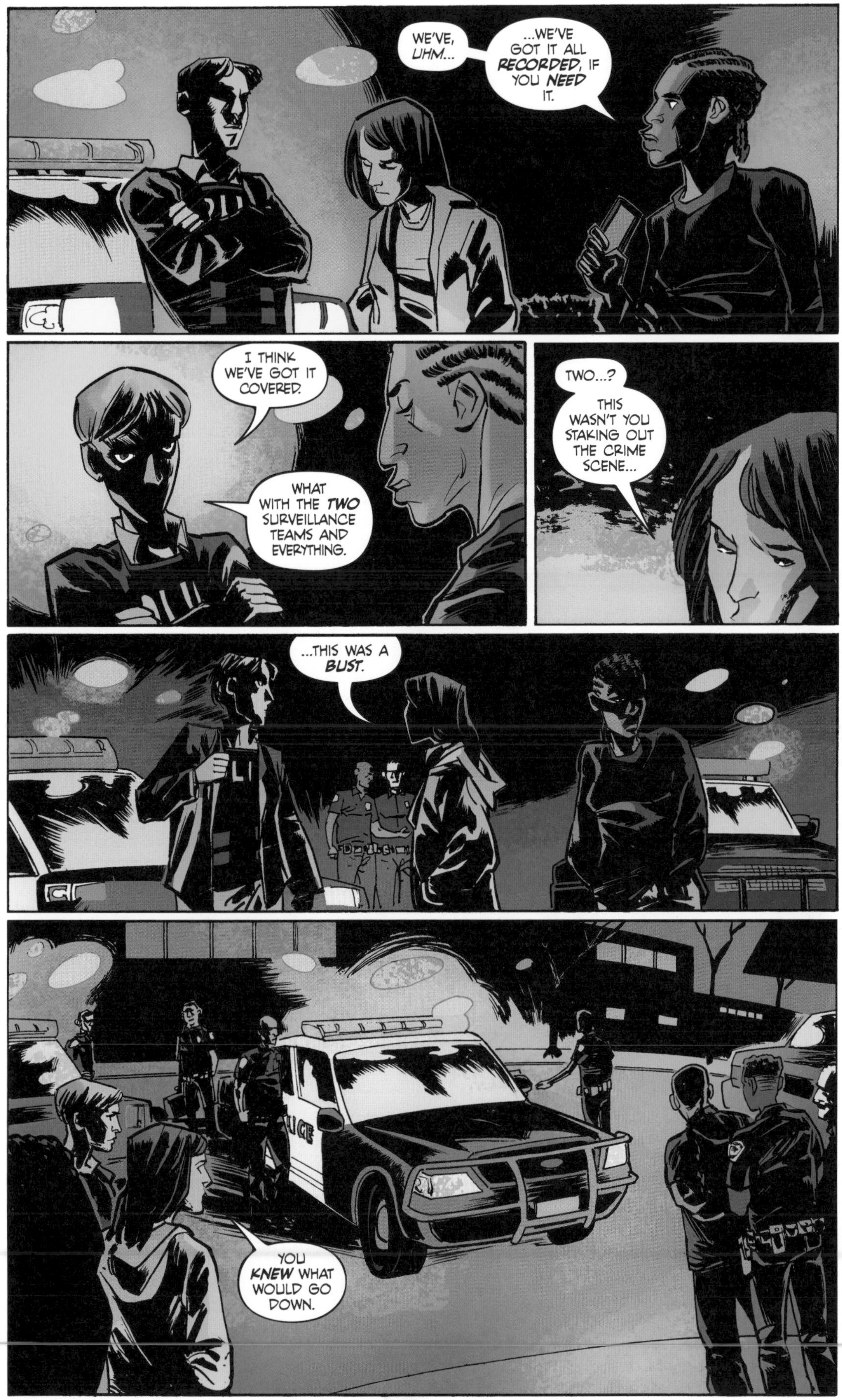
WE'VE, UHM...
...WE'VE GOT IT ALL RECORDED, IF YOU NEED IT.
I THINK WE'VE GOT IT COVERED.
WHAT WITH THE TWO SURVEILLANCE TEAMS AND EVERYTHING.
TWO...?
THIS WASN'T YOU STAKING OUT THE CRIME SCENE...
...THIS WAS A BUST.
YOU KNEW WHAT WOULD GO DOWN.

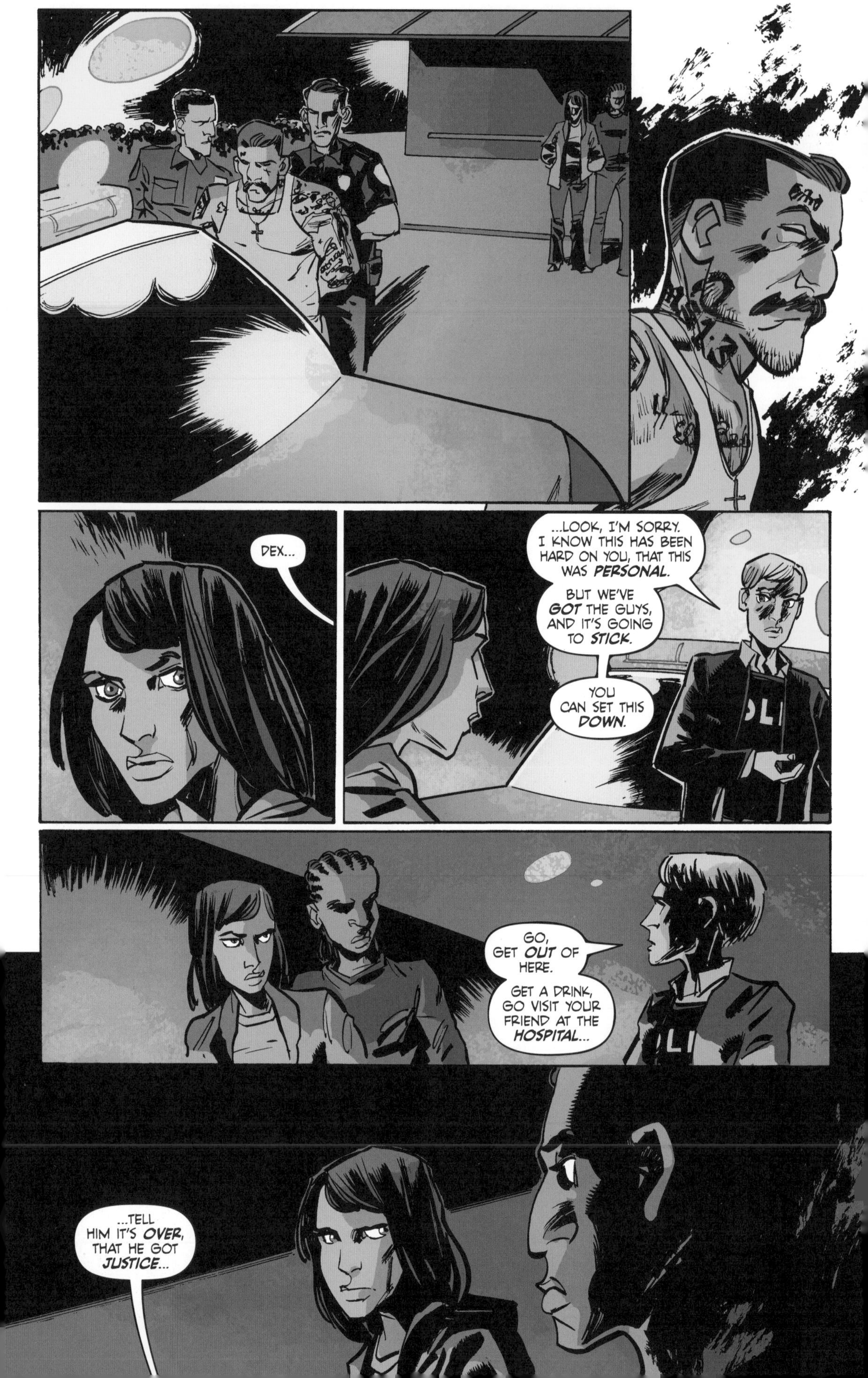
DEX...
...LOOK, I'M SORRY. I KNOW THIS HAS BEEN HARD ON YOU, THAT THIS WAS PERSONAL.
BUT WE'VE GOT THE GUYS, AND IT'S GOING TO STICK.
YOU CAN SET THIS DOWN.
GO, GET OUT OF HERE.
GET A DRINK, GO VISIT YOUR FRIEND AT THE HOSPITAL...
...TELL HIM IT'S OVER, THAT HE GOT JUSTICE...

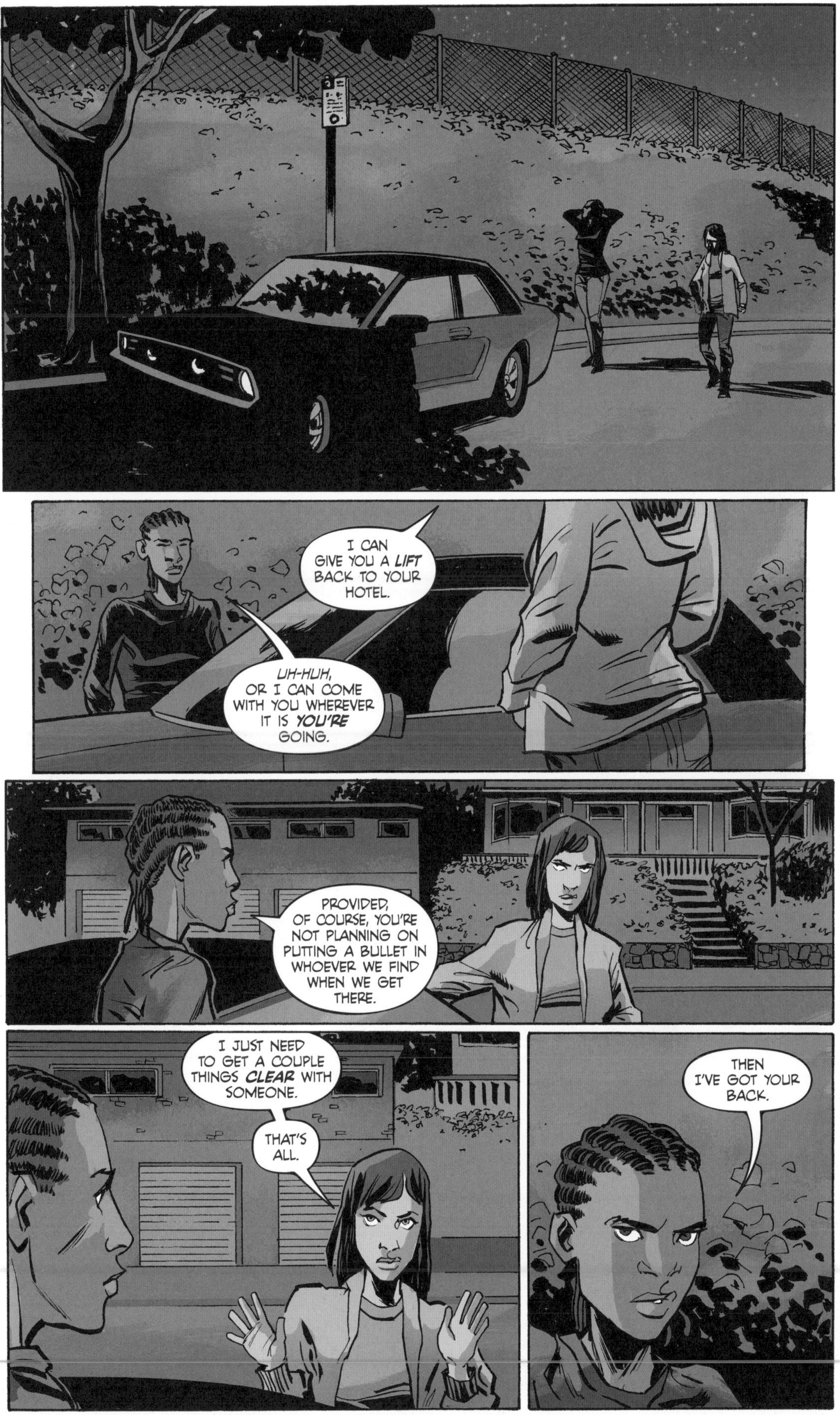
I CAN GIVE YOU A *LIFT* BACK TO YOUR HOTEL.
UH-HUH, OR I CAN COME WITH YOU WHEREVER IT IS ***YOU'RE*** GOING.
PROVIDED, OF COURSE, YOU'RE NOT PLANNING ON PUTTING A BULLET IN WHOEVER WE FIND WHEN WE GET THERE.
I JUST NEED TO GET A COUPLE THINGS ***CLEAR*** WITH SOMEONE.
THAT'S ALL.
THEN I'VE GOT YOUR BACK.

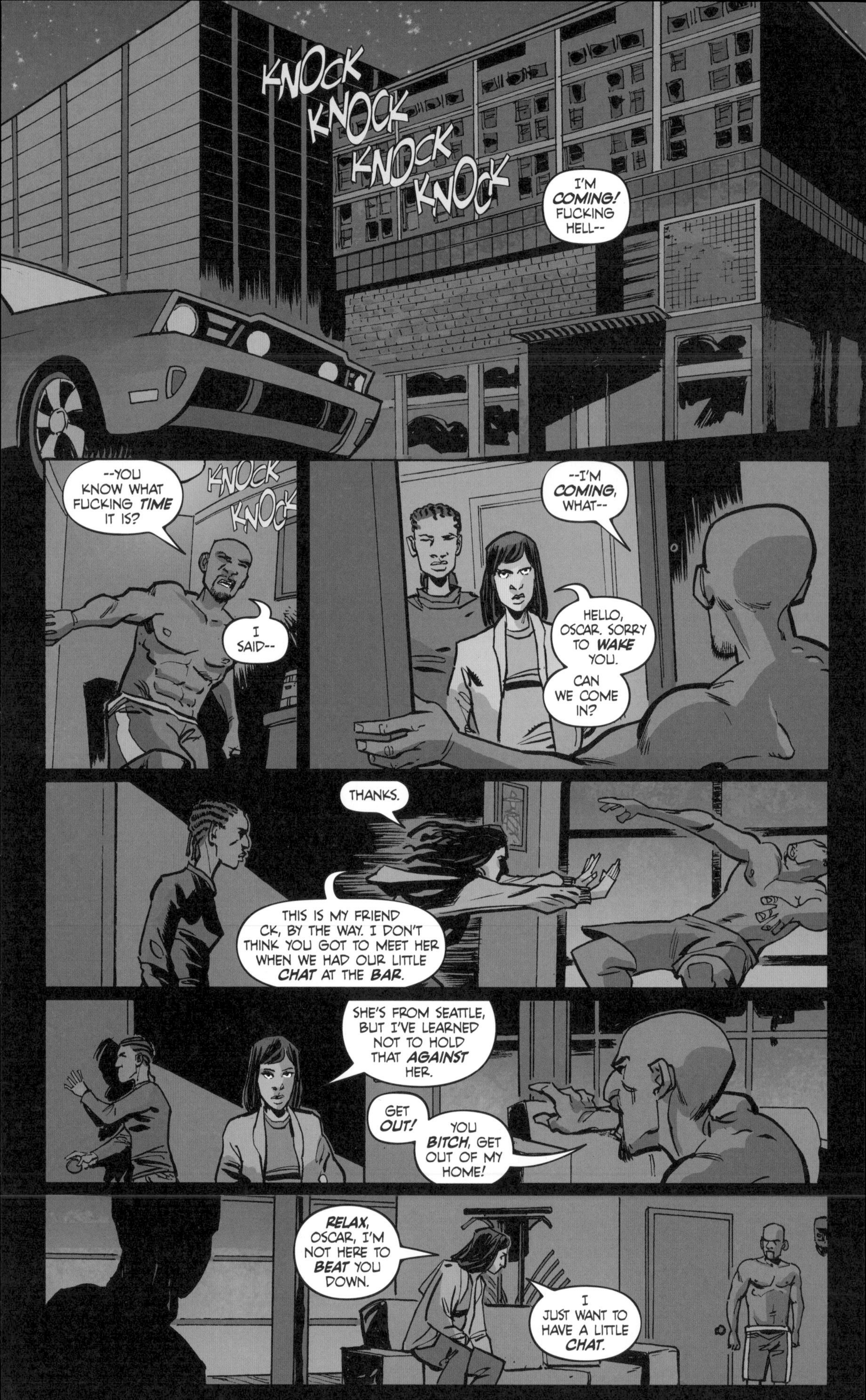
KNOCK KNOCK KNOCK KNOCK
I'M COMING! FUCKING HELL--
--YOU KNOW WHAT FUCKING TIME IT IS?
KNOCK KNOCK
I SAID--
--I'M COMING, WHAT--
HELLO, OSCAR. SORRY TO WAKE YOU.
CAN WE COME IN?
THANKS.
THIS IS MY FRIEND CK, BY THE WAY. I DON'T THINK YOU GOT TO MEET HER WHEN WE HAD OUR LITTLE CHAT AT THE BAR.
SHE'S FROM SEATTLE, BUT I'VE LEARNED NOT TO HOLD THAT AGAINST HER.
GET OUT!
YOU BITCH, GET OUT OF MY HOME!
RELAX, OSCAR, I'M NOT HERE TO BEAT YOU DOWN.
I JUST WANT TO HAVE A LITTLE CHAT.

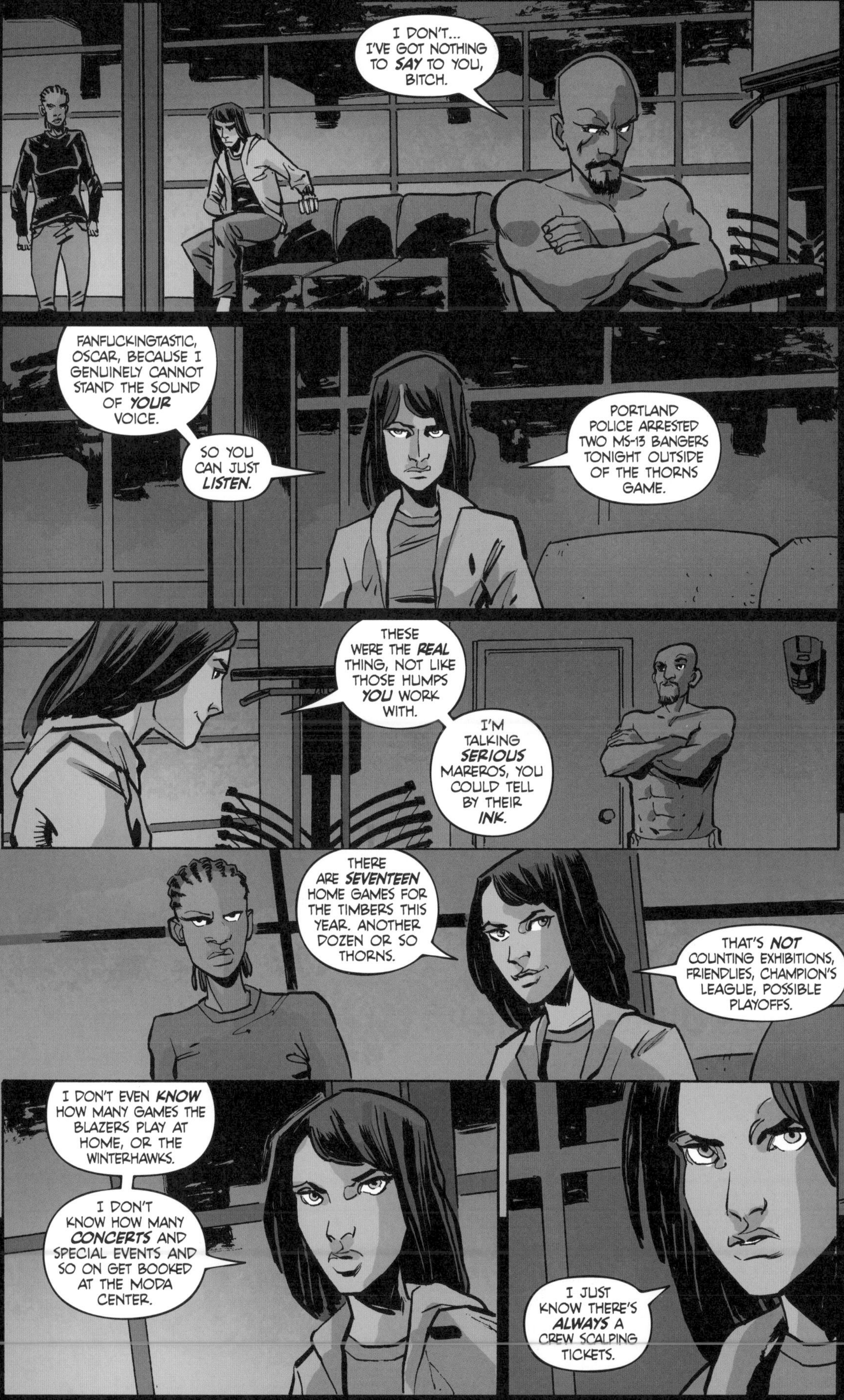

I DON'T... I'VE GOT NOTHING TO SAY TO YOU, BITCH.
FANFUCKINGTASTIC, OSCAR, BECAUSE I GENUINELY CANNOT STAND THE SOUND OF YOUR VOICE.
SO YOU CAN JUST LISTEN.
PORTLAND POLICE ARRESTED TWO MS-13 BANGERS TONIGHT OUTSIDE OF THE THORNS GAME.
THESE WERE THE REAL THING, NOT LIKE THOSE HUMPS YOU WORK WITH.
I'M TALKING SERIOUS MAREROS, YOU COULD TELL BY THEIR INK.
THERE ARE SEVENTEEN HOME GAMES FOR THE TIMBERS THIS YEAR. ANOTHER DOZEN OR SO THORNS.
THAT'S NOT COUNTING EXHIBITIONS, FRIENDLIES, CHAMPION'S LEAGUE, POSSIBLE PLAYOFFS.
I DON'T EVEN KNOW HOW MANY GAMES THE BLAZERS PLAY AT HOME, OR THE WINTERHAWKS.
I DON'T KNOW HOW MANY CONCERTS AND SPECIAL EVENTS AND SO ON GET BOOKED AT THE MODA CENTER.
I JUST KNOW THERE'S ALWAYS A CREW SCALPING TICKETS.

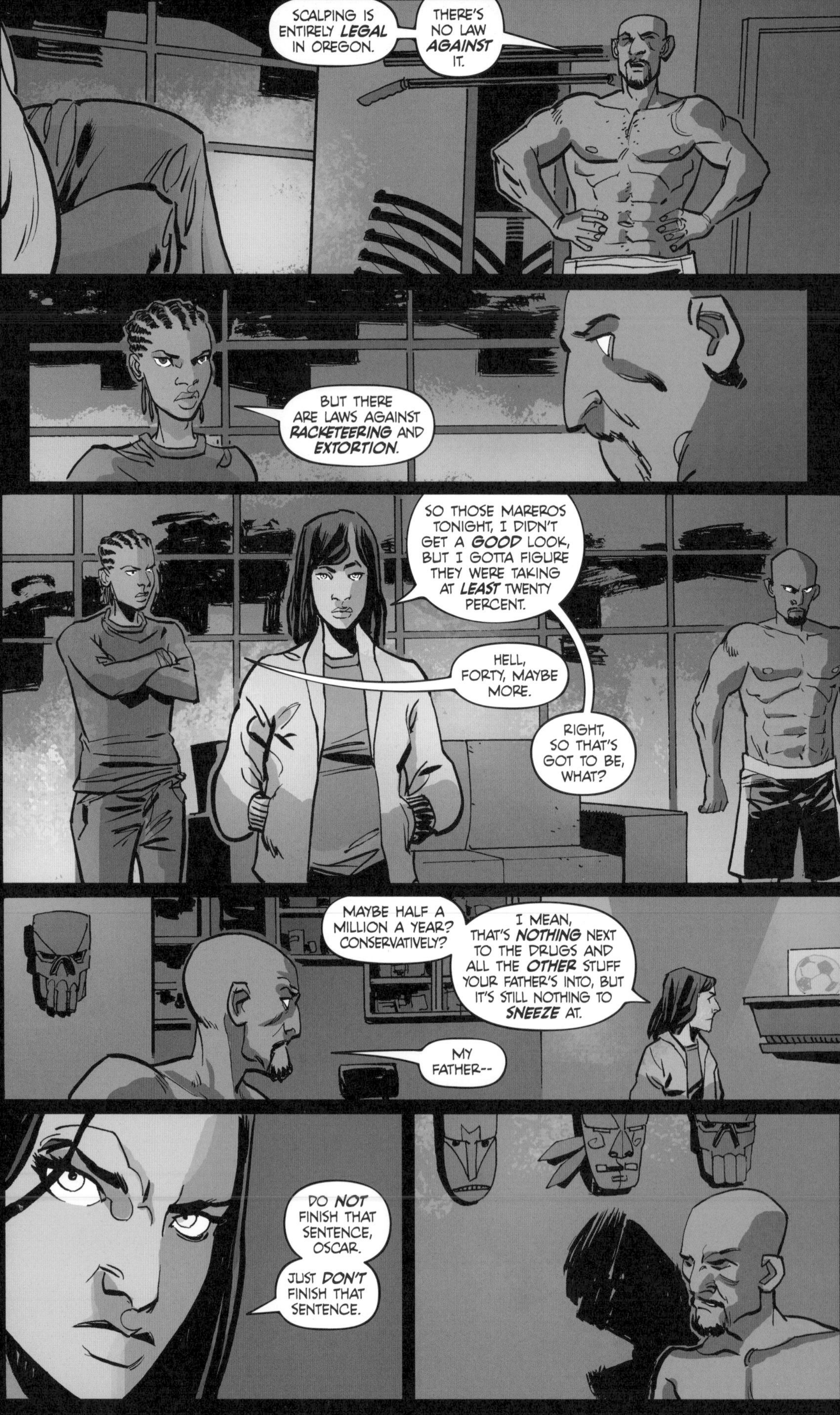

SCALPING IS ENTIRELY LEGAL IN OREGON.
THERE'S NO LAW AGAINST IT.
BUT THERE ARE LAWS AGAINST RACKETEERING AND EXTORTION.
SO THOSE MAREROS TONIGHT, I DIDN'T GET A GOOD LOOK, BUT I GOTTA FIGURE THEY WERE TAKING AT LEAST TWENTY PERCENT.
HELL, FORTY, MAYBE MORE.
RIGHT, SO THAT'S GOT TO BE, WHAT?
MAYBE HALF A MILLION A YEAR? CONSERVATIVELY?
I MEAN, THAT'S NOTHING NEXT TO THE DRUGS AND ALL THE OTHER STUFF YOUR FATHER'S INTO, BUT IT'S STILL NOTHING TO SNEEZE AT.
MY FATHER--
DO NOT FINISH THAT SENTENCE, OSCAR.
JUST DON'T FINISH THAT SENTENCE.

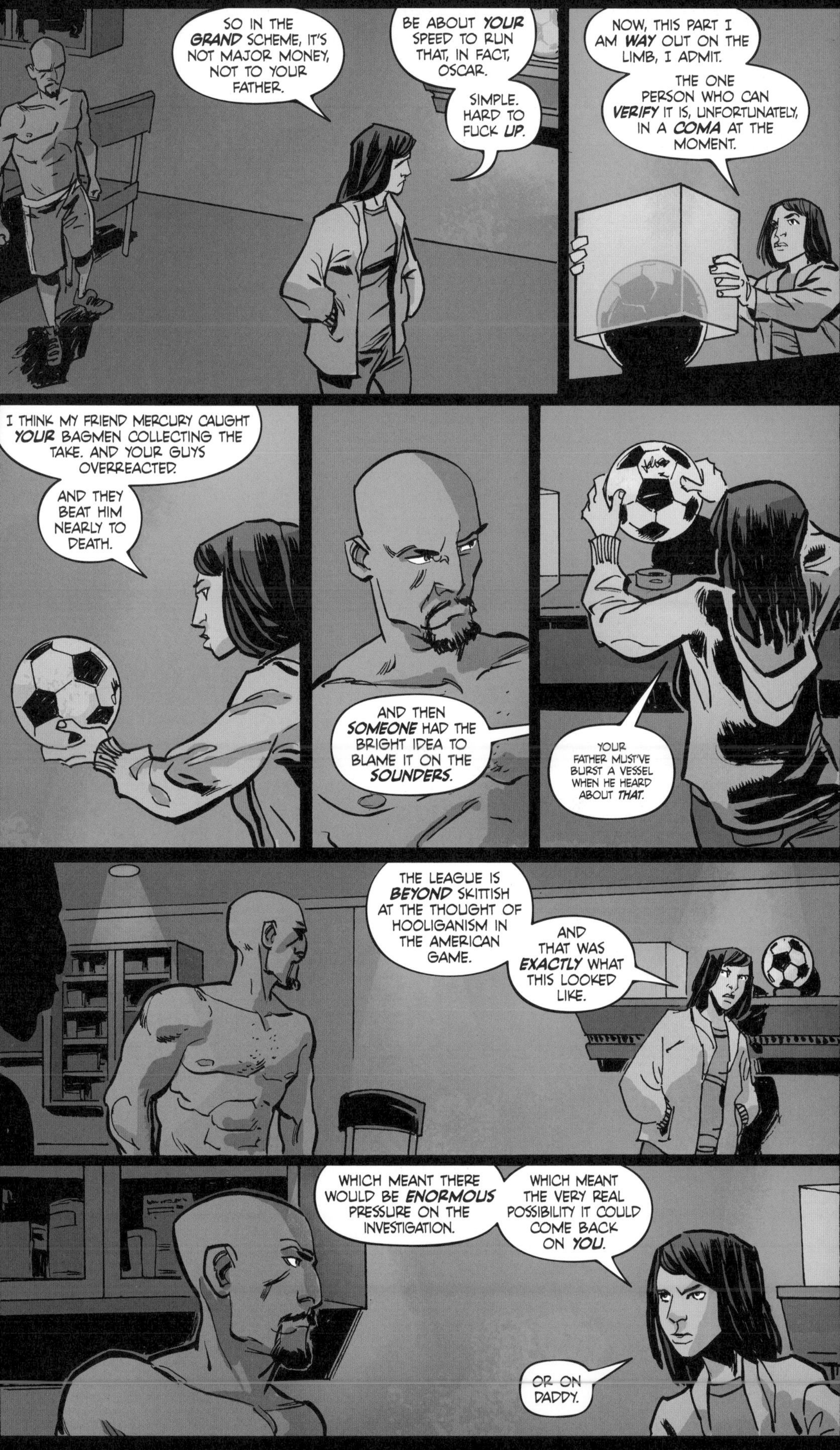
SO IN THE GRAND SCHEME, IT'S NOT MAJOR MONEY, NOT TO YOUR FATHER.
BE ABOUT YOUR SPEED TO RUN THAT, IN FACT, OSCAR.
SIMPLE. HARD TO FUCK UP.
NOW, THIS PART I AM WAY OUT ON THE LIMB, I ADMIT.
THE ONE PERSON WHO CAN VERIFY IT IS, UNFORTUNATELY, IN A COMA AT THE MOMENT.
I THINK MY FRIEND MERCURY CAUGHT YOUR BAGMEN COLLECTING THE TAKE. AND YOUR GUYS OVERREACTED.
AND THEY BEAT HIM NEARLY TO DEATH.
AND THEN SOMEONE HAD THE BRIGHT IDEA TO BLAME IT ON THE SOUNDERS.
YOUR FATHER MUST'VE BURST A VESSEL WHEN HE HEARD ABOUT THAT.
THE LEAGUE IS BEYOND SKITTISH AT THE THOUGHT OF HOOLIGANISM IN THE AMERICAN GAME.
AND THAT WAS EXACTLY WHAT THIS LOOKED LIKE.
WHICH MEANT THERE WOULD BE ENORMOUS PRESSURE ON THE INVESTIGATION.
WHICH MEANT THE VERY REAL POSSIBILITY IT COULD COME BACK ON YOU.
OR ON DADDY.

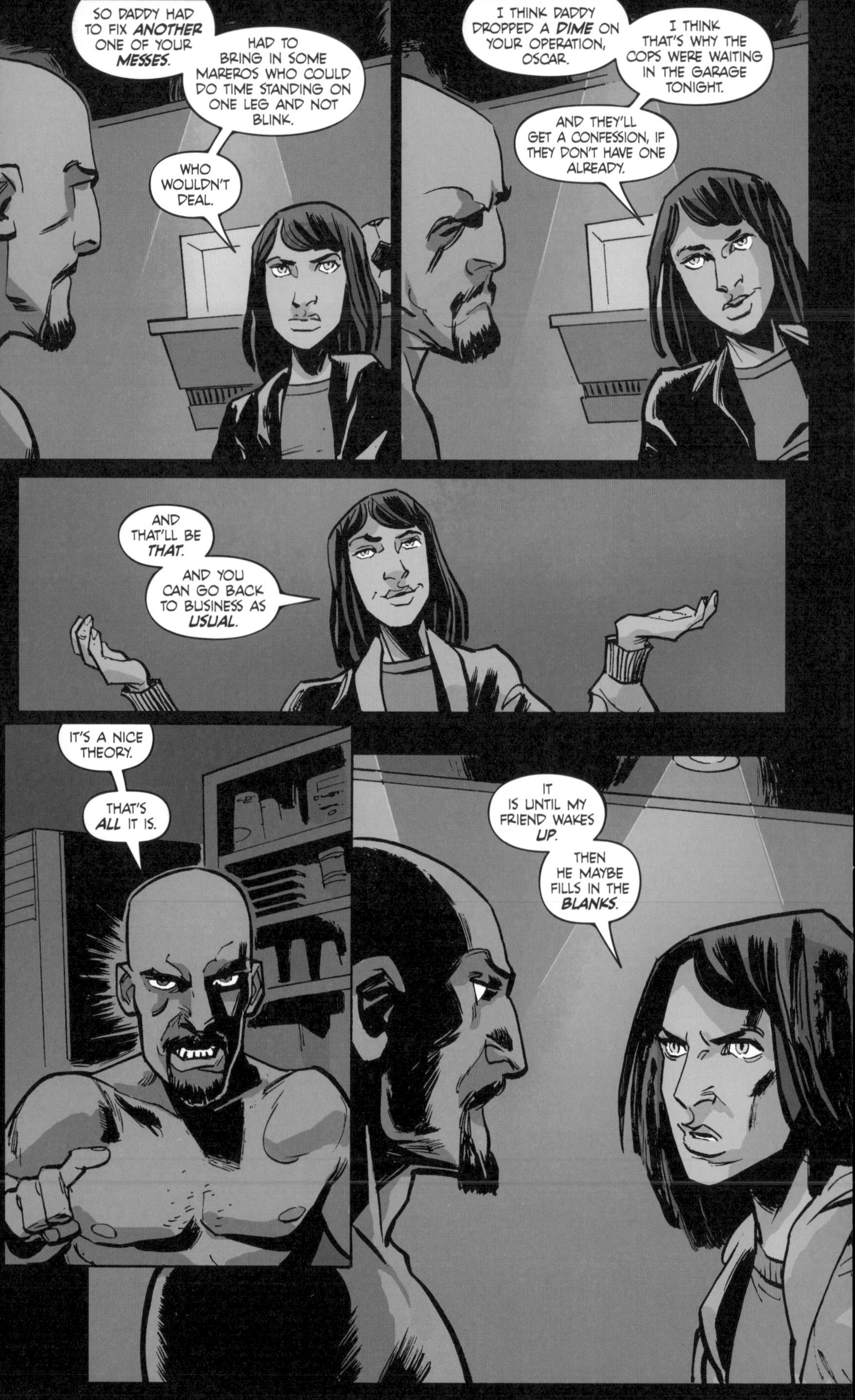
SO DADDY HAD TO FIX ANOTHER ONE OF YOUR MESSES.
HAD TO BRING IN SOME MAREROS WHO COULD DO TIME STANDING ON ONE LEG AND NOT BLINK.
WHO WOULDN'T DEAL.
I THINK DADDY DROPPED A DIME ON YOUR OPERATION, OSCAR.
I THINK THAT'S WHY THE COPS WERE WAITING IN THE GARAGE TONIGHT.
AND THEY'LL GET A CONFESSION, IF THEY DON'T HAVE ONE ALREADY.
AND THAT'LL BE THAT.
AND YOU CAN GO BACK TO BUSINESS AS USUAL.
IT'S A NICE THEORY.
THAT'S ALL IT IS.
IT IS UNTIL MY FRIEND WAKES UP.
THEN HE MAYBE FILLS IN THE BLANKS.

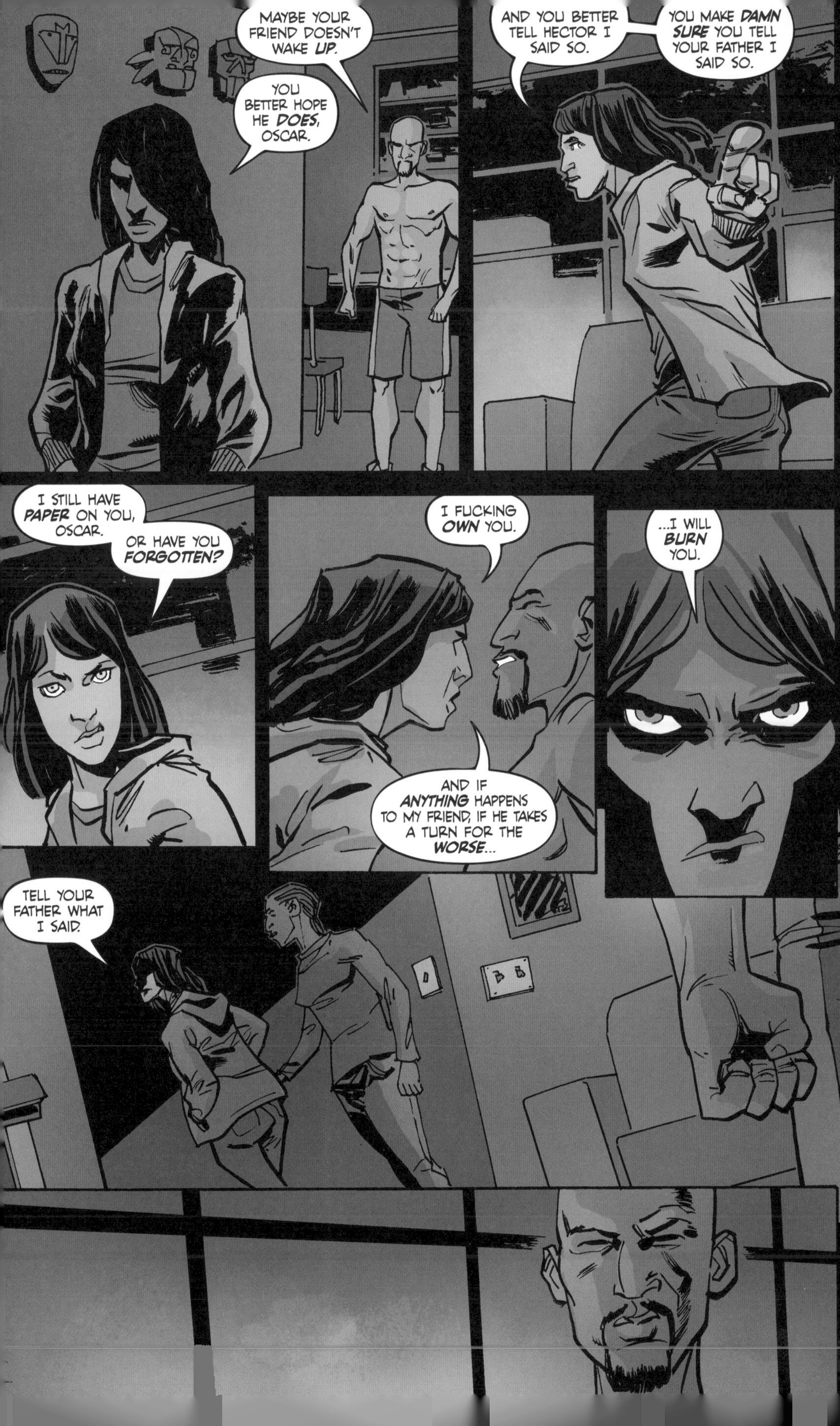
MAYBE YOUR FRIEND DOESN'T WAKE UP.
YOU BETTER HOPE HE DOES, OSCAR.
AND YOU BETTER TELL HECTOR I SAID SO.
YOU MAKE DAMN SURE YOU TELL YOUR FATHER I SAID SO.
I STILL HAVE PAPER ON YOU, OSCAR.
OR HAVE YOU FORGOTTEN?
I FUCKING OWN YOU.
AND IF ANYTHING HAPPENS TO MY FRIEND, IF HE TAKES A TURN FOR THE WORSE...
...I WILL BURN YOU.
TELL YOUR FATHER WHAT I SAID.

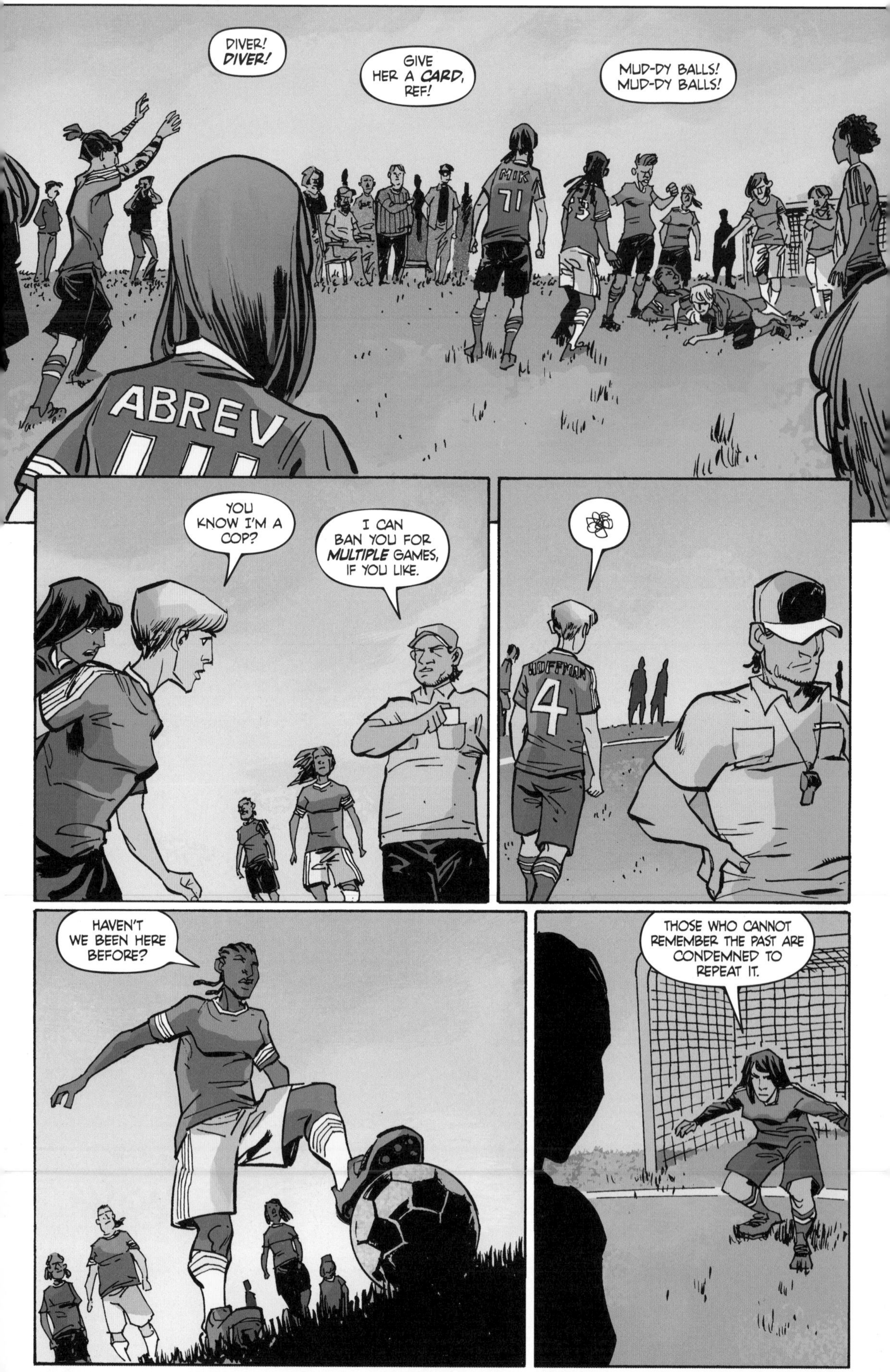
DIVER! DIVER!
GIVE HER A CARD, REF!
MUD-DY BALLS! MUD-DY BALLS!
ABREV
MIK 71
YOU KNOW I'M A COP?
I CAN BAN YOU FOR MULTIPLE GAMES, IF YOU LIKE.
HOFFMAN 4
HAVEN'T WE BEEN HERE BEFORE?
THOSE WHO CANNOT REMEMBER THE PAST ARE CONDEMNED TO REPEAT IT.

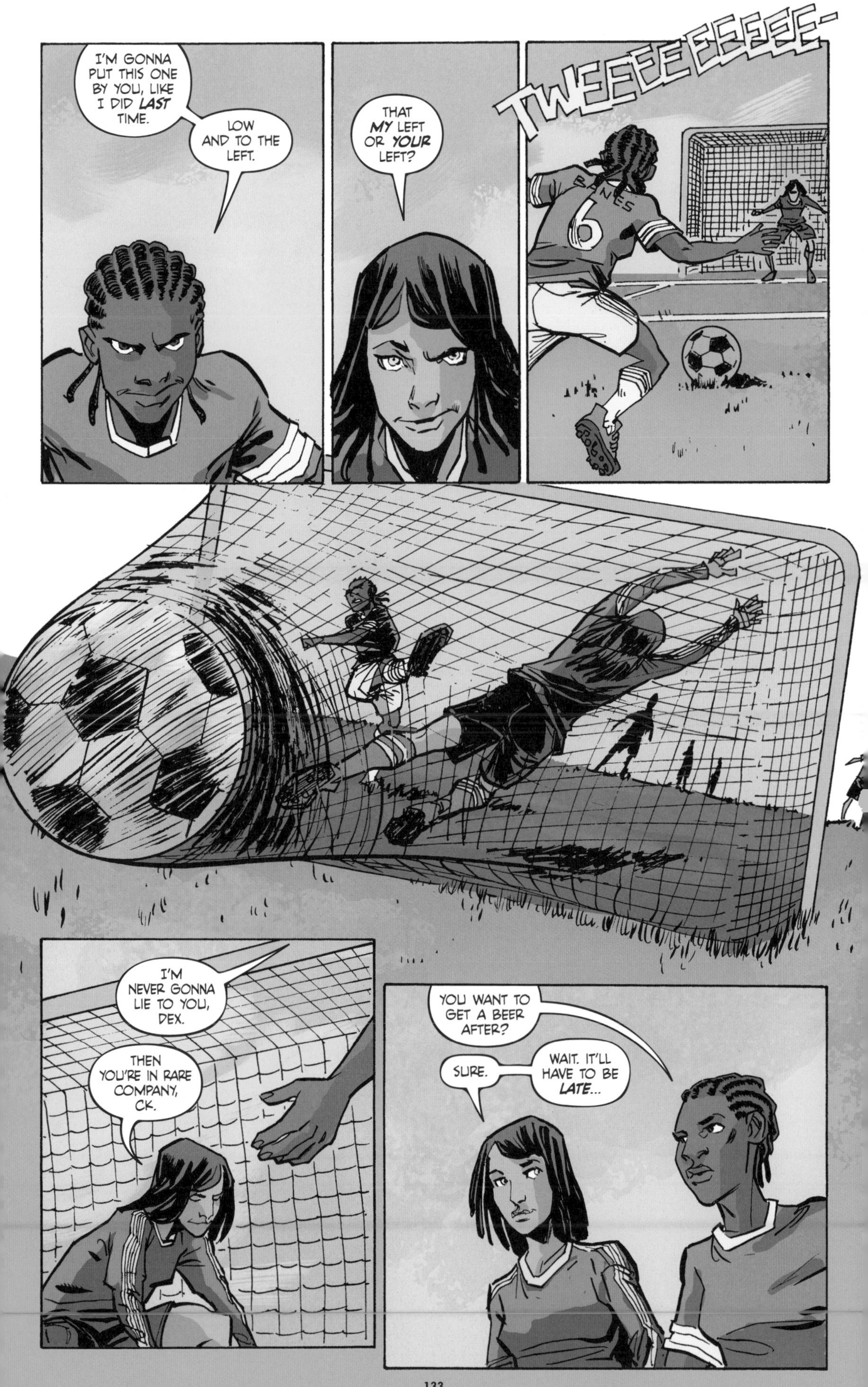
I'M GONNA PUT THIS ONE BY YOU, LIKE I DID LAST TIME.
LOW AND TO THE LEFT.
THAT MY LEFT OR YOUR LEFT?
TWEEEEEEEEEEE-
I'M NEVER GONNA LIE TO YOU, DEX.
THEN YOU'RE IN RARE COMPANY, CK.
YOU WANT TO GET A BEER AFTER?
SURE.
WAIT. IT'LL HAVE TO BE LATE...

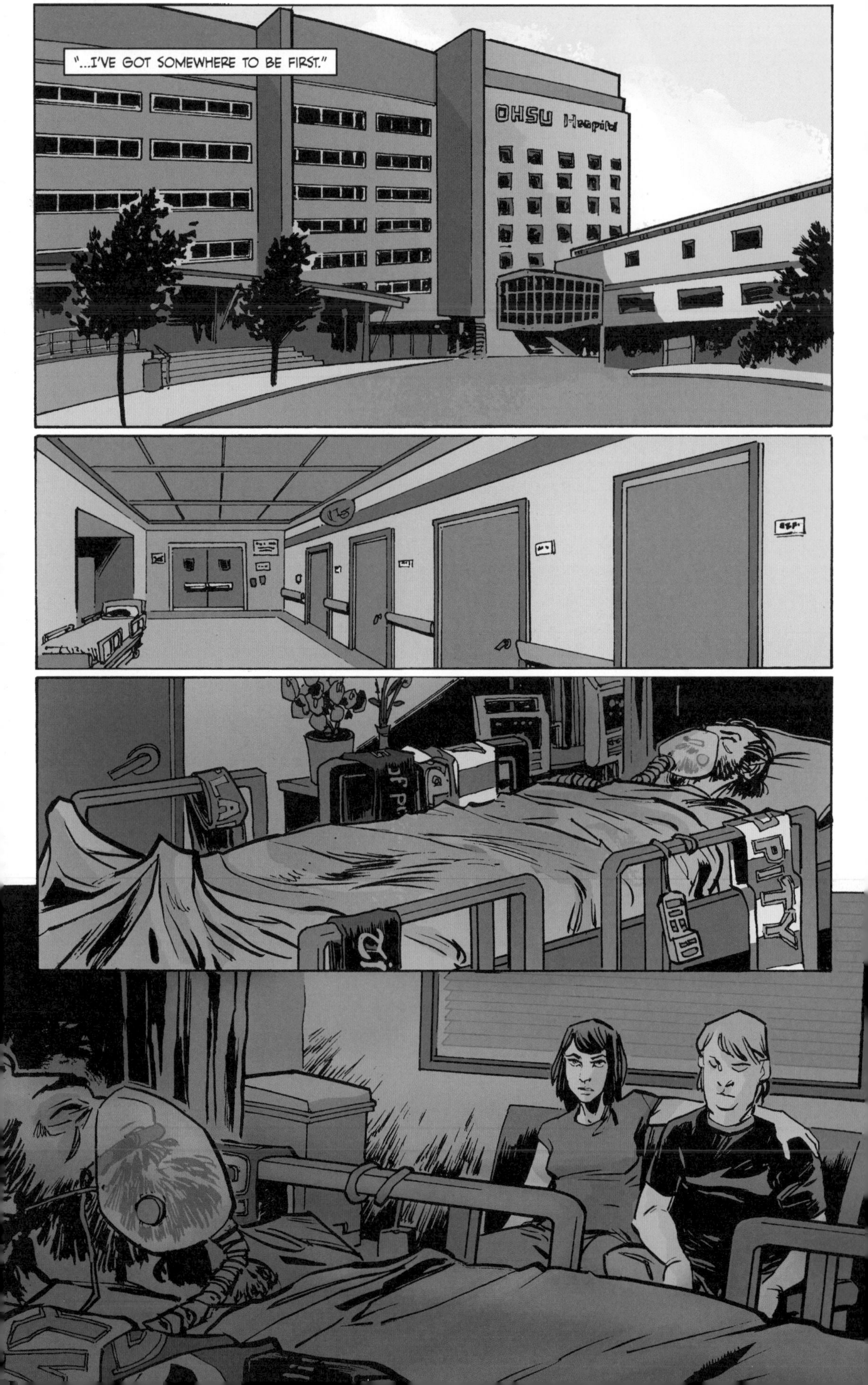
"...I'VE GOT SOMEWHERE TO BE FIRST."
OHSU Hospital
PITY